ALSO BY SEBASTIAN DE ASSIS

Nonfiction

Spiraling Madness

ZENior CitiZEN: Mastering the Art of Aging

rEvolution in Education

Teachers of the World, Unite!

Fiction

The Heat of the Sun

The Beast

The Alchemy of Time

Sailing Against the Wind

A Memoir

Sebastian de Assis

Blooming World Books

SAILING AGAINST THE WIND

Blooming World Books is a small press exclusively dedicated to publishing the work of its only author, Sebastian de Assis. Unabashedly proud to be solely responsible for all facets of the development and production of all Blooming World Books titles, i.e., writing, editing, typesetting, interior page layout, book cover design, indexing, and every relevant aspect of publication are the work of the author/publisher alone.

First Edition

ISBN 978-1-7323285-0-1

Library of Congress Control Number: 2023930070

Published in the United States of America

For Tali

AUTHOR'S NOTE

Most names and some identifying information about people in this book have been changed to protect individual privacy.

The Road Not Taken

Two roads diverged in a yellow wood,
And sorry I could not travel both
And be one traveler, long I stood
And looked down one as far as I could
To where it bent in the undergrowth;

Then took the other, as just as fair,
And having perhaps the better claim,
Because it was grassy and wanted wear;
Though as for that, the passing there
Had worn them really about the same,

And both that morning equally lay
In leaves no step had trodden black.
Oh, I kept the first for another day!
Yet knowing how way leads on to way,
I doubted if I should ever come back.

I shall be telling this with a sigh
Somewhere ages and ages hence:
Two roads diverged in a wood, and I—
I took the one less traveled by,
And that has made all the difference.

Robert Frost (1874–1963)

PART I

I came from a well-to-do family. I lived in a beachfront house with a swimming pool, sauna and all the amenities of an affluent life. I studied in the best private schools money can afford. I vacationed abroad, owned boats, cars and motorcycles, and was a member of a yacht club. Then, all of a sudden, I found myself homeless and alone in a foreign country hoping my living nightmare would end soon.

"Stop!"

I yelled with a trembling voice from the back of the substandard interstate bus. I wasn't sure whether it was an unexpected call to the bus driver or my mind screaming out for the inner turmoil to cease. The bus stopped but the emotional tempest raged unabated in the overcast horizon of my being; and it would continue on for some time to come.

Chugging my two canvas handbags through the narrow aisle under the scrutinizing eyes of curious passengers, I made my way to the front and off the bus after a five-hour drive. It was the longest bus ride of my life; not in terms of time or distance, but in the sum total of anguish and anticipation to I'd have to endure.

Watching the cloud of dust swirling as the bus drove off from the gravel road shoulder, I dropped my bags down to the ground with a thump as if they stored the heavy load of my battered self. Squinting while rubbing the dust off my eyes, I followed the sight of the bus until it disappeared in the semi-deserted road. Suddenly, the realization that I was alone, broke, and in the middle of nowhere in a country I did not know anyone hit me like an anvil falling on the crown of my head. Overwhelmed with feelings of searing sadness and crippling angst, I sat down on the pebbly ground, crossed my arms over my bent knees to ensconce my exhausted mind, and then surrendered to my despair. With no one around to witness my vulnerability, I wept and sobbed with unbridled abandon hoping that my tears would temporarily wash away my pent-up sorrow. They failed me.

"I can't just sit here all day," I said to myself after a long bout of crying. I dried up my eyes with my long sleeve covered forearm, took a deep sorrow-filled breath, and shook my head aware that dusk would arrive in no time and I needed to find a place to sleep before then.

Not even in my wildest nightmares had I ever thought that one day I'd experience something like this. For the first time in my life I was homeless and alone without any support system. The odds that one day I'd have to endure this inauspicious circumstance were close to nil at best. However, considering that I had to find my bearings around an unknown environment before nighttime, I could not afford to spend my time mulling over the absurdly low odds that befell upon me, for I had more immediate survival needs to take care of. I needed to scout the area to find a place to spend the night.

"Alright, dude, get on your feet and start walking," I said in a commanding tone to myself. It's interesting how loneliness compels one to talk out loud to himself.

I stood up and realized I had no idea what direction to go. Without giving it a second thought, I picked up my bags and began walking aimlessly; like a rudderless vessel drifting in a sea of uncertainty toward an unknown destination. I kept walking for what it seemed to be a very long time and distance without any idea of where I was going. With the traumatic memories of the past 36 hours still churning inside of me, I knew I had no other alternative. The decision I had made, as irrational as it might have seemed, was the right thing to do; and at least of that I was certain. Nevertheless, the anxiety of roaming about in a foreign country not knowing where to go occasionally made me question my choice. But at that moment there was only one thing for me to do: keep walking and shedding tears as if they were liquid bread crumbs marking the emotional path of my dolorous kismet.

After walking on the roadside for what it felt like an interminable time, I spotted from the distance a sleepy fishing village. I picked up my pace fueled by the hope of making an acquaintance, or at least finding a safe place to spend the night. Alas, neither one happened. Other than an old man riding a beat-up bicycle on a narrow sandy pathway by the cobblestone street, I didn't see another soul anywhere. The only other sign of life in sight was an emaciated stray cat foraging the grounds of a closed fish market. As for a place to sleep, I decided to walk along the beach and see if I could find a secluded and cozy nook to rest my exhausted body and emotionally drained self. For the next two nights, I sheltered myself under one of the several fishing boats resting upside down at the end of the beach. And once I rose with the Sun, I spent the day roaming about aimlessly dragging my sorrows along toward nowhere. I was both physically and emotionally lost.

On the third day my luck would take a favorable turn. As I strolled along the shore of the long white sand beach beholding the Sun coming down piecemeal, I started feeling very hungry. I needed to get something to eat or it would be an even longer night as a homeless man sleeping under a smelly fishing boat on the beach. Although I'd spent most of my money in my past 36-hour ordeal, I still had some cash left over for food and other basic necessities; at least for a couple of months. However, there was not any place in sight where I could purchase even a candy bar. Then, to my pleasant surprise, I spotted a large hotel not far inland from the beach. Like a famished beast that just spotted a helpless prey,

I charged for it determined to silence the ferocious roaring in my stomach before retiring for the evening to my improvised outdoor lodging.

"Excuse me," I said meekly while sticking my head inside the backdoor kitchen of the hotel by the parking lot. I waited anxiously as I heard sounds of banging pots followed by footsteps.

Then, walking toward me from inside the kitchen, a short and stout man wearing a grease-stained white apron and a chef's hat greeted me with a beaming smile. He interacted with me as if he'd encountered; not a stranger, but an old friend he had not seen in a long time.

"A piece of bread? That's what you want?" He reacted after I disclosed the purpose of my visit. "Come, c'mon in and I'll get you something to eat."

Next thing I knew I was sitting at a white tablecloth covered table in the kitchen devouring a succulent steak, baked potatoes, stir veggies, green salad, and, of course, bread. Also, he set on the table a carafe of red wine for me to wash down the dining extravaganza. Considering my circumstances and what I'd been through recently, that food and wine looked and tasted heavenly divine.

"Ah, you are from Rio de Janeiro," he said as we engaged in small talk while I chomped on the delicious food he served me. "I hear it is the land of beautiful women, samba, and soccer."

"It seems to be the city's international reputation, I suppose," I said barely pausing my eating with gusto.

"I suppose," he said curtly as his facial expression took on a serious look as if he'd suddenly realized something odd was going on.

"There's also an ugly side of the city that neither the rhythm of samba nor the excitement of soccer can hide," I said trying to disengage him from whatever was causing his brow to furrow. “They do not show shantytowns on the post-cards or advertise the widespread poverty and crime in the city.”

“What’s a young man from Rio doing at the backdoor kitchen of a hotel in a far away land asking for a piece of bread?” He asked me unexpectedly by-passing my sideline comment. With his elbows on the table, he leaned forward seemingly interested in hearing my answer.

After a brief and embarrassing eye contact with him, I lowered my head and kept chewing in silence. I wasn’t ready to share my recent trauma with anyone yet. However, if there was someone to be the first to hear what I’d been through—or at least part of my story—that man who welcomed me with friendly generosity deserved to be the one. I lifted my chin to look at him again before grabbing the wine glass to take a mouthful swig. Then, I let the dam holding my pent-up emotions break loose and gushed out more details about my anguish than I anticipated. Perhaps it was the empathetic look in his eyes that compelled me to speak out; or maybe I just had an irrepressible need to unload my heavy emotional cargo. Whatever it was, I felt lighter and relieved to digest my feelings while doing the same to my meal.

“I just had an idea,” he said standing up abruptly after we’d been talking for awhile. “Stay put. I’ll be right back.”

I watched him speedily walking toward an office space at the end of the kitchen. I noticed the peculiar waddling of his footsteps as he moved his short-statured plump body as if he were in a state of urgency. Despite his diminutive appearance and cumbersome motion, that man looked monumentally impressive to my eyes. What I saw in him was a colossal human being; a dignified soul existing among us disguised as a chef in a hotel kitchen.

"Alright," he said upon returning a few minutes later. "My boss told me he'll be here shortly."

"Did you call your boss?" I asked puzzled about his purpose.

"Yeah, he's a good man. He said he might be able to help you out," he said smiling at me with his bright brown eyes before engaging in small talk again. "What do you think about the last World Cup?"

It didn't take long for his boss to show up. The tall dark-haired man wearing jeans and a sports jacket stepped out of a pick-up truck and walked briskly toward us. I sized him up from afar as he headed in our direction and I immediately felt a sense of kinship and trust. Although physically opposites in appearance, the tall man walking toward me and the short one standing by my side shared a similar ethereal essence; as if they were branches of a common tree—and I felt trustingly at ease in the shade of their presence.

"I have a membership to a camping ground nearby and a tent in the bed of my truck," he said shortly after the perfunctory introductions. "You can spend the night there and we'll figure out a more stable housing situation for you at a later time. Meet me at the front-desk of the hotel tomorrow morning and I might have some work for you. As for the tent, just leave it there when you wake up and I'll come by to pick it up later."

The chef beamed with delight as if he were the one benefiting from the arrangement. I thanked him with deeply felt words of appreciation before hopping on the Food & Beverage manager's pick-up truck on the way to a much improved sleeping situation.

To this day, whenever I think of the chef's smiling face and the tall man's willingness to come to the assistance of a complete stranger, I send them loving thoughts of gratitude through the networks of the quantum field. And just as I am sure the electronic mails I send at the click of a button arrive at the intended recipients in a distant part of the globe, I'm equally positive that my gratitude-infused thought messages reach them wherever they happen to be in the time-space dimension at the moment.

Because of my fortuitous encounter with genuine human kindness, my short-lived brush with homelessness was curtailed; at least for the time being. But for a couple of days, I'd experienced firsthand what it's like to wander aimlessly alone without any support system. And that night, though I was lodged in a nice zipped up tent in a camping ground instead of under a boat on the beach, I shivered all the same and all night long as a thief-chill robbed me from a restful sleep. But I was grateful, indeed. The learning that those two men passed on to me through loving generosity of spirit, along with the empirical knowledge of scarcity and homelessness I acquired on my own, opened a whole new perspective in my awareness of what human nature is supposed to be. From that day onward, I was no longer afraid of the adventure I'd put myself into in the pursuit of a promising destiny. Whatever challenges awaited me on my long journey—and there would be plenty—I felt confident that I'd be protected and guided as I was that day. And considering what I'd just gone through, I experienced an unusual state of tranquility; and tranquility is courage in repose. Somehow I felt emboldened in the midst of intense emotional turmoil.

Using the same technique I applied sleeping under the boat, I curled myself into a fetal position hoping to amass some much needed body heat. With my mind racing inside my shivering body, I realized that as long as I never quit a challenging situation again, as I did in the worst 36-hour period of my life, my back would be covered and I would live to experience the opportunities that were promised to me. After all, perseverance is the key that opens the door of opportunity. But if the key gets rusty and warped by burning trepidations, the will to carry on the struggle can be severed and failure ensues. Alas, I had to learn this lesson the hard way before fulfilling my destiny to immigrate to the United States of America.

In the meantime, feeling cold in a transitional homelessness situation was where I was supposed to be.

❧❖☙

"That's it. I had enough of this heat," I said opening the door of the sauna and exiting it enveloped in a eucalyptus-scented steamy cloud. "I'm going for a dip."

"I'm following you," my half-brother said shadowing me all the way to the swimming pool for a refreshing splash.

Those family gatherings on sunny Sundays are the best memories I have from my privileged family life; my father's family that is. To me they felt like casual rituals of harmony and unity, neither of which I experienced on a regular basis. After enjoying a eucalyptus-infused sauna, we'd hang out under a parasol by the swimming pool savoring cold natural juices before a mirthful gathering around the dining table for a late Sunday brunch. With an abundance of food, wine, and laughter, I took great pleasure in those lovely moments and I still have fond memories of them. But it didn't always feel like that.

Considering my national origin, I've always felt fortunate for my bounteous upbringing. Growing up in a third world country with the unenviable reputation as one of the most iniquitous nations on Earth, I always had the best any kid in any part of the world would long for: the best education, international travels, boats, cars, motorcycles, and a household tantamount to a fall harvest cornucopia of abundance. Indeed, I felt lucky to have the best provider a son could wish for, though it came with a pricey trade tag. My contentious relationship with my emotionally wounded father was not an easy bargain. And it started out from the day I was born.

My father had been married to my mother for approximately eight years when I was born. As a young couple (he was 32 and she was 25-years-old), they already had two daughters when my mother began yearning for a son to complete the family. According to my father's account, my mother fantasized a future in which she'd walk on the street hand-in-arm with her grown up son filled with maternal pride. She wanted to name her son Sebastian, which my father vehemently opposed.

"It's a beautiful name," my father told me she often said. "It's of Greek origin and it means venerable and honorable. What's there not to like about it?"

"I've always hated my name," he'd reply to her. "If I ever have a son I will definitely not name him Sebastian Jr."

As a young military officer—and with an attitude to match—the armed forces administration moved him around the country as needed. Consequently, his first daughter was born in the Brazilian state of Minas Gerais. Then the next one was born in São Paulo. By the time he was transferred back to Rio de Janeiro, my mother was pregnant with me. And that's where I was born on January 20 at 12:20 pm on a sunny Sunday. It so happens that January 20 is a holiday celebrating Saint Sebastian; the patron saint of the city whose official name is City of San Sebastian of Rio de Janeiro. Hence, my mother's argument to name her son Sebastian gained significant weight against his resistance. And per my father's admission, he succumbed to both her wishes and his own superstition that if he were to continue objecting to my mother's determination, some ill-omened event would befall upon him. Unfortunately, to all concerned, his foreboding became a most traumatic self-fulfilling prophecy, even though he yielded to my mother's insistence to name her son Sebastian.

Almost four months after I was born my mother unexpectedly passed away at the tender age of 25. For years after finding out about her premature death when I was in my early teens, her *causa mortis* still remains a mystery to me. Although I never saw her death certificate, the obituary notice in a newspaper clip I found in one of my father's secret file folders made no reference to the cause of her death. And since it was not a subject matter to be brought up without some virulent emotional reaction on his part, I avoided broaching the topic in order to evade unnecessary conflict with my old man. It took me a long time to realize that my father had buried his past along with my mother; and talking about her death somehow unearthed the tormenting demons of his sorrows. Hence, I spent the early years of my youth quietly wondering what might have happened to my mother. Maybe the sporadic fainting episodes I learned she used to have played a role in her death; a heart condition, perhaps. What I do know is that her passing left two people deceased, albeit one only in an emotional and psychological sense of death. As it happened—and without any warning—my 32-year-old father became a widower with two grieving small daughters and an infant son named Sebastian he'd have to rear on his own.

In this bleak scenario of our collective family trauma, I always felt I was the one better off. After all, at 4-months-old I had no mental recollection of my mother's passing. However, even as a young child I realized that a potent emotional memory existed in every cell of my being; an incisively searing remembrance of abandonment. By the time I reached pre-puberty, I became unwittingly aware that my assumption of privilege of unawareness in the face of such a poignant loss was wrong. Somehow in the deep dark caverns of my father's unredeemable anguish, he acknowledged to me that he, unintentionally, associated the timing of my birth with the departure of his beloved wife. The son she was so eager to have and gave him the name my father detested had changed places with her. This subtle unconscious psychological underlying trauma set off a chain reaction of conflicts with my father that would mar our relationship for most of our lives. By my mid-teens our relationship had deteriorated so badly that I started fantasizing about one day leaving my country of birth and moving very far away. Not even the expanded family he created ameliorated the situation. In fact, as far as our relationship was concerned, it made it much worse.

A few months after my mother died, my father made acquaintance with a pretty 18-year-old girl who lived next door to his mother's house where his three children stayed while he went to work. In the evening when he came by to pick them up, he had to go next door where my sisters had befriended the teenager who gave them the attention they so desperately needed. As the frequency of the encounters increased, the cute teenage girl, whose father was a bohemian with whom she had a quasi-nonexistent relationship, became enamored with the young handsome father of three; a sort of Electra complex. In his turn, he appreciated how the attractive young woman gave both him and his daughters caring attention. It was a matter of time—a little over a year—for him to retire widowhood and become a married man once again.

Soon his family expanded. I was 3-years-old when my first half-brother was born; an event that significantly impacted my inauspicious relationship with my father; not because of my half-brother's birth, but the dynamic he initiated in the formation of a two-family tier. A few years later another half-sister was born, followed by another half-brother shortly thereafter. Now there were two branches of my father's family: my mother's three children and my stepmother's trio offspring. In the beginning when we were all children, everything felt normal, affable, and imperceptibly equalitarian from my naïve perspective. After all, I had no recollection of a mother other than the stepmother I'd known. And since my father made the unfortunate mistake to hide the truth from me and my half-siblings, we'd all pay a hefty emotional price for his blunder later on in our adulthood. Other than my older sisters, father, and stepmother, the rest of us were absolutely clueless that we lived in household of lies where two families coexisted under the guise of a harmonious and undivided one. It was a Dickensian situation of a Tale of Two Families within one spurious image of a unified happy family.

In the early years of his second marriage, doubling the size of his family put on a significant stress on my father's financial concerns. Although he managed to provide for his rapidly growing family over the years on a military salary and small businesses he created, he was an ambitious man whose aspirations to improve his socioeconomic status was fueled by an unswerving determination to make money. In addition to his unfettered desire to ride the gravy train, there was another equally poignant motivational factor catapulting him toward his goal: an enormous amount of unresolved pent-up sorrow that compelled him to become the proverbial "workaholic." Work became a palliative for dealing with the pain and trauma of unexpectedly losing, in his own words, "the love of his life." Thus, in his early forties when he reached the colonel rank and was entitled to retire with large enough pension to support his family, he embarked into the world of entrepreneurship with reckless abandon. Resilient and doggedly determined to be rich, after a series of disappointments and failures, eventually he'd establish himself as a very successful businessman, and made a lot of money in the process.

Although I greatly benefited from the fruits of my father's labor, my discontent and frustration with the discrimination within the family in time compelled me to leave the golden nest for good. I could no longer continue pretending that the bogus domestic bliss was genuine. Besides, the socioeconomic injustices and the political military dictatorship that afflicted Brazilian society were incompatible with my principles, even though neither of them affected me in any way; much to the contrary, I was the son of a well-to-do military officer. Thus, when the opportunity to leave the country arose effortlessly at a time I'd reached the nadir of my personal crisis—and the apex of my conflict with my father—I did not hesitate to embrace it willingly. I left my country of birth without looking back; except for an arduous 36-hour glance over the shoulder that caused me to stumble and fall hard.

Although growing up in Rio made me an eyewitness to abject poverty in the streets and ubiquitous shantytowns around the city, I never grew accustomed to a sight I considered to be an immorality of modern civilization. So, when I experienced homelessness, albeit very short-lived in a few interspersed occasions, my sense of empathy for those undergoing this decadent subhuman condition increased exponentially. However, it'd be a travesty to compare my fleeting experience of homelessness to those condemned to a life sentence of dispossession, for such sentiment would make a parody of poverty. And yet, roaming the streets in a foreign country without a home and not knowing where to go next can profoundly alter a man's outlook on life—and so can the encounters with loving people.

"Just go straight ahead to the front-desk and they'll show you where to go," the Food and Beverage manager said when I met him in front of the hotel in the morning. "I've already talked with the HR department and they're expecting you."

"Thank you," I said looking into his eye. "Thank you very much."

He simpered, shook his head, and walked away without saying a word.

Other than the day before when he came to drive me to the campground and that morning directing me to the front desk, I'd see him only one more time. I don't remember his name and not even what his countenance look like. But never; never, have I forgotten what he did for me at a time I was in dire straits. His caring generosity of spirit benefited me in manifold ways. Not only had I received much needed help, but also became empirically aware that there are some genuinely caring people in the world. Watching him vanish in the distance, I wondered whether there was some sort of natural law of encounters that brought people together by some mysterious cosmological force.

When a well-dressed older couple exited the hotel, my chimerical wonderings were suddenly interrupted. I greeted them with a smile and friendly nod when they passed by as I walked in to the front desk eager to find out what lay in store for me.

"Sebastian?" The pretty young brunette with shoulder length hair addressed me with a broad welcoming smile. The two men flanking her behind the counter didn't look as affable.

"Here, fill out this paperwork and take it to the HR office down the hallway to your left," she said ramping up her gracious demeanor in disguised seductive manner.

"Are you applying for the doorman job vacancy?" One of the men asked me abruptly barging in my pleasant interaction with his female colleague.

"Doorman? I don't know. I'm applying for a job, but I don't know what it is," I said intrigued by both his impromptu questioning and what apparently I was about to become.

"You're applying for a job you don't even know what it is?" He asked in a condescending tone of voice.

"Down the hallway to my left," I said returning my attention to the gracious girl while utterly ignoring her obnoxious male colleague. I took the papers from her hand, casually touching her soft manicured fingers before thanking her for her kindness and walking away. As soon as I turned my back, suddenly I had to stop and turn around to deal with a type of discrimination I would encounter many other times in the future.

"They always give the shitty jobs to these foreigners," I overheard the man who addressed me talking to the other at a volume clearly intended to reach me.

I stared at him as if punching him in the mouth with my eyes. I could feel my fist itching and my feet twitching to move in his direction to shred his prejudice with my bare hands.

"Down the hallway to your left," the young woman intervened in the tense silent moment that could have turned rowdy. I was grateful to her for rescuing me from a potentially troubling situation.

Although I was not oblivious to the existence of discriminatory behavior, I was not used to being a target of this common vice of ignorance. Perhaps, had I known at the time that I was going to endure similar biased conduct many other times in the future, I'd likely be thankful to that man's impudent comment, for it offered me the opportunity to practice self-restraint.

I did not know whether it was true that they gave the shitty jobs to foreigners. However, as much as I didn't like that man's attitude toward me, he was absolutely right about the shitty job part of it. And having just endured a very shitty job right before my 36-hour dreadful ordeal, I wasn't sure I would be able to handle another one immediately afterwards.

Dressed in full regalia; I mean, matching hat, white gloves, and golden braided locks cascading down from the shoulder pads of the oversized jacket, I looked and felt like a foolish soldier guarding the five star palace where the affluent came for vacation. As if it were possible, this job was even shittier than my previous one. Except for my half-hour lunch break and a couple of 15-minutes rest in the morning and afternoon, I had to stand on my feet all day doing nothing but open doors and greet the occasional hotel guests coming in and out. And since it was low season, there was not even much menial action taking place. The job was a boredom endurance test that, as it'd happened before, I failed miserably from day one. I spent all day longing to return to the miniscule room I rented next to a chicken coop in the nearby fishing village. It was there that I surrendered my emotionally and physically exhausted self to the solitude of the expatriate fugitive I had become. Thinking of the privileged situation I forsook to go after my dreams and what I'd been so convincingly promised, I cried myself to sleep with nothing good to dream about.

On my second day on the job, I'd figured out a way to manage the boredom of my new occupation. According to European tradition, even the hotel served red wine with lunch for all employees, whom I surmise, drank it responsibly as a pleasant accompaniment to their meals. I'm afraid I was an exception to the rule; but in fairness to my foibles, I wasn't European. Thus, as a foreigner doing an extremely tedious job, I didn't consider my indulging consumption of Dionysius' nectar an issue of grievance. However, on the fourth day on the job when the hotel general manager caught me tilting like a human Pisa Tower propping itself up against the wall, he reprimanded me for my unprofessional stance.

"This is not quite the way I intend to advertise the relaxing atmosphere of the hotel," he said after showing up unexpectedly accompanied by a V.I.P. guest who chuckled at the way he berated me. "Please, be aware of your duties and don't ever let me see you leaning against the wall again."

Although I was pleased to have been able to conceal my tipsiness, I knew my time doing that job was up. Either I quitted it or I'd be fired in a matter of time. Like the last menial job I had a week before my 36-hour ordeal, I knew I'd reached my limit of tolerance. I'd learned there are certain types of jobs I cannot do even if my life depended on them.

After five days of literally inebriating monotony, I took my day off to explore the charming marina right next to the snazzy hotel where I worked myself to deadly tedium. There were some couple of hundred plus yachts and medium-sized sailing boats from all over the world mooring in the idyllic marine setting. As I strolled along hearing the pleasant sounds of rigging gear banging against the masts of gently swinging vessels, I rejoiced in the atmosphere of that environment. With the Sun warming my blue jeans jacket-covered back while the ocean breeze brushed against my face, I was determined to make something happen. I needed another job and the thought of working in that environment appealed to me immensely. Perhaps I'd even be able to live there. However, it proved to be more difficult than I anticipated.

In spite of my unwavering determination, there was one major hurdle to overcome that was beyond my control: it was early April; the sluggishly-vacant season when the few people onboard were boat residents who took care of their own needs. It would take another couple of months before the beginning of summertime when the region supposedly sizzled with excitement of booming tourism. But I could not afford to wait that long. I needed another job right away. It was a matter of both psychological and financial survival. Thus, I spent the next two days knocking on every single boat's hatch looking for a deckhand job or any other work that did not involve standing up still all day long. By the end of the afternoon of the second day of my search, I'd already made contact with most inhabited boats in the marina to no avail.

Discouraged and dreading the next work day at the hotel, I headed to the small and quaint marina shopping area. As I walked around mindlessly, I passed by a marine supply store when I immediately halted my steps. It dawned on me that kind of business would be the most likely place to store valuable information about both the seasonal patterns and the who's who in the area. I turned around and walked in taking a last breath of hope. Alone behind the counter in the empty store, a lady welcomed me with a most friendly smile as if I were a regular customer she'd not seen in awhile. I began wondering whether I was attracting good fortune after having recently endured a traumatic experience. Perhaps I was being rewarded for my courage born out of despair. Regardless of how everything was playing out, I felt blessed with the continuous favorable serendipity.

Walking into that store marked the beginning of my almost one year sojourn at Marina de Vilamoura in the Algarve region of Southern Portugal; the departing harbor of my setting sail to the United States.

ଓ❖ଓ

I had just turned 13-years-old when a shocking revelation emerged from a degenerate mire of covered up falsehoods.

"Oh my God, he found out!" One of my older sisters blurted out covering her mouth with the palm of her hand. My puzzlement caused the skin between my eyes and the bridge of my nose to furrow with tense anticipatory curiosity. I felt as though I had inadvertently opened a Pandora's Box that would haunt me for the rest of my life. And it was exactly what I did.

Holding my birth certificate in my hands for the first time, I had just pointed out that the name of my mother was misprinted; in fact, it was a completely different name. It seemed unlikely that such a major blunder would happen in an important document. But after witnessing my sister's reaction, not even my pubescent naiveté could shelter me from the grievous lies I was misled to believe. I went to bed that night wondering what happened to my real mother, and why my parents lied to me and for what purpose. I felt betrayed by those I trusted the most, which triggered a lifelong skepticism in me. That day marked the beginning of one of the most difficult years of my life.

After that evening, I began understanding all the incomprehensible—and often times hurtful—relationship experiences I had as a child with the woman I believed to be my mother. There was one incident in particular that had left me flummoxed for years until that evening when I learned the truth. I was about 8-years-old when I came back from school to find all my toys scattered on the bedroom floor I shared with my half-brother. It was a royal mess. But when I noticed that the mischievous dimwit had thrown many of my toys out the window of the sixth floor of the spacious high-rise apartment building we lived in, I flipped out and naturally ran for the comforting support of my mother.

"Mommy, mommy," I knocked frantically on her bedroom door. I was in desperate need of some maternal loving.

"What?" She yelled from behind the closed door sounding somewhat irritated.

"Carl threw my toys out the window," I said with my face smashed against the door hoping she'd hear my sobbing.

The door abruptly opened and I almost fell forward. Just by looking at her pouting, I wished I had never bothered.

"Well, what do you want me to do? Why don't you go downstairs and pick them up. It's not hard to do, is it? Now quit whining and get moving," she said with dry indifference before slamming the door close in my face.

Suddenly, I couldn't care less for my toys; and yet, I went to pick them up as she told me to do. As I absent-mindedly gathered whatever toys had not fallen on the roof of the garage, I felt an enormous vacuum inside of my child self. I could not comprehend why my mother did not hug me and console me when I came to her in distress. And the fact she didn't berate my half-brother didn't help much either; not for the reprehension itself, but as a sign of fairness and equal caring. With broken toys in hands and a broken heart in my chest, none of it made sense to me; not until I haphazardly came across my birth certificate some five years later.

At a time when a flood of turbulent emotions inundated my befuddled mind, my first teen year was chaotic at best. I started experimenting with mind-altering drugs, getting involved in all kinds of mischief, and playing hooky on a regular basis until I dropped out of school altogether. But that was the good part. The real bad one was my father turning against me; not because I was getting into trouble, but for having found out the lie that sustained his false sense of family unity and happiness. It seemed to me that the unjustifiable resentment he harbored about the timing of my birth and my mother's death was exacerbated by a new threat. Somehow my finding out the truth generated disturbing waves on the placid lake of his new family life. In my turn, I felt as though a tsunami had crashed on the shore of the budding years of my individual development wreaking havoc on its path. Indeed, it was a year of existential pandemonium.

To my astonishment, my father was able to uphold the lies with dictatorial mastery. By imposing on both his new wife and children of his first marriage to address one another as mother, son and daughter, he was able to perpetuate his family revelry by not letting my half-siblings learn we were children of different mothers. Unbeknownst to him, he'd managed to aggravate and divide further his pseudo-unified family into two factions: the ones who knew the truth and the ones who didn't. As long as the legitimate truth was swept under the counterfeit Persian rug of appearance, he implicitly pledged to give his family all the good fortunes of material abundance he never had as a child. He definitely succeeded, but at a costly price to the individual members of his family later in adulthood.

But to make matters worse to my finding out that my relatively young mother was not my real mother, I unwittingly developed a disturbing psychological pattern that would haunt me for years to come. At a time my prepubescent hormones were raging in my body, a strong Oedipus complex began infiltrating my mind. Now that I knew she wasn't my real mother, the incest restrictive norms were slightly lifted and I felt freer to fantasize; except for the fact that she was still my father's wife. Thus, as I grew into my later teens, I had to wrestle with my mental and biological sexual drives fighting against my ethical and moral principles. I felt utterly hopeless, until I heard about a possible route to get away from the mess my life had become at the tender age of thirteen.

"It's super cool, dude, I bet you'd like it a lot," my oldest sister's boyfriend said to me as we chatted while he waited for her in the living room. "It's an experience like no other."

"Was it hard to be away from home on your own for weeks in a roll?" I asked wondering about the intrinsic challenges of what I imagined was a daunting change of environment.

"I'll tell you dude, once I got in the groove of it, I didn't even want to come back home even when I had to," he said displaying much enthusiasm for the place. "It's a life gig not to miss out."

A month later I was visiting the boarding school in the mountains in the outskirts of the state of Rio de Janeiro; a region colonized by Swiss immigrants who named the town New Fribourg. The elite private school named New Fribourg College had been modeled after the renowned Eton College in Great Britain. From the picturesque Gothic architecture of the building on the top of a mountain to the comprehensive curricula of educational activities, the school's founders envisioned to emulate the standards of Eton College to Latin American students. And like Eton catered to the developmental needs of the elite youth of British society, New Fribourg College fulfilled the same role for the privileged Brazilians and other Latin American students, as well as the children of foreign diplomats and businessmen.

Walking around the expansive quaint campus during the school break period felt like love at first stroll. The arboreal surroundings with brooks running down the mountain through the school grounds; the waterfall located a short hike away from the main building; the stereophonic music classroom; the swimming pool; the green soccer field; the large gymnasium with ample locker rooms; it was all very tantalizing to my senses. I was sold on the spot. As my sister's boyfriend said, "It was a life gig not to miss out."

"I want to come to this school," I said to my father who had accompanied me to visit the campus. "I think this is going to be really good for me."

"Are you sure you want to do this?" My father asked raising an eyebrow questioning my intention.

I felt a mix of concern and remorse in the tone of his voice. Perhaps he felt like he was the cause of my decision to wanting to enroll in the boarding school, which was partly true. I knew I had to get away from a home life I didn't feel able to fit in.

"Yes, I've got a strong hunch that this is the right place for me. I think I'm going to do well over here," I reiterated intuitively sure of my purpose.

"Alright, then," he said standing up. "Let's go to the administration office and get the white and green paperwork in order."

A couple of months later my father dropped me off for my first sojourn through what felt like a week in hell among mean-spirited fiends. Teenagers of all kinds roamed about like wild animals looking for rookies to haze. Long-haired wannabe hippies, muscular jocks, gangster enthusiasts, and even the nerd-looking ones carried a subtle threatening swagger about them. As a skinny 14-year-old student, I was a prime prey for the mob-like packs of famished hyenas. I spent the entire first week hiding around the building to avoid being tormented by the incessant hazing, which ranged from mild humiliation to physical hostility.

"If I stay here a second week, I might not make it to the third alive," I told my father over the phone while monitoring the foot traffic outside the phone booth in the school's main hallway. "This is not at all what I expected."

"Listen, stay one more week; and if you feel the same way, I'll come to pick you up," he said in a very calm and soothing voice as if he knew something I didn't, which he did because he attended the military academy. "Just another week to make sure this is what you want to do."

It was the best advice my father ever gave me. Albeit not nearly as dramatic and consequential as I would experience in a 36-hour period many years later in my life, eventually I realized that was the first time I attempted to quit a challenging worthy endeavor in the face of adversity. Considering how fundamental to my educational development my boarding school experience was, giving up that opportunity would have been costly to my personal growth. I ended up staying for the next three years of what turned out to be one of the most comprehensive educational experiences of my life. Once I got over the hump of the hazing craze, I started befriending many of my former tormenters. What at first felt to me like an elite of wild kids, soon I realized they were, as I was, troubled teenagers from well-to-do families who ended up at the school for various reasons. But for all their flaws and shortcomings, they were mostly good and smart adolescents who happened to have their own share of vicissitudes, which they acted out through aggressive behavior, meanness, and even occasional bouts of madness. And they were still there; they had not quit when it was their turn to undergo the trials of being a rookie.

In addition to the outstanding survival and self-reliance skills that the boarding school environment endowed me with, the traditional schooling I received was of the highest quality; the Latin American version of Eton education. From the best in arts and sciences to selective extra-curricular activities, I expanded my knowledge of mathematics, physics, literature, history, classical music, visual arts, theatre, and photography among other educational disciplines. But most importantly, my time at the boarding school was when I learned to love learning in a stimulating intellectual environment. Besides, in addition to the academic and empirical survival skills I acquired, I developed my budding young body through an exceptional physical education program.

However, as good as the traditional Eton-like education was, having to learn how to navigate a crowd of diverse wild teenagers in a confined environment was the ultimate self-preservation education a young man could get. It prepared me for what I'd experience a few years down the road when I left my country of birth for good.

☙❖❧

The serendipity of walking into the marine supply store at the marina's shopping center was a favorable turning point. Helena, the affable woman who welcomed me with a friendly smile, clued me in some most valuable information about the region's seasonal patterns, the movers and shakers, and life in the marina in general. She was in the know of everything and everyone who owned vessels and operated tourism-related business in the area.

"If you're trying to get some work, you're roughly two months too early before the season begins in earnest," she said when I expressed the purpose of my inquiries.

“Two months!” I repeated downheartedly thinking I wouldn’t be able to carry on the job at the hotel for another two weeks. I’d already experienced a similarly tedious job before my 36-hour tribulation and I was barely able to last a week. There are some jobs I know I cannot do even if my life depended on them.

She probably noticed the dejected intonation in my two-word statement, for her eyes glittered with empathetic expression that brought temporary solace to my discouragement.

“Wait a minute!” She said to herself as though she’d realized something unexpectedly. “Let me check something out and I’ll be right back.”

She went behind an open curtained area in the back of the store where I saw her opening a cabinet file and pulling out a folder she placed on the desk. Then, she jotted down some notes and came out with a piece of paper in hand.

“Here,” she said handing me a yellow index card with her handwriting on it. “This man is a Lisbon-based businessman who runs big game fishing and touring business in the summer. He always shows up this time of the year to set everything up and make sure his boats are ready to sail when the season starts. You might want to take a chance and walk by there in case he’s around since he usually comes down on the weekends. His fishing vessel is moored on pontoon H berth 7.”

“Thank you.” It was the only words that came out of my mouth, but they were infused with genuine appreciation.

“Good luck to you,” she said waving goodbye timidly as I stepped out of the store.

I immediately rushed to pontoon H where my hope for a positive change was harbored. As soon as I got there, I noticed that the bow deck hatch was lifted half-open. It was unlikely that the owner would have left it ajar unless he was around. He lived in

Lisbon, some five-hour drive down south to the marina; therefore leaving the hatch exposed to the elements for an entire week didn't make sense.

Having acquired much experience standing still for the past week, I stood up for a long time waiting for someone to show up. An hour-plus later, my patience paid off. A grayish sedan Citroën pulled over the parking space next to the pontoon. Two men got out of the car and headed down the ramp toward berth 7. The short one in the front smoking a cigarette walked with a subtle swagger; and the taller, older, and pudgy one seemed to stumble his cumbersome steps along trying to keep up with the other's peppery pace. I waited a few minutes, took a deep breath, and then walked down the metal wobbly ramp with the steadfastness of someone on a life and death mission. After introducing myself and cutting to the chase about the purpose of my unexpected appearance, I laid out my qualifications and job proposal for his consideration.

"What do you say?" I asked while he looked at me in the eye for a long time as if he sized up my character.

"Well, I suppose I could use some help preparing my boats for the upcoming season, and I don't have any problems with your sleeping onboard while working for me," he said zeroing in deeper into my right eye.

An unnerving pause ensued and filled the space with anticipation. He glanced at his taller companion, looked at me in the eye again, and then he said the words I longed to hear.

"I'm willing to pay you $80,000 escudos a month to carry out a list of tasks I'll give to you every week. If this sounds agreeable, you just got yourself a job."

"Excellent! I'm ready to get started right now," I said with cheerful disposition along with a friendly smile.

With the equivalent of approximately $500 dollars a month in wages but with no rent to pay, I figured it would keep my figurative boat afloat just fine; at least for the time being. Besides, I knew it would be a matter of time and I'd be making acquaintances and opportunities would come up once the season started. I was thrilled, until the other man witnessing my negotiation with the boss spoke up.

"That's impressive that you speak English and French. That will come in handy interacting with the tourists onboard," Manuel, the tall pudgy man remarked and the tone of his voice echoed subliminal envy.

"Yes, but my French is kind of remedial," I lied between my teeth trying to downplay my linguistic skills. I felt a compelling need to sidestep the envious energy darting my way, which it felt to me like a poisoned arrow. There was no reason for him to know that I'd studied French intensively for three years at the renowned—and expensive—Alliance Française and had just lived in French-speaking Switzerland before heading down to Portugal.

"Alright then," Afonso, the boats' owner, intervened probably picking on the awkward exchange between his buddy and me. "Let me show what needs to be done on this boat, and then we'll walk to *Celeste*, the touring vessel, for you to have an idea what needs to be done there."

"Let's do it," I said maintaining eye contact with a smile.

He replied with a half smile of his own and a subtle wink in the eye. Then, after inspecting both the fishing and touring vessels, we went through the list of chores before he handed me the keys to my new floating home.

By the time the stars dotted the night sky with their brilliance, I was all settled in the stern cabin of my new floating abode. The next morning I went to the hotel to submit my apologetic resignation to HR, but not before talking with the F&B manager who helped me get the job. His empathetic understanding made my cumbersome spiel slightly less so—and my gratitude immensely aggrandized. After taking care of my responsibilities with the hotel, I headed to the fishing village where I rented the small room next to a chicken coop in an old lady's backyard. I told her she could keep the balance of the rent money I paid in advance, picked up my two duffel bags with my worldly belongings, and eagerly headed to my new marine lifestyle; an experience that I'd treasure forever.

The southern region of Portugal known as Algarve is a major tourist destination for central and northern Europeans. With temperate weather, beautiful coastline, and friendly atmosphere, British, Germans, French, Scandinavians, and a slew of other nationalities flocked down to the region, particularly in the summer when the population doubled at a time when the Sun shone bright all day and nightlife burst at the seams. Lured by the beauty of the region, affordable real estate, and low cost of living, many foreigners were seasonal residents, including some of the boat owners. Among the latter group, a few were actually carefree itinerant sailors whose lifestyle appealed to me immensely.

I was first drawn to this way of life after befriending a young Scandinavian man I'd met in Switzerland. With unbridled enthusiasm, he shared with me his experiences in Spain's Costa del Sol during the sizzling southern European summer. He told me about the thrill of living onboard in the marina in Marbella and sailing all over the Mediterranean Sea. Because I was in the midst of a life-changing predicament at the time, his suggestion for me to give it a shot was an inspirational lifeline I desperately needed. I followed his recommendation and went to Marbella, but ended up in a different and yet very similar environment.

Vilamoura, the coastal town where the marina was located, was a budding hotspot for tourism in the early 1980s. As the highly touted Algarve region in the southern coast of Portugal was booming with both visitors and investors, developers got the whiff of profit in the sea salt air and built the marina, shopping centers, condominiums, golf courses, a casino, as well as the five-star hotel where I worked for five days. At the time of my almost year-long sojourn, the region seemed to be in the midst of a growing bust as more people and capital flocked to the area. But to me, the only thing that mattered was my new life at the marina. I never thought I would enjoy it as much as I did.

From the very first night I slept onboard I fell in love with the marine lifestyle. I remember lying on the deck wrapped up in a cozy wool blanket staring at the starry night sky feeling the best I had in a long time. The jingle of the sailing gears of numerous vessels gently hitting the masts sounded like symphony to my ears; a pleasant auditory sensation maximized by the olfactory delight of the intense sea breeze that permeated the air. After a long enjoyable multi-sensorial indulgence, I moved inside the cabin to retire for the evening. Ensconced in my bunk listening to the gentle sounds of the water softly bashing against the boat's hull, I felt like a happy infant being soothingly rocked to sleep in a special kind of water cradle. Having just gone through the most arduous and trying time of my life, a simple moment of utter serenity felt like a divine gift; some sort of recompense for overcoming the hardships I had recently endured. I felt as though Yemanjá, the Yoruba goddess of the oceans, had embraced me close to her bosom.

It was a matter of short time for the marina to feel like my home community. Although the hustling and bustling of the high season was yet to kick in, the excitement of living in that environment and making friends with the local boat residents felt like a primer for good things to come. Meanwhile, I worked diligently on the assignments that my boss designated to me in preparation for the upcoming season. And a few weeks before his boats were to be ready for business, he sent down from Lisbon the skipper of his 64-footer touring vessel to make sure everything was in order. As his deckhand, we sailed to the port town of Portimão for an engine tune up. It was my first experience at sea—and my first warning to what I should watch out for.

"Manuel is a cocksucker," the skipper said with a toothpick sticking out of the corner of his mouth while we sailed back from Portimão. "That fucker ain't good for nothing but trouble. The only reason the boss gave him a job is because they were friends back in Angola before the Communists took over the country. And because he suspects I'm a Communist, he gives me shit all the time. I tell you, you got watch out for that motherfucker."

"Since I'm not a Communist, he might leave me alone" I said jokingly trying to diffuse the intensity of his temperament.

"Are you a Christian?" He asked abruptly looking at me askance.

"Not any more than I am a Communist," I said.

"Manuel is a fucking Church-going Christian; and if you're not one, you're already in his wrong side," he said with his voice echoing distress. "Whenever people tell me they're Christians my defenses go up right away. They are the worst hypocrites of all."

After that unexpected exchange, I thought I probably should channel some Christian sentiment and pray that Manuel would be out of my way. I'd just landed a good gig I was very excited about that was still in its fledgling moments. I was beginning to get a good taste of what marine lifestyle was about—and I was absolutely loving it. Besides, the summer season had not even started yet and I was looking forward to it. The last thing I wanted was to be troubled unnecessarily; neither by Manuel nor any unexpected circumstances for that matter.

Alas, I was troubled by both.

My time at the boarding school was the most important three years of my adolescence. Undoubtedly, it was the defining formative period of my personal development. It established the foundation upon which I was able to grow into my full potential as an independent young man, an avid learner, and a survivalist. Having to fend for myself among a couple of hundred unruly teenage boys every day for three years was a special type of education in and by itself; one that bestowed upon me a unique set of skills that were to benefit me greatly in the future. Everything about that schooling experience contributed to the man I grew into being.

Located in an idyllic mountain setting some 3,000 feet above sea level, the ample campus itself offered an advantageous environment for living and learning. Surrounded by lush vegetation, mammoth boulders, and a gurgling serpentine brook running near the state of the art gymnasium, the school grounds were like an oasis of tranquility far away from the raucous city of Rio de Janeiro. As it was, the surroundings offered me a space of serenity even in the midst of the frenzy behavior of wild teenagers. And even though I'd always been aware of the high quality education the school provided, I didn't realize how much I appreciated the enormous environmental benefit of the campus until the year I decided it was time to leave and continue my education in the city. Perhaps it was an unwise decision, though one never knows the hidden purposes behind one's actions.

The truth is that at 17-years-old, I felt ready and motivated to experience new adventures beyond the confinements of the boarding school. Also, most of my close friends were moving on and leaving the school at the same time as well. Furthermore, I had an additional reason igniting my decision to move back to the city: love; yes, I was in love with my girlfriend whom in the past three years I saw a couple of weekends per month. The rest of the time, we exchanged passionate loving letters on a regular basis as our epistolary romance gradually grew into some genuine teenage love. We decided that it would be great to attend the same school and be with each other every day. It ended up being another ill-advised decision.

All of a sudden my life took an unexpected inauspicious turn. While in the boarding school I woke up to birds chirping, now the jarring sound of the obnoxiously loud alarm-clock jolted me out of bed every morning at 5:00 am. At the boarding school, the first thing I saw looking out the window in the morning was a magnificent mountain view. Now, I could barely see my own shadow in the dark wall of my bedroom. At the boarding school, I ate breakfast leisurely in the cafeteria with my friends, but now I ran a different schedule. After shoving down some peanut butter-smeared toast washed down with lukewarm *café au lait*, I rushed to the bus stop to wait for the next crowded bus to take me to the heart of downtown Rio. On a good traffic day, it was an approximately 45-minute ride standing up and crammed together with other somnolent passengers heading to their own daily misery. Once I arrived at my destination, I'd walk through busy streets to a building where my new college preparatory school was located on the fifth floor. Sitting at my desk distracted by the uninterrupted buzzing of city life, I used to look out and indulge in recollecting the sceneries of the boarding school's surroundings compared with the mountains of tall buildings before my sleep-deprived eyes. Then, at both recess and lunch break, I'd spend time with my girlfriend—every day! It was too dramatic a change; a traumatizing transformation I wasn't prepared for. It'd be a matter of time all of it had to come to a merciful end.

By mid-school year I had unofficially dropped out. Although I always enjoyed studying and had a genuine passion for learning, the changed circumstances in my life were acting like a fire extinguisher putting out the flame of my interest in education. The pressure to prepare for taking the highly competitive college entry exam was more about familiarizing with test-taking techniques than the actual learning of meaningful knowledge. I became so disturbed with that new way of life that I resumed consuming all sorts of drugs for therapeutic relief—and I took them before, during, and after school hours. The effects of my assiduous drugs consumption spilled over to my relationship with my girlfriend as we separated piecemeal. Notwithstanding, my precipitous academic performance—a blatant contrast with my stellar honor roll status in the previous three years—triggered an avalanche of conflicts with my father who now found a good reason to tyrannize me with presumptive justification.

Although I resumed my schooling in earnest the following year, my father insisted that it was time for me to start working with him in his business. Thus, for the next couple of years I went to school and worked every day—and did very well at both. In fact, I passed the highly competitive college entrance program and got to the university of my choice. Surprisingly, working with my father turned out not to be as bad as I'd fretted. Somehow the working together, the shared meals in the office, and the meaningful conversations we had on the drive home after work, all contributed to bridging what at times felt like an immeasurable chasm between us. Perhaps his sharing of the heartrending sorrow the sudden death of my mother inflicted on him sparked an enormous empathy for him, though not enough for my validating the emotional and verbal abuse he often dished out to me. But all things considered, our working relationship was thriving, and so were my college studies. I felt I was in a good space and going in the right direction, until my stepmother seemed to have felt unjustifiably threatened by my good working relationship with my father at a time his business was beginning to take off to the next level of prosperity.

Soon she decided she wanted to work in the business, too. Shortly thereafter, she insisted that my half-brother got involved as well, albeit with barely physical presence. In a matter of short time my relationship with my father—work and otherwise—went downhill fast and, if it were possible, got even worse than before. Cunningly able to control my father like a puppet on a string, my stepmother found a way into his emotional weakness and manipulated the situation with devilish mastery. Making all the decisions from behind the scenes while setting him up as the legitimate culprit and spokesperson of her wishes, she was in charge without having to assume any blame for the untoward changes taking place. Through his draconian edicts, she determined that I would carry the heavy load of duties and responsibilities at work while her son would have the privileges and special treatments. We were to be paid exactly the same wages regardless of our functions and hours of work, both of which differed significantly. Indeed, she created an unbearable situation for me to continue working with my father. Unable to cope with the growing disharmony of the unpleasant and unfair work environment, I quit.

Turning the focus to my education, I started methodically planning the livelihood path of my future. With a diplomatic career in mind, I needed to have at least two years of college credits under my belt and be fluent in two foreign languages before qualifying to apply for the diplomatic core. Thus, I amplified my already good knowledge of the English language, which I'd been studying from a very young age, and commenced my dedicated studies of French at the prestigious and pricey Alliance Française. In spite of all the troubles I endured with my father, I was always grateful that he didn't economize to finance my high quality education, as well as making sure I had the resources I needed to be an accomplished student. Perhaps because he didn't have the same opportunities he was able to offer his children, education was very important to him, which benefited me greatly.

Like many instances in my future would prove to be true, planning is often times a futile activity. Just when I thought I was finally heading in the right direction, the train carrying the hopes of my good fortune derailed in a disappointing educational detour. My goals of pursuing a diplomatic career abruptly stalled in the School of Social Sciences at the Federal University of Rio de Janeiro under a brutal military dictatorship.

❧ ❖ ❧

It was mid-May and the high season was just beginning to warm up to the excitement of the fast approaching summer. Soon, small parties of northern European tourists would start arriving and add brio to the Algarve region. Likely eager for a relief from the bitterly cold northern winter, they flocked down south as if hungry for an appetizer of the Sun before the summer banquet was open for business. In my turn, I got a preview of what awaited ahead, and I was noticeably excited about it. My maiden voyage as a crew member aboard the big game fishing vessel had arrived.

"*Bienvenue à bord,*" I greeted an attractive petite brunette French lady while holding her hand as she stepped on deck. "*Je vous souhaite une bonne journée avec nous.*"

"*C'est très gentil, monsieur. Merci,*" she said smiling with a playful glitter in the eye that I perceived as an appreciative return to my subtly flirtatious chivalry.

Standing on the pontoon a few feet away from the boarding ramp, Afonso, the boss, and Manuel, his acolyte, watched me attentively as I welcomed the customers alternating between English and French, or Portuguese according to individual needs and preferences. Afonso grinned at me and nodded as if to tell me I was doing a great job. Manuel, on the other hand, pouted his chicken ass thin lips as if he were experiencing digestive uneasiness. His face looked like a bad omen. I knew I should not have looked at him.

By the time we got to quite a few nautical miles offshore—far enough to barely be able to see land—the engine was turned off and the vessel was adrift in a supposedly fish rich sea region. Under my linguistic guidance, Manuel, the skipper, and I assisted the tourists with their fishing poles as they spread around the 58-foot fishing cruiser tossing their baits of hope in the water. Once they were all set up, I realized something was not well with me. It was a matter of time for the constant swinging of the boat to make me feel nauseated. I tried to avoid going into the cabin where it made me feel worse, but it was part of my job to prepare and serve the appetizers and drinks for the customers. It was a struggle, but I kept at it the best I could while making a great effort not to vomit. And just when I thought my situation couldn't get worse, it did.

"There's an issue with the head that needs immediate attention," Manuel said as I'm stepping down into the cabin. "You need to go there and do something about it. I'll take care of the folks on the deck."

Swaying and stumbling along toward the head, the stench coming from inside did not bode well; neither to my stomach nor to my anticipation of what lay ahead (no pun intended). I opened the folding metal door of the confining toilet area, and there it was staring at me in defying fashion: a ginormous fetid fat turd curving around the latrine. I pressed the flushing button but the water pressure didn't stand a chance against such a magnanimous human waste. My stomach convulsed and I was on the verge of losing it. I rushed up to the deck with a bucket in hand to gather some sea water in the hopes of sinking that stubborn monster to the bottom of the holding tank. As soon as showed up on the deck, the good-looking French lady approached me from behind.

"*Salut*," she greeted me with a mischievous tone of voice. "Would you help me set up my bait to the hook?"

"I need to fill this bucket with water and I'll be right back to assist you," I barely managed to reply while making an extraordinary effort to disguise my growing indisposition. Then, all of a sudden the urge to puke became irrepressible. Terrified of embarrassment, I quickly leaned overboard and vomited at the same time I tossed the bucket out at sea with my back to her. Somehow I managed to pull it off as she didn't seem to notice the state of my digestive distress; until she unwittingly aggravated it further.

"I'll go with you," she said not-so-subtly flirting with me.

"No…no, it's o.k. I'll be right back," I said wishing I could hang myself with the rope attached to the bucket. I was feeling terribly nauseated.

My pleading fell into deaf French ears, for she followed me down into the cabin smiling as though she had ulterior motives. However, her peppery manner quickly vanished as soon as the malodorous whiff assaulted our nostrils. And because I had left the head door open, she couldn't help but take a good unexpected look at the massive fetid culprit. She looked at me with undeniable disappointment; and since I was feeling and looking unwell, she probably thought that I was the creator of that magnum opus excrement. At that moment, I felt even more ashamed than I was sick.

"Did you take care of…," Manuel said barging into the cabin. When he saw the beautiful French lady there with me in such a compromising situation, he grinned and walked back up without saying another word.

The skipper was right: Manuel was full of shit; and I had no doubt that disgusting human waste fiend came out of his dirty ass.

Alas, my maiden voyage sank in a sea of embarrassment and disappointment. But worst of all was realizing that I had a serious problem to overcome if I were to pursue my newly found marine lifestyle. Seasickness was a tall order challenge that intimidated me in many levels. I know of no worse physical feeling than succumbing to debilitating vertigo—and I ended up experiencing countless episodes throughout my life. But now that my livelihood depended on it, the stakes were much higher than in the earlier days of my life when I'd been prone to motion sickness. All of a sudden, queasiness was much more than an unbearable neurological sensation; it'd become a survival issue. But how could I deal with a feeling that's like a knock-out punch capable of flooring even the toughest man? I had to find a solution to this pressing problem squashing my hopes to live the marine lifestyle.

My second adventure at sea was surprisingly pleasant. It was aboard the 64-footer cruising yacht that sailed along the shore of the Algarve between Vilamoura and Albufeira. Since the vessel was in constant motion in relatively placid sea conditions, my disposition was not disturbed by equilibrium-crippling sideway motions. Not only I didn't feel nauseated, I actually enjoyed the cruise. However, once I was back on the fishing boat, my navigational challenges resumed with a vengeance. After the third fishing tour, I knew I wouldn't be able to carry on my duties again in functional capacity. I had to work something out with the boss.

"But I need you on the fishing boat as much as I do on the cruise," Afonso objected to my suggestion to working on the cruise ship only. "You're going to put me in a bind."

"I can welcome the tourists aboard, explain everything they need to know before going out to sea; and from there on Manuel and the skipper can take over," I said in a desperate attempt to convince the boss that I was in a bind of my own. It was not only my job I was trying to hold on to, but my home as well.

Afonso looked at Manuel as if gauging his nonverbal reaction to my suggestion. It seemed to me that the boss was willing to consider going along with my compromising proposal, but the grumpy expression in Manuel's face conveyed opposition, which he did not hesitate to verbalize.

"This is not going to work out well," Manuel said addressing Afonso and ignoring me altogether. "You know we need someone to work onboard both vessels. This can't be a pick-and-choose what he wants to do. This is no way to run a business, Afonso."

"What do you suggest then?" Afonso asked Manuel as I stood there nervously watching the interaction deciding my kismet.

"If he can't handle the sea he shouldn't work on boats. It'll be a matter of time and he'll start getting seasick on the cruising tour, too," Manuel said in prosecutorial style.

"What do we do then?" Afonso pressured him again.

"It's early in the season and we can find somebody else who can handle the job," Manuel replied before turning around to look at me at last. "Just fire him."

And just like that, in the spur of an unfortunate moment, I was out of a job and homeless again.

❧❖☙

Dreams can dissipate in shallow expectations as quickly as they are fabricated in the depths of ardent wishes. Plans, too, often dissolve like cool ice cubes on hot surfaces they are not suitable to endure. And so my hopes of pursuing a diplomatic career washed away in another disappointment with a dysfunctional educational system. But unlike the boredom of high school where I'd endured didactic drudgery that threatened to stifle my passion for learning, in the School of Social Sciences at Federal University of Rio de Janeiro it became a dangerous affair.

"Did you hear what happened to Paulo?" I overhead a female student in pigtails whisper to a peer while staffing a political awareness display booth on campus.

I pretended to be aloof observing the banner draping the table they stood behind. On it, an image of Jesus Christ juxtaposed to one of Ernesto "Che" Guevara (1928–1967) had an intriguing inscription that called my attention. It read: "What do these men have in common? They were both revolutionaries who paid the ultimate price in the struggle for what they believed in."

"What happened to Paulo?" The bearded male student wearing large black square-framed eyeglasses inquired whispering in an even lower tone of voice.

"He was whisked away yesterday by undercover federal agents and nobody knows where he is," the girl replied almost inaudibly. "I'm scared. I wonder who's going to be next."

Although I was certain it wouldn't be me—not only I was not involved in any political activities, but I was the son of a military officer—the incident bothered me a great deal. And the more I heard of other kidnapping cases in different campuses, the more aggravated I became. I started wondering whether I wanted to join the diplomatic core of a country whose government abducted its young college students for exercising their freedom of speech, association, or political affiliation. But when I learned about the horrific torturing practices the agents of oppression carried out on their captured victims, I realized I did not want to represent an abhorrent criminal government that disregarded both the rights and welfare of its citizens.

Nevertheless, I managed to continue my studies focusing on earning an undergraduate degree in sociology. My career goal shifted to pursuing graduate studies to become a college professor. Unfortunately, my new plan did not go as I anticipated either. Uninterested in cultivating minds to think critically about socioeconomic and political issues, the Federal Government sponsoring the university system defunded schools they labeled as "infiltrated with subversive activities," which the sociology and political science departments sat on the top of the list. The ensuing precipitous drop in the already mediocre quality of education was the coup de grace that compelled me to drop out of college in the middle of my sophomore year. I put my schooling on hiatus and would not recommence it until many years later. Now I had to reevaluate my options for my professional future. I hit a wall of uncertainty and did not know what to do next.

With both my diplomatic and professorship career goals flushed down the military dictatorship toilet bowl, I reconsidered resuming working at my father's business again; but that option gave me the heebie-jeebies every time the thought passed through my mind. Then, an unexpected opportunity for comprehensive self-didactic education came up through my oldest sister's career change. Once she became a flight attendant for the German airline Lufthansa, a whole new world opened up to me.

Unbeknownst to me at the time, my passion for traveling was initiated a few years earlier when my other sister had married a Nebraska farmer she met while on a student exchange program. During the several times I came to the United States to visit her, I became earnestly enthused with traveling. Hence, by the time my oldest sister landed the Lufthansa job that allowed me to fly on a stand-by basis for only 15 percent of the airfare cost, I took advantage of the opportunity as I indulged in regular travels to Europe and the United States. In several occasions, I traveled for months throughout Western Europe. Hung out with my British friends in London's Piccadilly Circus; entertained myself with naughty girls in Amsterdam's red light district; had croissant, cheese, and wine—for breakfast—in Paris; and even flew out of Frankfurt airport in the cockpit of a DC10 jetliner, which would be impossible under today's security protocol. I happened to be in Frankfurt at the time of the famous Frankfurt Book Fair and all the flights out of town were booked up to capacity. Unable to get a seat with my stand-by ticket, I pleaded my case with the airline staff stressing my financial urgency to get to my next destination.

The captain of the aircraft took pity on me and let me fly in the cockpit, which was an amazing experience. However, it was a train trip from Lincoln, Nebraska to San Francisco, California that would prove to be a life-changing event, although I wouldn't know it until many years later when I faced a very challenging situation without knowing what to do with my life.

Bored stiff in the bone-chilling winter of Nebraska in one of my many visits to my sister and brother-in-law, I decided to board an Amtrak train to California to visit the Golden State for the first time. After a couple of weeks in the Bay Area spending a lot of time at the UC Berkeley campus (I dreamed of resuming my college education at the university I held in high regards), going to Marin County, Oakland, visiting Chinatown, the Golden Gate Bridge Park, Fisherman's Wharf, and all the tourist destinations of that extraordinary city, eventually it was time to return to what I used to call "the N land of the triple Cs;" that is, Nebraska, the land of cold, corn, and cows. Although I begrudgingly boarded the train back to Nebraska, that trip played a fundamental role in the shaping of my future many years later—and at a time when I had hit rock bottom.

"Is this seat taken?" The blond blue-eyed stereotypically beautiful California girl asked me.

"Not anymore," I said while removing a book I had placed on the vacant seat next to mine. Then I smiled at her aiming my brown arrows deep into the blue iris target of her eyes.

She winked at me mischievously, stowed away her backpack in the overhead compartment and sat down next to me.

"I'm Dawn," she said giving me her soft skinned hand. "Where are you heading to?"

"Lincoln, Nebraska," I said still holding her hand.

"I'm getting off in Denver," she said seemingly content to continue holding my hand.

From that moment onward there was quite a bit of holding happening—and some talking, too. We hit it off on all cylinders, which made the long travel a pleasant passing of time experience. By dusk we'd already established a nice bond and the making out went into higher gear. We moved to the back of the car where it was inconspicuously dark and allowed us to give in to uninhibited passion. We both wanted to go all the way, but the sleeper car was expensive and neither one of us could afford it. As it was, our own personal joyride could not be completed to the ultimate climatic destination.

Sooner than I wished, the train arrived in Denver and it was time for Dawn and me to bid farewell. We exchanged contact information and promises to keep in touch. Although our time together was relatively limited, the quality—and even more so the significance—of our encounter was boundless in manifold ways. Throughout the other leg of my trip to Lincoln, Nebraska, I kept wondering about how time can be measured beyond quantification, but even more so as a qualitative experience. That's when I understood Albert Einstein's (1879–1955) facetious explanation of his Theory of Relativity: "When you sit with a nice girl for two hours, it seems like two minutes. When you sit on a hot stove for two minutes, it seems like two hours. That's relativity." In fact, many years later I would learn that even love can be found, shared, and fulfilled in a short span of hours.

Dawn and I corresponded on a regular basis for the next years when I was back in Rio. Her last letter to me was a lifeline thrown to me at a time I was drowning in desperation. It not only rescued me, but the uncanny timing of her letter's arrival set me up for a series of events that were to transform my life forever.

For the next couple of days after being fired from my first boat job, I wandered about aimlessly unsure of what to do next. I went back to sleeping on the beach, but this time I found a sheltered cove on a different spot far from the fishing village. Dispirited and disillusioned with what seemed like a perpetual cycle of continuous challenges, I started spiraling down in a similar pattern I endured during my 36-hour ordeal. Both emotionally and financially, I couldn't afford to go through it again, for I didn't think I'd be able to survive it. I had to make it happen somehow. I could not quit again.

The morning I woke up with a tiny white crab tickling my face, I arose determined to stop moping and replace it with unwavering will to create something out of nothing. Stagnation is the preemptive kiss of death of action, for without motion no energy can be generated; and without energy nothing happens and it's back to stagnation in full circle. It's an inauspicious vicious cycle.

I wanted to swing by the marine supply store to pick Helena's brain again, but I felt embarrassed to come back to her after having already failed in such a short period of time. Instead, I decided to go to the marina's administration office at the harbor's entrance. I wasn't sure what I expected to find there, but I followed my gut feeling and went to check it out anyway.

As I walked in the lobby area I was immediately disappointed. Other than a small green couch, a coffee table covered with nautical publications, snack and pop vending machines on the corner, and a small office that happened to be closed when I came in, there was absolutely nothing else there—and not a soul in sight either. I was about to turn around and head out the door when I noticed a rectangular cork bulletin board near the office's door. I paused, frowned, and walked toward it with anticipatory curiosity. There, amidst pinned business cards, sale items notices, and a slew of miscellaneous messages, I found a handwritten index card that read: "Weekend deckhand help wanted. For information call…" I yanked the card off the board and searched for the nearest telephone booth in the marina shopping area. I was a man on a mission.

After talking with the boat's owner on the phone, we made arrangements to meet on Saturday morning at the pontoon address of his mooring vessel. Saturday arrived not a day too soon.

"I pay $6,000 escudos a month," the tall bearded young man said after we got acquainted. "I know it's not much, but it's for Saturday work only. I need help sailing some twelve tourists or so to a secluded beach for an all-day picnic. Is it something you'd be interested?"

"What about if I live onboard and you don't have to pay me at all?" I countered his offer without hesitating. More than piddly chomp change what I really needed was a home. Besides, I figured I might be able to find some odd jobs during the week to keep a cash flow stream.

Unlike me, he hesitated to answer. He looked at his 46-foot wooden schooner as if asking a woman whether she acquiesced allowing me to sleep with her. I took a quick glance at her thinking of the great nights we'd have together.

"Alright," he said. "But on Friday and Saturday nights when I'm here you'll have to find another place to sleep. Unless it is my girlfriend, I don't like companions when I sleep onboard."

"Not a problem," I said without a second thought. Ending my homelessness was my most pressing priority.

We shook hands and just like that I had a home yet again. Next, I needed to find any kind of work, which proved to be much more challenging than I'd anticipated.

Although my accommodation on his boat was not quite as spacious and comfortable as my previous floating home, I was delighted to be living onboard again. Bedtime was the best. The sleep-inducing swinging accompanied by the sounds of water gently bashing against the hull was a nighttime treat I looked forward every day. It was a simple pleasure of tranquility that nurtured my battered self immensely. Besides having a sheltered place to ensconce my loneliness at night, having access to a galley (kitchenette), a head (bathroom), and electricity were luxuries that added great value to my precarious situation. In all, it beat the dark and cold al fresco way of life of homelessness. Except for the lack of income, I was in a good space, until he started showing up on Friday nights.

The first sailing tour for the picnic on a quaint isolated beach was better than I expected, albeit it was a hard day's work. In addition to helping sail the boat while attending to the tourists' needs, I had to transport both people and supplies on a large inflatable dinghy from and to the vessel anchored in a horseshoe-shaped bay. After barbecuing and serving meals, I had to collect all the trash with large heavy duty plastic bags to take them back to the marina where I had to dispose of them in the dumpster. It was no wonder why by late afternoon when I could spot the marina's entrance starboard and portside lights blinking in the distance, I was already spent—and at night I could not sleep onboard. But I was content, and more importantly, feeling grateful that I didn't get seasick, which fueled further my determination to pursue the marine lifestyle. All was well, until an issue crept up on the following weekend that didn't bode favorable promises to my future circumstances.

"I noticed the varnishing on the edge of the bow's deck is peeling off and getting all cracked up," he said shortly before leaving on Sunday evening. "It'd be nice if you would take care of it. I keep some sanding paper, brushes, and a can of varnish in the tools cabinet."

I looked at him straight in the eye waiting to hear how much he was going to pay me for the job, but not a sound came out of his mouth. I didn't say a word either. Instead, I let my eyes do the talking while holding unwavering eye contact with him.

"Listen, I don't make much money with this Saturday gig," he said trying to validate his stinginess under the silent justifiable demand I made. "I do this for fun; something to look forward to on the weekend. And besides, mooring my boat in this marina costs me a lot of money."

"And yet you offered to pay me when we first spoke," I said maintaining a disapproving eye contact. "We have an agreement and I'm sticking to it. I hope you are, too. If you want me to do any additional work other than what we've agreed on, we're going to have to renegotiate our arrangement."

"Never mind. I'll take care of it myself at some later date," he said dashing away unreasonably miffed.

Watching him walking away muttering expletives between his teeth was my cue. I knew my days sleeping on his boat were counted. I surmised that he probably realized I had nowhere to go and wanted to make a serf out of me. At that moment, on Sunday, I felt more exhausted than I did the day before. Perhaps emotional fatigue is denser than physical weariness.

I woke up in the morning feeling downhearted and hopeless. It seemed like I was riding an unstoppable rollercoaster of ups and downs in a series of ongoing travails. Every now and then the thought of quitting jet-swept through my mind, but I made it sure to brush it aside at will. I'd already done it once and learned how miserably painful it can feel, At that point, I'd rather die persevering than feeling dead while still alive. Eager to quiet my mind and assuage my emotions, I decided to go to the marina shopping center to get a cup of coffee.

Upstairs in the marina shopping area there was an eatery that served good coffee; and the fellow who tended the store and I were in the process of striking a friendship. He was a very amicable man who flashed the most beautiful toothless smile I'd ever seen. A biracial Angolan refugee, José and I ended up becoming good friends. And that day my friend-to-be had a present for me.

"You should go check it out," he said with zest clearly wanting to be of help to me. I'd just shared with him my tenuous housing predicament when he filled me in on an opportunity he'd just learned about.

"It seems to be a good job in a charming hotel in Vale do Lobo; it's not far away from here. The pay is not shabby either, and it comes with room and board besides," he said while handing me the newspaper with the advertisement of the position circled in red pen ink. "It's a summer job only, but at least for a few months you can get something going."

I took the newspaper from his hand, thanked him, and walked out with mixed feelings. I was so gung-ho about pursuing my newly found marine lifestyle that the idea of working in a hotel again was slightly disconcerting to me. However, considering my circumstances and the nature of the job, I owed it to myself to check it out. After all, as enjoyable as living onboard felt to me, working as a lifeguard on a private hotel beach watching over northern European women with a proclivity to sunbathing topless sounded like the perfect summer job to me. Besides, I could always resume my pursuit of the marine lifestyle at a later date. The more I thought about it, the more enthused I became with the opportunity at hand.

Suddenly, I was beaming with excitement and anticipatory thrill about the possibility of landing the most ideal summer job. Then, as I turned around the corner, my exhilaration was magnified when I saw Heidi, the beautiful German girl I'd met a few days earlier. Gesturing and calling me over to where she sat at a table having tea on the terrace of a charming coffee shop by the promenade, I picked up my pace with a ear-to-ear grin thinking this was my opportunity to get a step closer to first base with her.

As Einstein facetiously explained his Theory of Relativity, spending a long time with a pretty girl can feel like a brief moment. After chatting for a long time over a cup of tea sweetened by Heidi's company, I realized I'd spent more time talking with her than I intended. Abruptly, I excused myself and rushed toward my original destination in the nearby resort of Vale do Lobo where a potential employment opportunity was at stake.

The hotel wasn't quite as fancy as the one I'd worked as a doorman some weeks earlier, but it was uniquely charming in a picturesque location with a pleasant atmosphere. I was confident that my work experience there would be infinitely more fulfilling than the drudgery of my previous employ. A spurt of excitement triggered my faster moving feet toward the HR office I had been guided to go. Then, even before getting the interview formally started, my anticipation turned into another heartrending disappointment.

"What a bummer! You would be a perfect fit for this job," the HR manager said after I gave him my elevator spiel about my background and qualifications. "A surfer that can speak English and French, and with international experience to top it off; now, that's the ideal candidate for this position I was hoping to hire."

I was flummoxed and I couldn't conceal my dismay. I felt the furrowing in my brow as my excitement was brusquely hijacked by his words that I could not comprehend yet.

"I just interviewed somebody else about 30 minutes ago; and I offered him the job," he said and the tone of his voice revealed his own disappointment, which was a quantum of disenchantment in comparison to mine. "If I had interviewed you before him; oh man, this job has your name all over it."

"Thirty minutes ago," I mumbled in disbelief.

"I'll tell you what," he said obviously noticing I was distraught. "Come see me again early next year and this summer job will be yours; guaranteed."

"Thirty minutes ago," I repeated quietly in my mind while shaking hands with him before leaving his office.

I walked out of the hotel feeling utterly deflated and stunned. I could not believe the insidious hard luck that seemed to shadow me like a haunting ghost in the foggy prospect of my future. I began wondering whether I was experiencing quitting in reverse; that is, the object of my pursuit quit on me every time I attempted to reach out for it. Overwhelmed by a flood of negative emotions, I realized the levy was about to burst with torrential tears. From the beach that could have been my summer outdoor office, I decided to embark on a doleful long walk back to the marina by the coastline. Alone and unobserved, I cried uninterruptedly while cussing intermittently. I felt as though I'd been hexed by some eerie occult force that hindered my progress with pertinent obtrusion. However, what was tormenting me the most was self-inflicted; the fact that the time I stopped to hang out with Heidi might have cost me a summer gig to remember. Had I not spent time with her, I would have likely been interviewed in time to get the ideal summer job.

As I cried, moped, and verbalized my uncontained frustration out loud to myself, I thought about the nature of time and how timing is of the essence in the outcome of events I could not control. How could I have missed such a perfect job at a time I was in dire straits? What an untoward consequence of bad timing—or so I conjectured without knowing better.

Unbeknownst to me at the time, not getting that "perfect job" was the greatest blessing in disguise. Although it seemed hard to beat watching topless babes sunbathing while hoping they might need to be rescued in the water, the real perfect job was just awaiting me around the corner. And had I been offered that summer job, which would end in three months, I'd never have landed one of the most exciting gigs of my life with no expiration date.

Drenched in tears of frustration while dragging my desolation with shuffling feet, I had no idea that I was on the verge of a turning point leading to my coveted marine lifestyle. My life was about to undergo a grandiose turnaround of good fortune at last.

Eventually the day arrived. After my traveling period in *laissez-faire* way of life, my savings ran out and I desperately needed to work again. The problem was the timing. The challenge of finding employment when a major economic downturn is rolling down the hill can turn into an avalanche of discouragement. And in Latin America it can be even more dispiriting. Hyperinflation was running amok in Brazil at the time and there was no work to be found. I had no choice but to ask my father for a job and resume working in his business. If I wanted cash in my wallet, I'd have to fold my pride and shove it in my trouser's pocket.

Hesitatingly, he gave me a job—along with a truckload of grief. It was a matter of short time for me to realize that, as I would learn later in my life, there are certain jobs I simply cannot hold. In this case, however, it was not the nature of the work itself, but the relationships in the doing of the work. With my stepmother solidly anchored in the day-to-day business, it was blatantly obvious to me that she felt threatened by my presence. She made me feel as if I were *persona non grata* in that working environment. Now, even my youngest half-brother, who would take over the business after my father's passing many years later, started showing up daily after school. Since it was obvious to everyone that my older half-brother was dimwittedly incompetent to carry out the managerial responsibilities of the business, she did not waste any time to plug in the one who might have a shot at succeeding. She—and my father at her petition—had to prime the youngest for the future. As for me, the only place I held in her plan was to be out. Turning routine interactions into daily conflicting drudgery seemed like an effective way to achieve the intended goal. They didn't have to fire me; they just made it so unbearable for me to endure the everyday ordeal until I had no reasonable option but to quit, again. But this time, my father issued a warning that it was a game changer for me. I believed then—and I still do today—that because he knew my character well, he spoke to make sure it was the last time he would have to.

"It's really hard finding a job out there these days," he said with a subtle smirk that bothered me to the core. "It's a matter of time and you'll be coming back begging for a job again."

As soon as he finished his assertion, we both knew it was the end of it. Sadly, I also knew that deep inside he wanted me to work with him, but he couldn't contradict his wife's will. She was in the control center stealthily calling the shots that he verbalized.

Out of a job in an increasingly worsening economic recession, I felt fortunate to land a part-time gig in a fledgling travel agency. A former classmate of mine at the Alliance Française had just started her business and I lucked out to have contacted her at time she needed help. Martha was a beautiful and intelligent young divorcée whom I had the hots for since the first day of class; and it was obvious to me that the attraction was mutual. However, once she hired me, she took on a professional stance and managed to create distance between the fine line separating the sexual woman from the sensible boss. Although I lamented the unexpected behavioral change, I respected her ability to not let her intimate personal interests interfere with business affairs. Besides, there was red-haired Ruth; the cute, petite, and sexy, office assistant with whom I spent a lot of sultry time after work—and sometimes even during lunch hour in the closed office. The hussy assistant and I did a fair amount of erotic overtime work.

The job itself was fun and the salacious perk was a welcomed unofficial employment benefit. My work involved taking foreign tourists on casual tours of Rio, assist with marketing strategies, and help out with some office work. Not only I enjoyed working there, but I was also glad to help Martha build her dream business from its fledgling stage. Although I was having fun on the job, the work was sporadic and the pay was not nearly enough to meet my needs. I knew that sooner rather than later I would have to make some changes. I just didn't have a clue of what to do, until Martha assigned me to take a septuagenarian Greek businessman on a tour of the self-proclaimed "Wonderful City."

"It sounds like you've done quite a bit of travelling," he remarked as we conversed while drinking a super cold beer at a sidewalk bar on Copacabana beach on a super hot Rio day. "And you speak English and French, too. It seems to me you're primed to take the next step."

"What do you mean by the next step?" I asked not understanding what the link was between my travels and linguistic skills with following initiatives.

"Well, not long ago you alluded to your current situation, which I assumed to be obvious that you're stuck in a dead-end job," he said making me regret having inadvertently self-disclosed too much information. After all, I'd just met him, though I felt trustingly at ease around him. He was one of those few elders who exude the wisdom of the years, whereas many older folks just seem to drag the years along the path of time.

"What does my dead-end job has to do with the next step?" I insisted on having a straightforward answer.

"Are you married?" He asked dodging my question at the same time frustrating my intent to get a direct answer.

"No, I'm not," I said curtly trying to camouflage my irritation. "What does my marital status have to do with next step?"

He placed his sweating beer mug and elbows on the table, and with his fingers interlaced he leaned forward toward me. Even before speaking, his penetrating gaze heralded the answer I was after.

"You are young, you don't have stable work, and you don't have a family to support. There's nothing holding you back from adventuring into life's extraordinary possibilities. Maybe it's time for you to embark on a different kind of travelling," he said while running his indicator finger around the brim of his beer mug.

"What do you mean by a different kind of travelling?" I asked still confused but now very interested in specific details.

He took a good swig and wiped off the foam from his thick white mustache before answering. "Travelling as a tourist is a convenient way to see the world. However, it's not nearly the same as travelling as a wanderer; a world vagabond. You can learn a lot about what you're made of when you're on your own in survival mode."

As soon as he finished his sentence, a book from one of my literary heroes, Hermann Hesse (1877–1962), came to mind right away. *Knulp*, the book's title and the main character of the story, chronicles the life of an amicable, drifting vagabond who wanders about refusing to tie himself down to any trade, place, or person. Even at his advanced age, his quest for freedom leads him to eschew the settled life in favor of the road. *Knulp* is a child of the spirit who at the end of his time realizes his life's purpose was to bring "a little homesickness for freedom" into the lives of ordinary men.

Then, he went on sharing with me his travelling adventures when he was a young man. He told me about the time he had quit his own dead-end job to travel throughout Europe and going as far east as Asia for a number of years. Eventually, he went back to Greece, resumed his schooling, got a good job, raised a family, and felt as though his life was complete. He pointed out that many of his friends had what he called "freedom longings," which he felt immune to.

"If you don't do it when you're young and free, then when will you ever be able to do something daringly meaningful in your life?" He remarked as I stared at a pretty girl walking by on the sidewalk toward the beach. "When you're lost not knowing what to do is often the right time to take chances. Sometimes taking the plunge is the only viable option."

His words had a tremendous impact on me and I thought about them daily since. He talked about a different kind of travel; one in which the focus is on the self-development of the traveler, rather than the experience of visiting different countries and cultures. I'd done and enjoyed the latter, but the former called for some serious chutzpah and a particular set of survival skills I wasn't sure I possessed. But as my situation was at the time, it was a moot point for me to wonder about quixotic adventurous possibilities. I was running out of money while the economic recession deepened almost as fast as my apprehension about my future. And as my uncertainties and troubles grew to a crescendo personal crisis, I reached rock-bottom and saw myself entrapped in a web of confusion I felt unable to escape. Only a miracle could reverse the downward spiraling vortex my life had succumbed to. There was not a glitter of hope in sight.

As the weeks went by quickly so did my savings. Having exhausted my hope of landing a steady full-time job after numerous fruitless attempts, I resorted to going to the beach every day to pass the time. But I had no fun in the Sun. Either surfing in the green-blue water or prostrated on the white sand, I felt black-spirited as though my life had reached a dead-end; and a dead-end life is infinitely worse than a dead-end job, for you cannot just quit a life and go on looking for another one. I felt utterly lost and dejected. And yet, had I known at the time that my life was in the liminal state of a positive transition, I would have enjoyed my precious days on the beach with gusto. In hindsight, I've learned the valuable lesson of staying in the moment while flowing with the perpetual motions of change—flowing with the Tao, as I'd say later in my life when I became a dedicated student of Taoism.

After spending the previous day in an exhausting and fruitless job-searching effort smack in the middle of a deep economic recession, I decided to go to the beach to air out my stifled mind. Sprawling on the warm white sand on Barra da Tijuca beach in a beautiful late afternoon, I felt so glum that I was indifferent to the myriad of colors that a glorious sunset painted on the canvas of the horizon. I was so preoccupied with my precarious situation that all my eyes could see was a nebulous future. Something would have to give but I had no idea what that could be.

With my head aching, my heart throbbing, and my stomach growling, I got to my feet, walked to my car, and drove to a nearby shopping center where there was an eatery that served delectable sandwiches. However, being Friday evening, the parking lot was jammed packed, which forced me to drive around quite a few times looking for a vacant parking stall. Suddenly, walking out of the ground floor supermarket pushing a loaded shopping cart, a most stunning golden tanned goddess rendered me helplessly smitten at first sight. Wearing tight low cut blue jeans and a short yellow top that exposed her curvaceous mid-section, the tall brunette with straight waist-length hair paraded through the parking lot as if she were a female feline prowling through a concrete savanna. I watched her agape thinking she was the most voluptuously beautiful woman I'd ever seen. I knew I'd been hexed.

"Hey you, watch out!" Someone yelled at me as I swerved off center while looking sideways. I wasn't sure whether I was following her or just magnetized by that woman's magical allure. Consumed by an uncontrollable drive to approach her, I realized I was under some spellbinding effect. I'd seen countless gorgeous women in Rio in the many years I lived there, but that particular female specimen held a unique power of her own. I feverishly yearned to find out what she got.

As luck and destiny would touch base, a car pulled out from a parking space in front of me. I hastily parked, got out of the car, and dashed out through the thronged parking lot searching for the woman that rendered me besotted. When I finally located her, she was about to place the last bag of groceries in the trunk of her car.

"I'm sorry if I come across rudely, but I had to meet you," I said looking into her eye as she's about to shut the trunk closed.

To my pleasant astonishment, she smiled welcomingly, and one of the most important encounters in my life came into being at that moment. The more we talked, the more I realized that what started out as a sexually driven motivation was transforming piecemeal. Suddenly, I started feeling an eerie metamorphosis in both my thoughts and feelings that had extrapolated beyond the realm of sexuality. It was as though an esoteric switch had been turned up to a much higher frequency of interaction. As I gazed into her wide green eyes, I felt hypnotized by some mysterious energy. I could feel an alchemical process unfolding as the dynamics between us gradually transmuted carnal attraction into soul connection. There was some hidden purpose in that seemingly serendipitous *rendezvous*.

We spent hours talking in her car that evening. What had been ignited by fervent sexual magnetism turned into a most fortuitous encounter. It felt as though two good friends who had not seen each other in a long time unexpectedly crossed paths. As our conversation unfolded, we both started sharing intimate details of our lives and circumstances of our current challenges. I told her about my life's dilemmas and she disclosed the miseries of hers; the unhappy marriage, the loneliness, and the low self-esteem that had plagued her since childhood. Looking at her beautiful face it was hard to fathom someone like her could have lost the sense of self-worth. Apparently, self-assurance lies beneath deeper layers from the surface of an attractive appearance—or whatever the nature of the facade may be.

After that evening, I never laid eyes on Lucia again, though we spoke on the phone several times for a few months until I left Brazil for good. As it so happened, she was the one who always called me, most of the time to vent about the misfortunes of her marital misery with her wealthy abusive husband. I was happy to oblige with supportive attention and willingness to be a sounding board for her, until the tides turned and I was the one who needed to be in the receiving end of her attention.

One gloomy rainy day, I finally reached the bottom of my dried up well. I felt utterly hopeless watching my savings fade away piecemeal without the slightest possibility of landing even a mediocre job. With my bank account dwindling fast, unable to find employment, interminable conflicts with my father, and no friends to rely on, I'd reached the nadir of my bleak horizon. Suddenly, it occurred to me to call Lucia. The time had come when I was the one in need of a sounding board. That day would prove to be the most extraordinary manifestation of the unexplainable coming into being. It was the day that magic happened.

"I just don't seem to catch a break," I grumbled on the phone feeling my heart beat in my head. "I'm sick and tired of trying over and over and getting nowhere. I've reached my rope's end and I won't be able to hang on to it for too much longer."

The line was eerily silent. She didn't utter a single word.

"I've been thinking about selling all my personal belongings and run away somewhere; but even that I'm out in the dark, for I have no idea where to go," I said intending to fuel her reaction.

The permeating uncanny silence began perturbing me.

"Aren't you going to say anything?" I asked feeling both annoyed and antsy for a response; any kind of reaction. Then, when she spoke, I was stunned with what she had to say.

"You'll be leaving the country very soon," she said softly and with conviction as though she spoke of a well-known fact. "And it'll happen much sooner than you can imagine."

"You really think so," I said sardonically thinking she was just trying to assuage my tempered emotions. "I am jobless and going broke. I couldn't leave town much less the country. Besides, I would have no idea where to go."

"Brazil is too small for you," she said making me wonder how the fifth largest country in the world could be too small for anybody. "You are not meant to live the rest of your life in this country. Your future is abroad and your life is about to undergo radical transformation in that direction."

All of a sudden she got my attention. Her voice was imbued with a paranormal authoritative tone, as if it echoed millenary wisdom and knowledge of past, present, and future. Both her words and the intonation of her voice caught me by surprise. It was almost as if I were listening to somebody else; someone I'd never met before. I chose to remain silent and waited, with much anticipation, whatever she was going to say next.

"You are going to leave the country very soon and you'll live abroad for the rest of your life. There will be extraordinary opportunities for your personal development and growth," she continued speaking in a quasi-supernatural tone of voice as if she read from future chapters of the book of my life. "But before you get to your adopted motherland destination, first you'll go to different countries and undergo challenging situations that will require a great deal of determination, resilience, and courage on your part. But once the turning point is overcome, your life will blossom like a flower in the springtime. Then, you'll settle down in a beautiful paradisiacal place and your life will be completely transformed."

I was speechless. Was that woman a supreme pythoness or a deranged lunatic? How could she talk about my promising future with such conviction at a time the circumstances of my life evinced otherwise?

"You just wait and see. Later on in your life you'll remember my words at a time when you thought the world was tumbling down on you," she said as if she could read my mind. "But if you remember only one thing of what I say to you today remember this: it is of paramount importance that you never give up, no matter how unfavorable the circumstances may be."

As much as I liked hearing her prophetic statement, leaving the country any time soon was such a farfetched possibility that it was hard for me to grasp. Although I desperately wanted to believe her vision of my future, the awareness of my current situation nullified my inclination.

"Now go get some rest and don't think about it anymore. Much sooner than you think, you'll be leaving the country and your life will change for much, much better," she said as I noticed her voice slowly fading away as if she were departing in the distance. "Go to sleep now and immerse yourself in your dreams."

Then, she hung up abruptly. Awestruck, I didn't know what to make of what I'd just heard. Exhausted, I decided to heed her advice and tuck myself in bed for a restful night sleep.

The next day I woke up feeling relaxed and collected like I had not felt in a long time. I spent the day at home reading and listening to J.S. Bach. I did not want to do anything or go anywhere that could disturb the pleasant state of serenity I was immersed in. It was not until early afternoon that I decided to go check the mailbox, mostly to get some leg movement. Inside, there was only one letter addressed to me. It was from Dawn, the Californian girl I'd met on the train trip from San Francisco to

Lincoln, Nebraska, a couple of years earlier. We'd been corresponding on occasion for quite some time. I opened it expecting to read the same casual exchange of information we shared in our letters. But the content of this one was life changing. In her stylish cursive handwriting, she shared that her mother had been hired as the principal of an American high school in Switzerland and that she was moving to Europe. Then, she said the school was hiring international personnel bilingual in English and French. She mentioned me to her mother who included an official letter of her own offering me the school boy's dormitory supervisor position. In essence, it was a job offer with an invitation to move to Switzerland.

Holding the letter in my hand in awe and agape, my emotions fluctuated between total exhilaration and mind-spinning bewilderment. Less than twenty-four hours ago Lucia—or whoever spoke to me through her—emphasized that I'd be leaving the country much sooner than I could imagine. I was in utter disbelief. I'd witnessed many inexplicable accounts in the mystical Afro-Brazilian culture, but the uncanny precision of both the timing and content of Lucia's message were unprecedentedly paranormal.

Within one month from receiving the letter, I had sold all my personal belongings, which included a couple of surfboards, my stereo and vinyl collection, my books, my old car, and Magdalene, my motorcycle that I rode around Rio with great pleasure. Turning the proceeds into a one-way ticket to Geneva and exchanging the remaining cash into dollars—at considerable loss due to high inflation—I departed my country of birth never to return again; except for a 36-hour expiation interval that forever transformed my life and sealed my kismet.

Unarguably, crossing paths with Lucia has been the most consequential event that forever changed the course of my life. Because of the timely accuracy of one of her predictions materialized in an invitation letter to move to Switzerland within hours of our conversation, I unswervingly believed in everything she'd shared with me about my destiny. My taking to heart her words with utmost confidence would play a fundamental role to reclaiming my future when I had given it up.

❧❖❧

After a few days mourning over the perfect job that never happened, I picked up the pieces of my disappointed self, dusted off the accumulating frustrations, and resumed the home and job hunting all over again. Now that I knew about the bulletin board in the marina's administration building, I decided to check it out again hoping to find updated opportunities. Although there were no new announcements pinned to the corkboard, my timing was a stroke of luck.

"Young men who check out this bulletin board are usually looking for work," a bearded and bespectacled man walking out of the adjacent office remarked.

"Yeah…as a matter of fact I am," I said surprised by his unexpected utterance.

"Well, then this is your lucky day. I'm looking for someone to take care of three boats I manage while I go to England to pick up another one," he said. "It's temporary and I can't pay much, but it might lead to more work when I come back with the new boat from Southampton in a couple of weeks. Would you be interested?"

"Yes," I blurted out instinctively without thinking twice.

"Good. You're hired," he said smiling at me while stretching out his right hand. "I'm Mario."

"I'm Sebastian," I replied reciprocating the smile with a firm handshake.

"Well, let's get started right away," he said. "Let me take you to the pontoons where the boats are docked."

And just like that I had a job again—and another comfortable floating home, for he let me stay onboard a powerboat whose South African owner would not be coming down that summer. Suddenly, the possibility of having long-term housing was real. As for the pay, I didn't even ask how much he paid or what work I was supposed to do. I was glad to have a stable home again.

After showing me the vessels under his care and telling me what I needed to do, he walked me to the pontoon where my new residence was docked.

"In a couple of weeks I'll bring her right here," he said pointing to the vacant berth right across my new home where the yacht he was sailing from England would be moored. "She's a brand new beauty and I'm looking forward to sailing her this summer. The owner told me he's thinking of cruising on the Mediterranean Sea with his family; and since my Brit deckhand will return to the U.K., I'm going to need help. Are you up for it?"

"Sure," I said in disbelief of the fortunate turn of events.

"Awesome. Let's see how it all plays out when I come back. In the meantime, I already showed you what to do and you're on your own. See you when I come back," he said before dashing off the squeaky pontoon.

That moment marked the beginning of my extraordinary marine lifestyle experience. Mario, the pleasant young skipper who gave me a job and a home, unwittingly inaugurated a whole exciting new phase of my life. Within the short time he was gone I befriended a number of residents in the marina community. In fact, I even got myself a beautiful blond English girlfriend who, appropriately, lived aboard a sailboat she cared for called *Fair Mistress*. With the connections I was making on a daily basis, I felt very confident about the opportunities that might arise, especially with the summer season picking up steam. Gradually, I was becoming a popular character among the members of the floating community; the jovial happy-go-lucky Brazilian dude whose smile could not be wiped off his face. At last, I'd set sail to a fun-filled time in my life.

After devouring a salami with Swiss cheese sourdough baguette sandwich washed down with a cold dark Guinness for lunch, I relaxed on the deck of my floating residence getting some Sun while reading the local newspaper. Suddenly, I noticed a large double-decked yacht mooring at the marina's customs pier. I didn't make much of it until the vessel started moving toward pontoon L where I was and I recognized the skipper. I immediately got up to my feet and walked toward the vacant berth to help Mario and his deckhand with the lines. As he skillfully backed up the sizeable vessel perfectly in place, I grabbed the stern lines as I read the shinning golden letters protruding from the burnishing wood: *Lady Promise*. I was surprised how I instantly thought of Lucia, the woman who'd made extraordinary predictions about my life; and by doing so, changed the course of my destiny in 36 hours. The yacht's name felt like a good omen.

"Isn't she a beauty?" Mario said standing on the pontoon next to me after she was securely moored. "The boss wants to bring his family over this weekend to play with his new toy. I'm counting on you to be my deckhand and help his family with whatever they need."

"Of course," I said right away. "Who's the boss?"

"Dr. Kazar Hamil is a powerhouse finance attorney based in Lisbon. He's a Portuguese citizen of Pakistani descent who works with international financial institutions. The man is loaded and swimming in the dough," he said with a chuckle. "Well, I must get going now. Here's my card. Call me before the weekend."

The weekend arrived not a moment too soon. It was around 10 o'clock in the morning when I woke up to the sounds of young girls' talking and giggling on the pontoon. I peeked through the thinly faded curtain covering the porthole of my cabin and I saw the Hamil family arriving for their coveted weekend. Oddly, I felt nervous. After delaying my getting out of bed hindered by temporary angst, I mustered my inherently good human relations skills and stepped out to meet whom I hoped it would be my long-term employer. Since Mario told me on the phone that he'd given the boss the heads up about me, I felt at ease approaching the Portuguese-Pakistani humdinger.

"I've been to Brazil several times on business trips," Dr. Kazar Hamil said after our casual introduction when he commented on my distinct Brazilian accent. "Good food, good weather, and good people."

Paying particular attention to the last two words, I felt like I had a good head start. Then, he invited me aboard to meet his family.

Lady Promise was even more beautiful inside than her curvaceous hull, protruding bow, and salient stern revealed. A spacious well-furnished living room, three cabins plus the master suite, two heads (bathrooms), a good size galley (kitchen), a broad windowed wheelhouse, and a large open upper deck—all smelling brand new. Hanging from the upper deck like an ornament on a maritime Christmas tree, a large rubber dinghy with an outboard engine looked as decorative as functional. And on the deck below, a small 125cc Honda motorcycle was firmly attached to its parking spot on the starboard side. *Lady Promise* was gorgeous and I felt very attracted to her. I couldn't help fantasizing about one day; perhaps, establish a live-in situation with her.

"I told Kazar that on the weekends I just want to cruise by the Algarve coast," Maria Hamil said standing next to her husband who had just introduced me to his wife. "But sometime in the summer, I definitely want to sail the Mediterranean Sea and go to Costa del Sol and Ibiza."

Oh boy, and so would I! But at that time all I had to do was to step up to the plate and make a positive impression on the boss and his family. That first cruise by the coastline was my opportunity to prove to both Mario and the Hamil family that I was going to be an asset for all. Then, I might have a shot to go sailing on the Mediterranean Sea all the way to Ibiza. The stakes were high.

Soon Mario arrived and by early afternoon we were already out at sea. I was expeditious and efficacious with the assistance I provided to both Mario and the members of the family. In their turn, they were pleasant and friendly toward me, which made the development of our relationship a smooth transition from stranger to welcomed acquaintance. I quickly realized that the two preteen girls were his children only. It was a self-evident assumption, for they had the physical traits of their father and referred to Maria Hamil by her name. The infant boy was the couple's only child together, and Maria had two young adult children of her own. Later I'd find out interesting details about their blended family that reminded me of my father's.

By the second weekend I felt completely acclimated and comfortable with my well-established position. I was learning the ropes—literally—of helping sailing *Lady Promise* and Mario seemed to be appreciative of my assistance. And in another crucially important matter, I was elated that not once I experienced even a mild case of seasickness. As for the family, Kazar, Maria, and the girls seemed to be quite pleased with me. And the more they learned about me, the more they opened up—and vice-versa. I was surprised as to how in a quick span of time, I started feeling more like a friend than an employee. But like sailing on the Mediterranean Sea, the weather can change on a dime.

On the fourth weekend the blue sky turned gray. Watching the Sun ensconcing behind the horizon shooting up crimson-color light at sea's end, Kazar, Maria, and I were conversing with sociable ease as we returned to the marina after a lovely day cruising on the coast. We shared our experiences in different parts of the world we'd been to among other culturally enriching topics. Suddenly, I felt a strong urge to turn around to look behind me. I was stunned to see Mario staring at me with piercing eyes that looked and felt like a disgruntled expression. He didn't budge his gazing at me when our eyes met. It was a creepy feeling that threw me off and I didn't understand what was going on.

Shortly after the Hamil family drove back to Lisbon, Mario approached me while I hosed off the boat. I tried to ignore his presence by focusing on my task, but he clearly had an agenda he wanted to address.

"You're getting way too cozy with the boss and his family," he said in a sudden verbal jab that carried a real intonation punch.

"They don't seem to mind," I said curtly to avoid discussion.

"But I do," he replied looking me in the eye without saying another word.

"I'll make a point of keeping to myself next weekend," I said trying to appease the subtle tension.

"There will be no more weekends for you," he said as I shivered inside. "But I'm not going to drop you on your head. I'll let you sleep on the other boat under my care on the other side of the marina. I don't want you living across *Lady Promise* anymore. In fact, I don't want to see you on this pontoon again."

"Are you firing me?" I asked in disbelief.

"I'm letting you go," he said. "I realized I'll be better off if I handle this boat with someone else onboard."

And just like that, he torpedoed my aspirations and sank my hopes of sailing the Mediterranean Sea. As I'm packing my stuff getting ready to move to the other side of the marina, I realized his petty jealousy got the worst of him and set a wedge between us. Sad and disappointed, I walked away with the consolation prize that at least I was not homeless, yet.

Switzerland struck me as a mountain paradise; the equivalent of Polynesia to the Pacific Ocean. And everything about it was different from the place I came from: the weather, the environment, the culture, the people, and even more strikingly so, the organization of society. For me who had always struggled adapting to the utter lack of organization in Brazilian society and culture, moving to a country where the train schedules operated with timely precision was a welcome change from a place you don't even know if the train will show up at all. That sense of order and propriety suited me quite well. However, the most thrilling aspect of my moving to Switzerland was the moving itself. But before going up the mountains where the school was located, I decided to stay in Geneva for a couple of days to explore that exciting European city.

Among the twenty-two cantons (counties) of the Swiss confederation, Geneva is one of the most fascinating. It lies in the

Rhone Valley at the extreme southwestern corner of the Lake of Geneva—or Lake Leman—and borders the canton of Vaud in the extreme north. Geneva was admitted to the Swiss confederation in 1815, and therefore is the junior of the twenty-two cantons. Walking through Geneva's streets is like strolling through history itself. Rue de la Cité, Grand Rue, and Rue de L' hotel de Ville are popular streets in town. The latter has beautiful 17th century buildings and a very simple house where the greatest philosopher of the Enlightenment movement—and one of my most respected thinkers—Jean Jacques Rousseau (1712–1778) was born. But once my playing tourist days were over, it was time to embark on the adventure that my life had unexpectedly become.

After a long time agonizing over my bleak future, a most unforeseen turning point in my past had catapulted me to an auspicious present. In an immaculate moment in time, my life shifted in the right direction without any conscious effort of my own. One day I lay dreary on the beach moping about the untoward circumstances of my life, the next I'm literally on the top of the world with an open sky of possibilities surrounding me.

As I'd soon find out, with opportunities and forward-looking expectations challenges come along for the ride. The first day I arrived at the American School, Dawn and her mother made arrangements for an introductory welcoming dinner at the matriarch's quaint chalet. That evening it was clear to me that both women had certain expectations of their own—and they were not in sync with mine.

"I'm so glad you're here," Dawn said gently touching my forearm with a subtle amorous twinkle in her eyes. "I think you'll really enjoy living in this lovely town in this amazing country."

"And who knows, he might like it so much that he'll want to stay here for good," Dawn's mother remarked with a sly smile that subtly disclosed her hidden agenda.

Soon I got the whiff of the purpose behind the invitation for my coming to Switzerland—and it wasn't quite like what I had in mind. It didn't take me long to realize that whatever I'd experienced with Dawn on the train trip from San Francisco to Lincoln in the past had no bearings with the present. I suppose it was my first realization of how time and space are intrinsically connected. Not only you cannot replicate one without the other, they are in perpetual changing mode affecting everything and everyone in a continuous transformational process. And it so happened that within the motion of change, whatever attraction I felt for Dawn years before was non-existent at the present space-time. However, her experience was seemingly opposite to mine; as if the present exacerbated what she experienced when we first met years back. The contrast didn't bode well.

As soon as it became clear to everyone concerned that the cupid had flown south, the unrequited romantic aspirations turned sour and my relationship with both Dawn and her mother became chilly at best. And when I started dating a cute red-haired girl from New Zealand who lived in town, my rapport with Dawn and her mother deteriorated with expedience. As it became obvious that I was losing ground with the ones who brought me over to Switzerland, I found hopeful solace in the excellent rapport I established with both students and staff at the school. Nevertheless, I was aware that my job was hanging in the balance and my future in the paradise of mountains was in jeopardy.

The *coup de grace* came when one of the owners of the private school arrived shortly before the Thanksgiving holiday. The ungainly, bespectacled, and scrawny tall man and I didn't look eye to eye even before we were officially introduced. Then, on the day of the school Thanksgiving celebration party he showed up unannounced. And as he's walking toward me with a frown hiding behind his thick black frame glasses, I could feel the wavelengths of change oscillating in my direction.

"How come you're not wearing a suit?" The dapper dressed-to-kill goodie-two-shoes asked me askance. Clearly, he was more interested in harassing me than an actual answer.

"Because I don't have one," I replied nonchalantly.

"Well, you should. Attending a celebratory event at a private school of our caliber requires proper attire," he rebuked me with an air of pseudo-superiority before walking away.

For a moment I wasn't sure whether I should leave the party or stay. I looked around the room and a few of the more conservative students were wearing suits, but most were not. I also noticed that a couple of teachers were not wearing suits either, though I didn't see the hoity-toity boss approach them. I felt so uncomfortable that I eventually left the party alleging indisposition. As I walked to my room, I knew I'd been tagged by a power figure.

By early December as the school prepared for the Christmas break, the inevitable happened. There was a clause in my contract that stipulated a mid-term renewal option, which they exercised by not renewing it. I thought my Switzerland sojourn was over; and worse yet, I had no idea of what to do next, until I shared the news with some of the local school staff I'd befriended and they came to my rescue. I was gladly surprised to see how quickly they mobilized in effort to help me out.

"I talked to Madame Bochard and she's expecting you to come by this afternoon," one of the local ladies in charge of the school's housekeeping said. "I think she might have a job for you."

Indeed, she did. Madame Bochard ran the only industrial laundry facility in town, which supplied services to all the hotels in the popular ski resort region—the *Sommet des Diablerets* (10,530 ft.) is one of the most popular skiing destinations in the Swiss Alps. I knew absolutely nothing about industrial laundry operations, but at that point I'd take a job as a butcher if one had been offered to me. The only problem was that the job wouldn't be available for another two months, and I couldn't wait that long in a high cost of living country like Switzerland. In time, I had a brilliant idea: I would fly to New York City to spend Christmas with my oldest sister who had just been hired by a large Brazilian investment bank in Manhattan. After the New Year, I'd go to Nebraska to visit my other sister, and then I'd come back to NYC and fly back to Switzerland to start my new job. Not having to pay for room and board while working at the school, I had saved enough money to afford my travel expenses.

It was with great anticipation that I landed on JFK airport for a short break between jobs in Switzerland. Unbeknownst to me at the time, some 16 months later I'd be arriving at the same airport on my way to becoming an American citizen.

✤

I was sitting at an ice-cream parlor in the marina shopping area when two young girls came dashing toward me.

"Why did you do this?" The older of the two protested.

"Yeah, it was definitely not cool," the younger one segued.

"What are you talking about?" I asked Kazar's daughters who had rushed in my direction as soon as they spotted me.

"You quit and you didn't even tell my dad you're not coming back," the elder sister said in a prosecutorial tone of voice.

I looked at her and it made me feel good to notice that they regretted my unexpected departure. However, I was confused and interested in learning the details of their story.

"I didn't quit. I was fired and told not to come around again. I'd never quit without talking with your father and saying goodbye to you girls," I said attempting to let them know how much I appreciated their subtle disclosure of caring.

"Well, that's not what Mario told my dad," the youngest said as her eyes stretched wide open by surprise. "He told my dad that you quit because you didn't want to work for us anymore."

Some thirty minutes and a couple of chocolate ice-cream waffle cones later they knew the truth; and as some biblical passage says, the truth will set you free. According to the girls' story, Mario, the skipper who became oddly jealous of his deckhand getting the boss' family attention, told their father a dishonestly deviant narrative that had nothing to do with the truth. I was outraged that he portrayed me in such a low behavioral level that was not conducive to my character. All of a sudden I found myself in a ticklish situation: I had to let Kazar know the truth directly from me; but by doing so, Mario certainly would kick me out of my boat home. Nevertheless, my choice was unhesitatingly obvious: I could handle homelessness again, but I would not allow the integrity of my character to be left unsheltered.

My decision to talk with Kazar and tell him the truth proved to be a defining moment. From that day onward I developed a solid bond with Kazar and his family, and they provided me with everything I needed. I was rehired on the spot and invited to move in and live onboard *Lady Promise*—my fantasy come true. Then, as Mario was coming down the pontoon visibly discombobulated to see me standing next to the boss, I was flabbergasted to eyewitness Kazar fire him as unceremoniously as I'd been fired. As I watched Mario gather his belongings before walking away, I felt justified and redeemed from his calumnious behavior. But as I watched the skipper walk away, it dawned on me that Kazar had incurred a significant problem upon himself. He must have read my mind at the time.

"Don't worry about it," he said. "We'll find another skipper."

I was deeply moved that in detriment to his own interest, he chose to fire the skipper and keep the deckhand instead. After a long searching process in which *Lady Promise* was unable to go out to sea, eventually he identified a good fit for the position and soon we were sailing again. Meanwhile, Maria Hamil started planning in earnest her coveted cruise to Ibiza, which thrilled me with anticipatory excitement.

As my relationship with the entire family deepened, both Kazar and Maria Hamil became more opened to me as if I were a long lost trustful friend. For reasons that have always defied my comprehension, people who get to see beyond the outer layers of my being tend to self-disclose their innermost angst to me. I believe it was at that time that I noticed this life-long pattern for the first time. Maria Hamil was the first one to show me that beyond the external appearances of every individual lie deep-seated sorrows and dark secrets.

"It was the saddest day of my life," she said holding back tears as I helped her put the clean dishes away. "Losing my husband unexpectedly in a car accident and left behind with two children to rear on my own was a very hard blow. Then, when I met Kazar a few years later felt like a God-sent gift. He is wealthy, witty, fun to be around, and he liked me. Besides, he has his own share of grief to deal with. We are a match made in …; well, we are a good match."

I was caught off guard by the extemporaneous revelation and I didn't know what to say. Thus, I listened; until she concluded with a poignant statement.

"But if I could have my first husband back, I wouldn't even think twice. He'll always be the love of my life," she said while heading to the playpen where her son with Kazar whimpered; a son that was of enormous significance to the healing of his father.

Watching her picking up the infant to take him outside, I reflected on her words and wondered whether my father would have felt the same way she did. Since more than once he shared with me that my mother was the love of his life, I could only surmise that he'd relate to Maria Hamil's sentiments. However, when it came to me, his first born son, I knew for sure there was not a shadow of semblance to the positive impact Kazar's son had in his life. As far as my father was concerned, my birth was inextricably linked with the timing of my mother's death and his ensuing grief, whereas Kazar's son was a source of healing to a man's broken heart.

On a Saturday night after everyone had retired, a dejected-looking Kazar asked me to go for a walk around the marina with him. It was on that evening he shared with me the version of his secret agony. He'd been married to whom he also deemed to be the love of his life and the mother of his two daughters. Running a thriving law practice firm with his childhood best friend, his life seemed to be heading in the right direction, until it careened off track mercilessly when his wife and best friend eloped. As if such a disappointment and betrayal were not devastating enough, his erstwhile best friend and ex-wife had a son together; a son Kazar had long yearned to have. Once I learned about this painfully poignant aspect of his past, it made sense to me that when he and Maria met they resonated with each other's needs and sorrows.

And having a son of their own was a welcoming bond that kept them contently together.

After self-disclosing their innermost angst to me, I thought about all the people, like the Hamils, who are perceived to be happy according to misguided measuring systems of success. I realized the perceptually deceiving aspect of appearance that strives to camouflage what is not wanted to be revealed. Like a multi-layered onion covering up the core, when the layers of appearance are removed, a forlorn self bathed in lacrimation is often exposed. I also became aware that I was a magnet for those yearning to open their wounded hearts out for me to take a peek at the depth of their sorrow. Perhaps I elicited a sense of trust that turned me into a source of comfort for them. As it happened, my meaningful and intimate interactions with both Maria and Kazar significantly strengthened our relationships. I felt as though I'd been upgraded from employee, to friend, to surrogate relative in a very short period of time—and they treated me accordingly.

Now I was living my dream life. In addition to paying me very well for working mostly on the weekends, they let me live onboard their brand new yacht with a motorcycle and dinghy at my disposal. I was cruising the marina by land and sea in style. I had friends from all over the world and a beautiful English girlfriend with whom I shared passionate evenings—and occasional daytime escapades. Sometimes on full moon nights, I'd be on the rubber dinghy chopping through the illuminated lunar lane in the water to go to friends' boats to have dinner, wine, and fun till the wee hours of the morning. I felt as though I was being compensated for having endured challenging situations with adamant determination and unwavering resilience.

As most of my international friends had to leave the country at least every six months to renew their visas, Gibraltar was the preferred destination, especially for the British. Thus, in one of those necessary getaways to Gibraltar, I joined my English girlfriend and other members of the visa renewing crew on a sailing jaunt. It was my first taste of what real sailing experience was about; and its tantalizing appeal seduced my senses making me long for more. That carefree lifestyle suited my adventurous spirit and I was determined to pursue it, though the dread of unexpected seasickness always haunted me like a threatening ghoul. But after sailing through the Bay of Cádiz and spotting "The Rock" from the distance, I knew I was willing to take the risk.

After returning from Gibraltar, I began looking forward to Maria Hamil's planned trip to Ibiza.

❧❖☙

Christmas in New York City was a memorable occasion. The speedy crowd moving up and down Fifth Avenue couldn't affect my tourist-infatuated slow stroll. I let them zoom by while standing still beholding the Christmas decorations in shopping windows near the Rockefeller Center. Soon, the tantalizing aroma of toasting pretzels would sneak in through my nostrils making me move again in the direction of my appetite's demand. I was excited to be in NYC before transitioning back to Switzerland to a new work situation I didn't know what to expect.

After the New Year celebration in Time Square, I went to Lincoln, Nebraska to spend a week visiting my other sister. When I returned to New York, the anxiety of going back to Switzerland to work in an industrial laundry facility began disturbing me. I even noticed that the excitement of being back in NYC had vanished in the haze of my preoccupation with what lay ahead—and when the excitement of being in NYC was gone, I knew something was not right with me.

Out of the blue, I felt a strong urge to resume practicing hatha yoga and meditate daily. It was as though I intuitively knew that there were some hard times ahead I needed to prepare myself for. Unbeknownst to me, I was in active training mode for a cataclysmic emotional event that was going to rattle the foundation of my being and change the course of my life. Every morning upon waking up, I stayed in bed in a state of restlessness as if my sleep had aroused uneasiness instead of repose. After lounging in apprehension for an hour or so, I'd get up and do my yoga asanas hoping to boost inner relief that my sleep failed to provide. I felt like a warrior preparing for a very distinct type of battle; one in which I had to face the most daring foe of all: myself.

Soon the day to return to Switzerland arrived. Although the yoga and meditation practice helped me cope with my anxiety, on the actual day of leaving I realized I was running low in confidence. Not knowing what I was up against in my new employment and living conditions in Switzerland, I caved in to the inner pressure of my trepidations. By the time I shut my sister's apartment's door closed leaving the key inside, the thudding sound reverberated through the hallway like an eerie death knell announcing the end of a time in my life. Locked out and with only one way to go, I felt my false sense of security melt away as it percolated through the sweaty palms of my hands.

Chugging my luggage along the crowded sidewalk at rush hour only aggravated my already amped up state of mind. Running late while nervously checking the time, I realized I was in a kind of peculiar street fight trying to snatch a cab from fierce competitors with similar goal. By the time I flagged a taxi successfully, some twenty minutes had gone by and the congested traffic seemed to hold the clock back further. The stress of being trapped in gridlock traffic with a sense of time urgency made me feel nauseated. The carbon-monoxide infused fumes, the flickering cars' headlights, the changing traffic lights, and the continual blaring horns pushed my nervous system over the edge of distress. Cold sweating while looking at my watch every five minutes, I barely made in time for my flight. Later, buckling up my seatbelt with rickety hands, I could still feel the perspiration moistening my brow. I felt tense and exhausted. Somehow I was intuitively aware that a new challenging phase in my life had just begun. My second sojourn in Switzerland was not going to be a mountain paradise experience—and it wouldn't last long either.

"*Bienvenue, monsieur,*" Madame Bochard greeted me on my first morning on the job. She was a mid-sexagenarian lady of short stature and rotund shape. From the very first time we met before my going to NYC, we had established a positive connection as soon as we made eye contact. Unfortunately, her welcoming disposition and friendly demeanor were not enough to help me endure a gruelingly mind-numbing job that would turn into an unsalvageable situation.

From an employment standpoint, the laundry facility job seemed like an ideal situation for a young foreigner out of work. It offered everything needed for a modest living: a clean and comfortable private room, three tasty daily meals seven days a week, and a good salary for Switzerland's standards. Upstairs from the main floor where the industrial laundry operated, there were several rooms where most of the working crew resided. The meals were served at a nearby hotel cafeteria that had a contractual agreement with the laundry business. And considering the nature of the menial work, the wages were good enough to attract workers from abroad for the busy winter season. My fellow-workers were men and women from the former Yugoslavia, a couple of French women, a Turkish man, and Paolo, the mid-twenties chill Italian chap who happened to be the floor manager. They were all simple and amicable folks who were easy to be around, which made it for a pleasant working environment. But it was the work itself that proved to be an impossible task for me to endure; and it took me only one day to realize I would not be able to carry on.

"There's no way in hell I can survive this dreadful job another day," I said to myself looking in the mirror in the evening after the unbearable drudgery of a long first working day. To my stupefaction—and out of my survival needs—I managed to stay on the job three more days.

The morning after my first day on the job, I dreaded waking up and have to resume doing what felt like an impossible task. From eight in the morning until five in the afternoon—minus a half-hour lunch time and a couple of 15 minutes coffee breaks—I tried to survive doing the most tedious work I'd ever done in my life. Standing in front of a long and wide table, I spent the day straightening crumpled damp pillow cases getting them ready for the rolling ironing dryer. It was a terribly repetitive motion that ended only when I pushed the piles to the side for the next worker to take them away for the next step of the process. But as soon as the heaps were gone, another large container on wheels would stop right next to me with another load of wrinkled damp pillow cases ready for an encore of drudgery. And to make matters much worse, there was a large round clock on the wall right across the table where I stood all day doing the same repetitive motion. Although at the time I was unfamiliar with Einstein's Theory of Special Relativity, today I am convinced that I experienced some sort of time dilation; that is, the "slowing down" of a clock as determined by an observer who is in relative motion with respect to that clock. Time had come to a standstill in the most inauspicious situation. Another pile pushed away along the table, another large wheelbarrow-like container with a fresh batch showed up to be done. It was a Sisyphean task that felt like Chinese torture annihilating my spirit with tedium.

"Hey, why don't you take a shot at the sheet ironing machine?" Paolo said with his eyes exuding empathy. My exasperation must have been conspicuous. "Let's just change the motion a little bit to spice things up."

Half hour later the different monotonous pattern became all too unbearably familiar. Now, instead of spreading my hands across moist pillow cases, I placed my forearm to fold warm sheets coming out of the drying machine every time a green light beeped—uninterruptedly! I recalled Charles Chaplin's (1889–1977) magnum opus, *Modern Times*, and realized that I, like his character in the motion picture, was about to lose my mind. At one point, I became so disconnected from the wearisome process that I missed the green light warning and I messed up the timing of the conveyer belt progression. All of a sudden, unfolded clean sheets started falling down on the dirty floor one after the other in royal disarray.

"Don't worry about it," Paolo said after shutting down the machine to fix the messy problem I unwittingly created. "Maybe you should go back to straightening the pillow cases."

Embarrassed, I moved back to the table where my Yugoslavian co-workers looked at me with empathetic eyes. In my turn, I looked at them wondering how in the world they could manage to have been doing this work for many seasons. I'd survived one day and I was barely holding my own on the second. I knew it was time for me to have a *tête-à- tête* with Madame Bochard.

"*Bien sûr*," she said sympathetically after I shared my inaptitude for the job peppered with some made-up reasons I had to leave by week's end. "I noticed yesterday you were struggling to fit in the system. It's just not your nature, I suppose. I'll have your paycheck ready for you on Friday."

At night, alone in my room, that's when I realized what I was up against. I had just quit my job—a job I couldn't do if my life depended on it—along with my room and board. By week's end I'd have to be somewhere else, though I had no idea where that somewhere was. Suddenly, my anxiety about having to survive this job a couple of more days was overshadowed by much more pressing concerns. At least for the next two days I would have a place to sleep, eat, and even make some money. But what would happen afterwards? I had a hard time falling asleep that night.

The next day I didn't even notice I was straightening pillow cases for the rolling ironing machine. My mind was racing around itself as I wondered what I would do next. The temptation to take the easy way out and return to Brazil began infiltrating the strength of my resistance. Every time I contemplated the idea I experienced sheer terror inside of me. It was not the fact that there was nothing worthwhile in Brazil for me, for that I could have handled. But the prospect of being denied the promising prophecies Lucia had made for my life was not something I was willing to forsake. Because of the uncanny timely precision of her very first foresight into my future, I didn't have a scintilla of a doubt that I was going to live the rest of my life far away from my country of birth, as she had foretold me when we spoke on the phone. I couldn't conceive the idea of foregoing what had already started as an unfolding possibility that happened to hit a major obstacle. And yet, other than going back to Brazil, there were seemingly no other alternatives, especially within the very short timeframe at my disposal to act.

For the next two days during my breaks and after work, I walked to the only travel agency in town to inquire about the cost and schedules of flights from Geneva to Rio. After having come in routinely asking related questions without taking any action, the pleasant lady tending the business looked at me with compassionate eyes as if she could tell that I was in a state of inner despair. I couldn't pluck the courage—or the cowardice, depending on the perspective—to purchase the airfare ticket that would put an end to my dreams. And yet, by Friday I would be out of the laundry facility with nowhere to go but back to my homeland where I didn't feel welcome. Then, as the serendipity of luck that has shadowed me all my life would have, I came across a young Swedish man I'd met when I worked at the American School and he attended the *école hôtelière* in the same building. My brief conversation with him on the street resolved my urgent quandary.

"It might be a little early to start scavenging the area for work," he said as I shared with him my dilemma of not knowing where to go. "But on the other hand, you'll get ahead of the crowd before the season begins. You might even be able to find a temporary situation onboard until the summer action takes off."

"Costa del Sol," I said out loud after listening to him.

"Yep, it's the place to be in the summer. I spent three months working on a yacht moored at *Puerto José Banus* in Marbella and it was an awesome experience," he said speaking with great enthusiasm about his summer adventure. "I'd give it a shot if I were you. Besides, it doesn't sound like you have options to choose from anyway."

The next time I walked into the travel agency, I surprised the lovely lady by purchasing a train ticket to Spain instead of an airfare to Rio de Janeiro. It was the logical thing to do, since I would be able to buy time while keeping my dreams alive. At that point, I was willing to try doing anything that would not involve foregoing what it'd been prophesized for my future with paranormal precision.

After travelling through France to Spain on a third class train ticket, I stayed a couple of days in Seville before heading down to the renowned Costa del Sol. At every stop along the way, I hoped to find something or someone that would help anchoring me to a stable situation. Being out of work was nothing new to me, but not having a home was an unprecedented situation. And having been a homebody all my life, homelessness was a disturbing prospect that frightened my imagination. The anxiety created by the slightest possibility of being threatened to fall into what I dreaded the most terrified me; and yet, not as nearly as the possibility of returning to Brazil and having my dreams obliterated. Although I still had some saved money, it was a limited amount that I wouldn't be able to stretch very long.

Once I made it to Marbella, I went straight to *Puerto José Banus* as my Swedish friend suggested. The place looked like a coastal ghost town. A small but quaint marina, there were several vacant berths; and the few mooring vessels seemed to be locked up. Evidently, as my friend warned me, I arrived quite a bit earlier before the season started. I felt a growing sense of urgency, for I needed to find both work and a place to live soon. Although I was staying in economical *pensiones*, I knew my meager personal budget was going against time. Suddenly, I saw a man coming out of the cabin of a nearby sailing boat. I rushed toward him like a hungry animal that spotted a potential kill.

"You're not going to find much around here this time of the year; not even the restaurants and stores are hiring," he said in the course of our conversation after I self-disclosed the predicament of my situation. "But because you speak Portuguese, you might want to check out a new marina in the Algarve region of Portugal. You might have a better chance there."

The next day I was on a wobbly locomotive toward the south border of Spain and Portugal. After hopping on a barge to cross the Guadiana River that functions as an estuary border between the two countries, I arrived in what felt like another space-time dimension. Not only was the Portuguese town of Vila Real de Santo Antonio reminiscent of medieval times with ladies wearing black garments under a blazing Sun, my experience of having crossed some liminal portal was eerily tangible. I tried to pretend I did not feel it, as if by ignoring it the sensation would vanish as mysteriously as it'd showed up.

Shortly after disembarking the barge, I made acquaintance with some fellow foreign travelers with whom I caroused and partied as we moved into southern Portugal until we dispersed in different directions. Soon I was alone again; left with my worries about my uncertain situation. And because of the partying traveling troop I'd temporarily joined, I never made it to the marina the man in *Puerto José Banus* had suggested. Suddenly, I felt like the medieval-looking women I saw in the small town of Vila Real de Santo Antonio: I felt cloaked in darkness.

With despondency creeping into me like a sluggish worm eager to consume my moribund spirit, I began to cave in to the pressure of having to make something happen—quickly. After two days looking for work and housing to no avail, I noticed my moxie deflating along with my flagging determination to endure. There was nothing even remotely promising panning out in my efforts; neither outside nor inside of me. As my discouragement incremented with crescendo acceleration, it was a matter of time for my mind to succumb to the treacherous temptation of giving up what I believed to be the promises of my destiny: to build my life abroad. By the time I went to sleep, I felt as though my dreams were about to fade away in oscillating delta waves heading to a terrifying nightmare.

"Oh, shit!" I blurted out waking up abruptly at the same time my body was jolted upright to a sitting position in bed. Huffing and puffing, I ran my hand through my hair and noticed I was soaking wet. My heart raced inside my chest as if it were a fugitive running away from menacing huntsmen eager to slash it into pieces. I knew I'd experienced a horrific nightmare, though I didn't have the slightest recollection of it. I'd wakened up to the strangest morning of my life.

I checked out of the *albergue* around 9:00 o'clock in the morning. For the next few hours I wondered about aimlessly in an utter state of stupor. Without thinking clearly and quasi-unaware of what I was doing, I got on a bus to Lisbon and headed for the airport. It was late afternoon when I arrived. By early evening, I'd already walked back and forth to the airline ticketing counter several times; like I did at the travel agency in Switzerland. The cost of one way ticket to Rio was more than half the amount of money I had left; but it was the costly consequence of purchasing it I feared would leave my spirit broke. Then, aware that I'd reached the point of no return, I handed a wad of cash to the airline clerk and walked away from the counter as if enveloped in a cloud of despondency. Holding the ticket in my hand, I paced around vacant-mindedly oblivious to my surroundings. When emotional exhaustion overwhelmed me into submission, I sat down and fell asleep at the departure gate.

"Excuse me, sir," an airline employee gently nudged me awake. "Are you Mr. de Assis?"

"Yes," I replied wondering whether I was dreaming.

"Your flight is about to take off, sir. We need to get you on-board right away."

He helped me carry my luggage to a van and drove speedily toward the aircraft whose engines were already revving up on the tarmac. As I walked on the plane under the disapproving eyes and disparaging words of annoyed passengers, I didn't even bother to care. Nothing mattered to me anymore. I fastened my seat belt to what was going to be a very emotionally turbulent flight to the most agonizing and life-changing 36 hours of my life.

❧❖☙

Excitement was the dominant emotion of the day. All packed up and ready to set sail to the Mediterranean Sea, everyone onboard was beaming with joy. With the Sun shining bright in the azure sky, a placid sea expanding through the horizon, and a gentle offshore breeze cooling off the hot summer air, the ideal nautical stage was set for the beginning of an exhilarating voyage. As *Lady Promise* left the harbor with her bow tilted up powered by dual Cummings turbo diesel engines, to my eyes she looked like the mythological goddess Amphitrite, the wife of god Poseidon, who was eager to pursue new adventures in the realm of her beloved husband. Standing on the upper deck feeling the warm breeze blowing through my naked chest and face, a wave of bliss flowed through me triggering an ineffable feeling of happiness. That moment alone made everything I'd gone through recently worthwhile.

After sailing through the Bay of Cádiz, we spent the night in Gibraltar where I woke up to the loud sounds of the British Royal Air Force Harrier jets landing vertically on the runway next to the marina. Leaving "The Rock" in the morning, we set sail through the southern coast of Spain on the way to Barcelona with an overnight stop nearby the small coastal town of Motril. At dusk, as we were anchoring at a haven inlet, we all noticed in awe—and with some degree of apprehension—a couple of sharks flitting around in the vicinity. In the morning, I faced my first challenge of my long anticipated cruise to Ibiza.

"The anchor is not reeling up," the skipper said while revving up the motor to retrieve it. "The chain must have got tangled up around a rock or something. You're gonna have to dive down there to see what's going on. Do you think you can handle it?"

"How deep is it?" I asked more concerned about the sharks I saw prowling the night before than the depth I'd have to reach.

"The echo sounder indicates it to be around 30 feet," he said. "Do you have good lungs?"

"I guess we'll find out," I said still thinking of the sharks.

"Good. Let's get to it then," he said reaching inside a large blue rubber bag to hand me the snorkeling gear.

With the Hamil family watching me jump in the water as if I were some sort of a superhero, I dove in pulling myself down to the bottom by holding the anchor chain. Mid-way down, I spotted the dreaded beasts of the sea at a distance and I freaked out. However, knowing they were all expecting me to show both my merit and mettle, I sped down as my fear drained my energy even more than the holding of my breath. By the time I managed to dislodge the chain from under a rock, I realized I was more likely to die of asphyxia than from a shark attack. In a state of extreme anxiety, I moved the fins as fast as I could to propel myself up with the urgency of survival. I barely made it to the surface.

"Did you get it?" The skipper asked me as soon as my head popped out of the water.

Huffing and puffing in disguised distress, I could not reply with words. Instead, I gave him the thumbs up signal and the smile of satisfaction in the Hamil family members' face made it all worthwhile. But as soon as I climbed onboard I rushed to the head and vomited pints of salt water. Little I knew then that was a minor prelude to a much more challenging event yet to come.

The rest of the cruise on the way to Ibiza was a pleasant sailing experience. After a stop in Alicante and an overnight in Valencia, we headed to Barcelona for a couple of delightful days in that exciting city. From there we set out to the Balearic Islands with a quick stop in Minorca, a day in Majorca, and then to the much anticipated hotbed of European summer: Ibiza.

Ibiza did not disappoint. It was everything I'd heard about from those who had spent time there. Heavily populated with young tourists from all over Europe, the island was a social gathering paradise where day and night mingled into one party extravaganza. With the Sun shining during the day, the beaches were crowded with topless sunbathing girls and guys hanging out as if they were bird watchers. Once the Sun ensconced behind the crimson horizon, the silvery moon took over the center stage to dictate the second half of the summer fun. As the evening progressed, the suntanned youth congregated in the bursting at the seams nightclubs where the party continued until the Sun rose again. It was an around the clock bacchanal that would make Dionysius proud of his devotees exuding ecstasy.

After spending a few days in that exciting orgiastic island, the skipper, of all people, began to display signs of saturated impatience. His characteristic grumpy mood seemed to have been elevated to a higher plateau. Eager to return to Portugal for reasons of his own interest, he talked the Hamil family into leaving one day earlier. According to him, the weather forecast divulged a bad storm was developing in North Africa and heading to the Mediterranean Sea. Curious, I decided to do my homework to ferret out the details of the weather report on my own. He was right about the storm, though his timing was suspiciously miscalculated.

"I heard on the radio that the Spain National Meteorological report is anticipating the storm to arrive tomorrow, not the day after," I said subtly questioning his judgment of wanting to sail before the storm passed through. "Wouldn't it make more sense if we wait for it to blow by and depart in two days instead of tomorrow?"

He looked at me with a raised eyebrow and a faintly delineated smirk on his thin lips. Obviously, he was not amused with a deckhand telling the skipper what maritime common sense conditions ought to be.

"Wouldn't it?" I insisted not intimidated by his glaring.

"Not if we leave the Balearic Islands toward the coast before the storm leaves North Africa. As I told Dr. Hamil, we're leaving tomorrow morning," he replied in an authoritative manner that put an end to the conversation, if there was ever one.

Later that evening, he accidentally let me know that he was having some serious marital problems. Apparently, he had a confrontational telephone talk with his soon-to-be ex-wife, therefore his urgency to get back to Portugal.

The next morning the sky looked somberly grey. In fact, it was the first day in Ibiza that I didn't see the Sun shine. But to me, besides the lead-colored clouds in the atmosphere, there was something ominous in the air. Furthermore, a morose skipper behaving hastily on a dark cloudy day did not bode well for smooth sailing. In spite of my preoccupations, by 8:00 o'clock in the morning we were heading out the harbor toward the Spanish coast hoping to evade a storm that was tracking us from behind.

A couple of hours later, when we were well out on open sea between the Balearic Islands and Spain's mainland, the billowing sinister-looking clouds and fast moving winds caught up with us. Soon the sea turned into a tempestuous agitation of rising swells. Before long, it got so gnarly that peril was imminent.

"Make sure to tie up everything on the deck," the skipper shouted from *Lady Promise's* wheelhouse. Both his scratchy voice and the tension in his facial expression made me feel increasingly uneasy.

As I'm rushing through to secure loose items on the deck, I was abruptly hurled down by a crashing wave as I hit my forehead on the iron hatch frame. With blood oozing out the cut, I hurried inside to get the emergency medical supplies box. As soon as I walked in, I was stunned to eyewitness the chaotic sight. The furniture, lamps, decorative items, stereo, television set, and everything else in the boat's living room was in total disarray. With the Hamils' infant child screaming nonstop, the girls curling down on the corner holding each other as if each were a life vest to the other, and Kazar and Maria's terrified expression upgraded my already troubled state of being to desperation mode. I could feel the vessel's bow rising and piercing through the oncoming high waves before landing with thunderous impact. I thought the hull would be splintered into smithereens at any moment. Feeling terribly seasick, I rushed out of the cabin in search of solace that was nowhere to be found.

"Is everything secured?" The skipper yelled from the wheelhouse when I walked by outside. His tense voice revealed both the level of his stress and the gravity of the moment.

I wanted to tell him to fuck off but I didn't have the energy to utter a single word. I was seriously sick and pissed off. His irresponsible selfishness had put all of us in a life-threatening situation and I resented him for that. It reached a point when I became convinced that day was my last day on Earth. We were all going to die at sea. Then, overwhelmed by debilitating nausea like I'd never experienced in my life, I lay on the bow's deck vomiting nonstop until my empty stomach convulsed involuntarily. I began longing for the next wave to crash over the boat and wash away my moribund body along with my misery to the bottom of the sea. When formidable vertigo takes over a helpless victim, death can be welcomed as the ultimate reward of a life not worth living.

After hours of grueling existential misery in which I longed for my imminent demise, we miraculously made it to a small fishing village on the coast of mainland Spain. After the skipper moored the vessel at a rinky-dink dock—without any help from me—it took me several hours to be able to stand up from incapacitating prostration. Later when I tried to walk, my wobbly legs were able to waddle a couple of feet before succumbing to the deck forcing me to lie down again. Dizzy, dazed, and done, my undulating mind yearned for a modicum of physical stability. Suddenly, the recollection of an infinitely more turbulent time reminded me of my ability to bounce back from extreme adversity. I remembered the only time in my life when I felt much worse; and the recollection somehow made me feel better at that moment. Just a few months ago, I'd knocked on the door of bedlam and almost walked in for good.

Eventually, I fell asleep and the next day my indisposition ameliorated. But there was a time when it happened in reverse: I'd just woken up from a surreal sleep and a debilitating instability ensued.

I couldn't fall asleep the entire transatlantic flight. My mind was racing as though attempting to avoid getting sucked in a spiraling down vortex of despair. Overwhelmed by the anxiety of returning to Brazil where all my hopes and dreams would come to an end, I tried to distract my troubled mind by thinking of positive ways to rebuild my life. Maybe things would be different this time around. And yet, I knew that my optimistic thoughts were but subterfuges of my concerned mind yearning to disconnect from the reality that what I really wanted the most had now gone in the opposite direction.

As I walked out of the airport from the baggage claim area, I felt oddly out of place; almost as if I were in a foreign country I'd never visited before. Although the surroundings, language, and customs were clearly recognizable, my experience of being in an unfamiliar place was at odds with the fact that I was, after all, in my homeland. By the time I got in the taxi to go to my father's vacant weekend home not far from the airport, I realized I was in a state of slumber. It was as though my brain waves were moving at a slow theta frequency; the threshold between different perceptions of consciousness. I chatted with the cab driver as if he were a character in what felt like an inconsequential night dream; except that when I woke up, I realized it was a living nightmare.

As soon as I got out of the taxi and walked into my father's house, I noticed something wasn't right. I didn't even notice the housekeeper who'd let me in and carried my luggage while welcoming me home. As he walked by my side, his voice faded away piecemeal until I could not hear him at all. Then, a deafening silence completely obstructed my auditory sense until a boisterous alarm clock went off inside of my head overwhelming my hearing from within. I'd been brutally awakened from the most bizarre sleep-like experience of my life.

"What the hell am I doing here?" I uttered out loud to myself placing my hand over my mouth in disbelief. "This is not where I'm supposed to be."

"Excuse me, sir," the housekeeper said not understanding what was going on. His voice was now audible to me again as I was back to the place I didn't belong.

Seemingly, since crossing the Guadiana River separating Spain from Portugal, I'd been in some strange sleep state of being, as if existing in a parallel dimension. And as soon as I walked through the gate of my father's house, I seemed to have entered—or exited—another liminal line of existence. I'd wakened up into a terrifying real life nightmare.

My half-brother, who'd been spending time in the house with his girlfriend, came out to greet me looking as puzzled as I felt. I couldn't even try to disguise the overwhelming awe that had hijacked my senses. Something surreal was happening to me. I was irretrievably afflicted by despair and he couldn't help noticing it.

"Maybe if we smoke a big doobie you'll loosen up," my half-brother said trying to mitigate the palpable tension exuding from me. Alas, I'd already reached the point of no return; the event horizon of a frightening black hole that hauled me into an existential world of darkness.

Oddly, the more I smoked the more tense I became. I could not feel any effect of the excessive amount of tetrahydrocannabinol I consumed. Instead, I was being devoured by an overwhelming sensation of hopelessness ignited by my awakening to an unfavorable reality I was not supposed to be living. Suddenly, I realized I was back in a trapped situation I had managed to escape.

My high hopes of creating an exciting life abroad, as it'd been prophesized to me with uncanny precision, was now a crushed dream under my own boots. Why did I abort my aspirations? What would I do now? I started pacing around the house in a state of panic as if I were lost in a maze of madness unable to find my way out back to sanity. Mumbling hokum statements and cursing the woman who deluded me into believing I was destined to live an adventurous life abroad, I began losing my mind to unbridled despondency. I urgently needed some answers or I would never escape out of the mind trap I'd fallen into. I felt like I was in the verge of going crazy—literally crazy.

Likely disturbed by the way I looked and behaved, my half-brother and his girlfriend sneaked out of the house and left me alone with my tormenting commotion. As soon as I realized they were gone, I released an ear piercing scream that echoed in the depth of the bleak cavern my soul was hiding within. This never should have happened. I'd been led to believe that I was supposed to live abroad, and now I was smack in the middle of a real life nightmare from which there was no awakening. Feeling angry and vindictive, I picked up the phone determined to demand some explanation from the one who made me believe, convincingly, in inexplicable divination.

"You fooled me into believing that an exciting life was coming my way," I shouted at Lucia not holding back my uncontainable rage. "Look at me now. I'm back to the same place and condition I was before. You lied to me and made me believe in all sort of things I should have not. You really fucked up."

"No, you did it all by yourself. You acted like a coward quitting the game just because you fell behind in the scoreboard," she said admonishing me as if she were a sports coach talking to an apathetic player who'd just fumbled the ball. "It was just the first half of the game and you had plenty of time for coming back from behind. But instead, you chose to act like a wuss. Now, don't you dare to call me to bitch about your self-inflicted failures. You are the only one who fucked up."

"But you said...," I tried to justify a self-defense argument but she stopped me on my tracks.

"Whatever I said was what I saw in the realm of possibilities where many options are present in the future. But before a vision can shape the likelihoods of the future, one must act to trigger the forward motion of the promising prediction. And because you behaved like a pussycat and did not persist in your efforts, you ended up emasculated and in the same place you were before," she chided me with utter indifference to my emotional plight, and even a certain degree of disdain for my lack of courage. I felt ashamed, embarrassed, and much worse than before calling her.

"You quit in the first half of the game when there were still so many possibilities ahead for you to win the match. The truth is that you blew it in the worst possible way," she said continuing to excoriate me as if I needed any additional comeuppance. "I told you at the time there were two phases in your journey, and you didn't even complete the first. I have nothing else to say to you but to wish you good luck pulling yourself out of this mess you got yourself into."

Then she hung up on me rather snappishly. Now the self-loathing began torturing me from within. I felt significantly more dejected, hopeless, and helpless. I thought of her analogy of two halves game and remembered when she first told me that I'd first go to a country and undergo challenging situations before moving on to the country of my final destination. Of course, I surmised Switzerland as the first and going to Portugal as my second and final settling place. Although I had gone to the U.S. after Switzerland, since I had no intentions of staying there at the time, I never thought of it as my ultimate destination. But at that moment of regretful anguish, nothing really mattered any more.

Alone in the haunted house of my past where all my disappointments and fears lived, I paced back and forth mumbling agonizing sounds produced by a mind overcome with the guilt of self-defeat. I began sliding down a slippery slope of self-contempt. I could feel myself standing on the edge of the abyss of irreversible dejection that I was about to fall into at any moment. Regret may well be the worst self-inflicted punishment.

"She's right. I'm the one who fucked it all up. Now I'm stuck in this country where there's absolutely nothing for me but disappointments and heartaches. What am I going to do now?" I spoke out loud in crescendo desperation. Banging my tight fists against the wall while uttering anguished jumbled words, I felt as though I was about to cross the fine line between reason and madness hoping to find solace in insanity. Then, in the midst of my inner chaos, a paranormal dialogue ensued inside my head without my noticing how it happened.

"What am I going to do with my life now?" I verbalized my inquietude of spirit. "I'm snared in a wretched web of my own weaving. It's just a matter of time for the deadly poisonous spider of madness to devour me."

"At this point, there's only one thing for you to do," a serene voice spoke inside my head as if some ethereal being was partaking my mind without my recognized consent.

"What?" I blurted out loud stunned with the unexpected intrusion in my thoughts.

"You must go back," the voice whispered exuding ineffable equanimity.

"What?" I exclaimed again beginning to feel disturbed and wondering whether I'd already gone insane.

"You must go back to Portugal and start it all over," the voice clarified leaving no room for ambiguous interpretations.

"Go back to Portugal? Are you fucking kidding me?" I yelled at the voice inside of my head feeling sure my mind had already collapsed under the weight of my distress. "I just spent more than half of my money to get here and you're telling me to go back to a country where I know no one and there was nothing happening for me when I was there? And not only I have less money, I'm now carrying a heavy load of mental and emotional anguish with me. Are you fucking out of your mind?"

"You either go back or you go crazy," the voice whispered succinctly in my inner ear.

"How could I embark on such a seemingly impossible journey when I just got here? I don't think I could make it," I said fretting the inconceivable challenge of such undertaking.

"You must go back," the voice repeated curtly, but this time in a commanding tone.

"I don't think I can do this," I mumbled picturing the dreadful scenario of returning to a place I knew no one, and with significantly less money to get by.

There was a sudden lull of silence in my mind that momentarily placated my emotional turmoil. Then, the voice spoke again for the last time; a five-word statement that changed everything.

"You are not going alone," it said assertively.

For some mysterious reason, those five words had an enigmatic effect on me. It was as though I'd been encouraged to take a leap of faith straight into the cesspool of my fears. And even though I felt energized by the reassuring statement, I shivered at every thought of the daunting task at hand. But in the tug of war game taking place inside of me between the panic of staying or the dread of going back, I knew which one represented a second chance to a second half of a different game I'd quit and therefore lost. It was my only and likely last chance for redemption. Jittery and cold sweating, I dashed out of the bedroom to make an important phone call.

"Let me see what I can do," my stepmother said when I called her pleading to get me a one-way ticket to Lisbon.

"No later than tomorrow, please," I entreated. I knew time was of the essence or I'd risk changing my mind.

"I'll do what I can," she said. "As soon as I have it in hand I'll let you know when you can come to pick it up."

"Oh, no, no, you don't understand. I came from the airport straight home and I must go straight back to the airport from here. I cannot go anywhere else but back to the airport. This was never supposed to have happened. I beg you, please, bring this airfare ticket to me no later than tomorrow, please," I insisted.

"I'll do my best. In the meantime, try to get some rest," she said obviously noticing my distressed state of being.

My eyes remained wide open all night long. The anxiety and anticipation of what I was about to do were wreaking havoc on my nervous system. I couldn't stop wondering where I'd be spending the next night. I was frightened; and yet, oddly excited about a second chance for redemption. As for my stepmother, regardless of the ulterior motives she may have had to get me a one-way ticket out of the country, I've remained immensely grateful for her stepping up to help me when I needed the most.

The next day late in the afternoon my father and stepmother showed up with my one-way ticket to Lisbon. By early evening they drove me to the airport to send me off. My half-brother and his girlfriend came along, too. As I'm about to cross the departure gate, I turned around to look at them one more time and I was touched by the sympathetic expression in their eyes. I could feel they knew how difficult and necessary what I was doing was for me. In the last 36 hours I'd gone from the airport to home and back as if time had stood still with no interruptions in the continuity of my destiny. Something of paranormal nature that confounded my sensorial perception of space-time had taken place within three dozen hours. Befuddled, anxious, and yet feeling oddly relieved, I walked onto the airplane to resume a most daunting challenge that would put my mettle to the ultimate test.

Physically and emotionally exhausted, I fell deeply asleep—a coma-like sort of sleep—as soon as I fastened the seatbelt and leaned my head against the closed airplane window. Then, to my utter astonishment, I dreamed about the dream I could not remember when I woke up in distress the morning of the day I left Portugal. It was one of the most surreal dreams I've ever experienced. I was wandering through pitch-black dark streets not knowing where to go. I could feel the chilling temperature prompted by an anxiety-ridden turmoil that harassed me as I shivered from the inside out. Suddenly, I reached an intersection where a dim lit light post nearby flickered as if it were a moribund lightning bug in the twilight of its ephemeral existence. As I approached it, I noticed there was something right at the center of the intersecting streets. Puzzled, I gingerly moved toward it to find out what it was. As soon as I got closer to it, the flickering light post went off and only the object at the center of the crossroads was visible. I screamed when I realized it was my own pulsating heart bleeding on the asphalt with a wooden stake in it. I was terrified.

"This is your own doing," the sounds coming from my hemorrhaging live organ resonated. "If you want to survive you'll have to remove the stake, learn your lesson, and make sure that you'll never quit again."

As I interpreted the dream I'd not been able to remember the day I left Portugal, I immediately realized what the stake pierced through my heart represented: there was so much at stake; my life was at stake. But instead of having the heart (the etymology of the word courage comes from the Latin root *cor* or heart), I forfeited all that was at stake in my heart's desires. I'd quit out of weakness and now I had to remove the symbolic stake in order to bring my heart (courage) back to life again. As excruciatingly painful as the experience of going back to Brazil was, it became a most valuable life lesson that would serve me well as I moved toward my promised destination. Never would I quit a worthwhile endeavor again—never!

"I've been travelling on business trips around the world for decades," an older man donning a silver pinstripe suit sitting next to me said when the plane landed in Lisbon. "I've never seen anybody sleep soundly through an entire transcontinental flight."

I simpered looking at his stunned face without saying a word. He had no idea what I'd been through in the last 36 hours—and I had no idea what I'd still have to go through in the hours ahead. Removing a stake from a bleeding heart is not a task for the faint of heart.

After going through customs, I walked by the airline ticketing counter where hours earlier I had spent more than half of my money. How I wished I had that money back in my pocket, but there was no time for regrets. The only thing for me to do was to get on the interstate bus and ride back to the Algarve region; the place where I'd abandoned my efforts to make something happen. I thought of Lucia's analogy of two halves game and I was aware I was further down on the scoreboard, and still in the first half of the game. And even though I had no idea where I was going or what I'd do next, it was eerily comforting to feel that I was not going alone.

By the time I got off the bus in the Algarve region, I realized how badly battered I was. However, in spite of the high anxiety and deep sorrow I was experiencing, I was determined to remove the stake from my bleeding heart at any cost.

⁂

After cruising the Mediterranean Sea, many sailing jaunts to Gibraltar and throughout the Algarve coast—and having a grand time living the maritime lifestyle—my enthusiasm for all of it suddenly began waning. Perhaps it was the change of season that affected me. By the time late fall settled in bringing along the rain, fog, and chilling weather, I started craving something new. But underneath the layers of excuses I found to validate my discontent, I realized that at the core of it was an emerging need for change. As good and fun as my time in Marina de Vilamoura had been, I began feeling a growing urge to pursue different opportunities, though I wasn't sure exactly what I wanted. Somehow I knew the time had come to change the course of my life toward a new direction. I just did not have a clue what that might be.

By early winter the Hamil family invited me to spend Christmas with them in Lisbon. I was touched when they insisted that I joined their family for the holiday season. I gladly obliged; and in an act of reciprocal consideration, I decided to let Dr. Kazar Hamil know what I'd been bearing in mind of late.

"If what you're concerned about is making something of your life, then you're going to have to be more specific about what exactly you want to do," he said after I disclosed my latest yearning for change.

"To do or not to do; that is the question," I said pulling off a lamely constructed *Hamlet* line. "But I can't do what I don't know what it is."

Touching the tip of his elongated nose and with his eyes looking upward, he paused for a long moment as if he gave consideration to some thought or idea.

"How would you like to move to Lisbon and work in my law office?" He asked me unexpectedly.

"Wow! This is an unpredicted and generous proposition," I replied dismayed by his thoughtful blindsiding offer. "I don't know what to say."

"Well, you don't have to say anything right now. Take your time thinking about it and we'll revisit it at a later date. Now, let's go inside and get a bite of that sumptuous-looking chocolate cake that I haven't tried yet," he said putting his arm around my shoulder and leading me in from the balcony to the living room.

I was deeply grateful—and deeply confused. I wasn't sure that was the kind of change I thought I wanted. Moving to a big city and working in an office building was not exactly what I had in mind. However, it was a legitimate opportunity to take a giant leaping step in the building of my future. To work for a renowned attorney who'd taken me under his protective wings bode favorably to the prospect of starting a flying high career. Besides, his family was so loving and supportive of me that it all sounded too good to pass up. Nevertheless, his offer would entail more than just a mere change; it was a radical lifestyle transformation I had not considered even remotely. I had a lot to think about.

The next few days I found myself in the midst of some serious quandary. Although my life in the marina was getting as dull as a rubber knife, moving to Lisbon to work a desk job was not the kind of change I had anticipated. What I'd envisioned was spending some time elsewhere; perhaps in Gibraltar, Marbella, or another port town in the Mediterranean Sea; maybe even going back for a long sojourn on Ibiza. What I had not given any thought to was the idea of embarking on an unexpected career path, which I not only didn't anticipate, but also wasn't sure I was ready to pursue at the time.

As the rainy, cold, and gloomy weather settled in to stay, my mood attuned with the new meteorological environment. A sense of urgency to make something happen became insidious, which moving to Lisbon to start a new career was a viable option on the table. However, every time I gave the seemingly golden opportunity serious deliberation, I felt emotionally squeamish as if sailing in rough seas. As it had happened many other times in the past—and it would happen many times again in the future—I did not know what to do,

As unexpectedly as Dr. Kazar Hamil's offer came about, in the span of a few days two exciting new possibilities emerged; and both almost identical in nature. One morning when I was walking down the pontoon toward the marina's shopping center, I stopped by Dan's boat as he engaged in what in the next season I'd have called spring cleaning. Dan was a retiree from Seattle who sailed around the world with his wife on their 48-foot ketch.

"Going on a fishing expedition?" I quipped as he stood amidst strewn gear of all sorts.

"More like crossing the Atlantic," he said. "I got to get rid of some of this junk. If you see anything that fancies your heart's desire, by all means, help yourself."

"Crossing the Atlantic," I repeated with yearning curiosity.

"Yep, we're going back home to Seattle," he said moving toward me. "And by the way, we're looking for some deckhand help for the trip. If you know any trustworthy sailor who might be interested in crossing the Atlantic Ocean, have him come talk with me."

I spent the rest of the day wondering what would be like to sail across the Atlantic Ocean all the way to the West Coast of the United States. I started imagining the freedom of being out in the ocean without seeing land for days while breathing the invigoratingly fresh sea air round the clock. And going to the United States again suddenly felt more appealing than ever before; almost like a calling. At a time I wasn't sure what to do, an unanticipated opportunity popped up like a virtual particle from the quantum realm of possibilities. But as the trade winds of excitement blew into my sails of hope, a stormy thought came to mind disrupting my pleasant mental sailing image. From the shadowy caves in the deep ocean of my fears, I recalled my terrifying recent seasickness experience. What if a similar situation were to reoccur while in the middle of the Atlantic Ocean for weeks away from land? I'd die either of dehydration or by throwing myself overboard. The intrusive dire memory put a damper on my fleeting excitement. Like the life span of a virtual particle, it disappeared as quickly as it showed up.

A couple of days later, on the opposite side of the marina where my pontoon was located, I met someone who would validate the serendipitous occurrences of late. I had gone to a Norwegian friend's boat to return a tool I'd borrowed when he was talking with a mid-forties looking man. He was the owner of the recently arrived American flagged yacht mooring next to my friend's berth.

"David is on his way back to Los Angeles," my Norwegian friend said. "He and his wife are looking for deckhand help to cross the Atlantic."

I was stunned. For the second time in three days nearly identical opportunities had showed up by chance. I took it as an omen; a message from a genie out of the bottle of opportunities offering me options for change. This couple had been sailing the Mediterranean Sea and were now heading back home to L.A. Portugal was their last stop before the transatlantic crossing. David was a wealthy Hollywood movie producer and his wife was a lovely young woman. Both were very affable and we hit it off from the get-go. Once I revealed undisguised enthusiasm with the possibility of sailing across the Atlantic Ocean, the welcoming invitation came up right away.

"How would you like to join us in this journey?" David asked me point-blank.

"When are you leaving?" I asked without knowing how to answer his question regardless of his answer to mine.

"Next week," he said. "I know it's kind of short notice but we need to be back in L.A. by the end of next month."

"I'm afraid I'll need to renew my visa to the U.S.," I said. "I assume it'll take longer than a week."

"You can get it done at the U.S. consulate in the Caribbean, or in Panama before we cross the canal," he said undeterred. "Think about it and let me know ASAP."

Henceforth, all I did was to think about it. It was plenty obvious that the Universe was communicating with me in some kind of esoteric language of serendipity. All of a sudden, going to the United States seemed like the right thing to do. As alluring and generous Dr. Kazar Hamil's offer to me was, which would likely lead to a promising career in his powerhouse law firm, the mysterious messages coming to me through the natural law of encounters indicated a different direction. I'd come to a crossroad in which my analytical mind conflicted with my visceral feelings. But the most disturbing issue wedged between the opposing forces battling for my decision was the haunting anxiety that my fear of seasickness created. After the frightening experience in the Mediterranean Sea, I'd become traumatized and leery of ever sailing in rough seas again. Although my intuition seemed to be getting ahead in the tug of war against my mind, my apprehension was weighing heavily on my decision-making process.

Another critical detail was the timeframe. Although I had two viable options at hand, David and his wife were a much better fit to be stuck with on a boat for weeks than older cranky Dan and his aloof alcoholic wife. But one week was a very tight window of time to accommodate, whereas Dan's intention was to depart within a month. But in either case, the most important decision was contingent on leveraging what to do about my legitimate angst regarding seasickness. The answer came to me when I learned about the wonder drug that seasickness-prone sailors raved about: scopolamine. The drug is administered in the form of a transcutaneous patch placed behind the ear and is widely used for prevention of motion sickness. One patch provides therapeutic levels of scopolamine for up to three days. This was the turning point in the making up of my mind. I bought a dozen doses on the marina black market from a bona fide scopolamine drug dealer—who happened to be a medical doctor—and was determined to take my chances in an adventurous transatlantic voyage.

Although joining David and his wife was by far my preferred option, I felt like I owed Dr. Kazan Hamil and his family a timely announcement of my decision. I could not leave in a hurry and give them a short notice of my departure; I just couldn't do it. The enormous appreciation and gratitude I felt for them would not allow me to leave in a week without showing consideration and a proper farewell. Thus, I made a special trip to Lisbon to let the Hamil family know of my plans. But before heading north to the country's capital, I set up a young couple friends of mine to sail with David and his wife to Los Angeles. I also wanted to let Don know of my interest to sail with him to Seattle, but he was out sailing the day I left. I thought I'd talk with him when I came back from Lisbon in a couple of days. And now with more time at my disposal, I made sure to renew my visa to the U.S. before leaving Portugal.

"I'll have it ready for you to pick up tomorrow," the U.S. consular employee said after asking me a barrage of pro-forma questions regarding my visa request. However, after noticing the multiple U.S. entries and exits stamps in my passport, he didn't hesitate and obliged to my sense of urgency.

Having done my due diligence with the Hamil family and with my extended visa granted, I got on the bus back to Marina de Vilamoura with mixed feelings of excitement and trepidation. I couldn't help recalling the tear-jerking circumstance when I took that same ride from Lisbon to the Algarve region after my 36-hour ordeal. Almost a year later so much had changed—and in a much better direction—though I still felt as apprehensive as I did on that day following the turning point and most challenging time of my life. But this time the uneasiness I experienced was of a different nature. This time around I knew where I was going and how—and the latter was what inflamed my angst.

Being loaded with a supply of scopolamine was like having life vests for my stomach butterflies. Nevertheless, the bad sensorial memory of my last seasickness episode raised my level of concern to the thin surface of my skin. I could not fathom going through something similar again, especially in the middle of the Atlantic Ocean. And yet, my desire to embark on the exciting adventure was so robust that I was willing to take my chances. I knew many people in the marina community who'd welcome opportunities to cross the Atlantic Ocean just for the sheer fun of sailing. Some would make arrangements with other vessels to sail back home, while others would fly back to the point of origin. And there were a few like me who had challenges with motion sickness and still did it anyway. I was not going to be the one to chicken out of a unique adventurous opportunity.

The next morning of my returning from Lisbon, I went to Dan's boat to announce my intention to join him on the transatlantic crossing.

"Oh jeez, I just made arrangements with Patrick yesterday and he's going to be coming along," Dan said as I immediately recalled the hotel summer job incident.

I was very disappointed. This was not what I expected to hear. I knew Patrick well; the inveterate Irish sailor who would sail anywhere for a bottle of whisky. But his drinking habit aside, he was an experienced sailor and a good person, too. For all practical purposes, he was definitely much better suited for the task than I was.

"I suppose I could take you along as well," Dan said breaking the silence my disappointment had created. "But I want $100 dollars to cover your food expenses."

Not only I would not eat $100 dollars worth of provisions, it was a lot of money in the early 1980s; a money I was reluctant to part with when I wasn't expecting to make any for a long time. Besides, I would help navigating the vessel and hold night watch shifts. But it was the asking for the money itself—and the timing in which it took place—that left a bitter taste in my mouth. It was not a good way to begin a long transatlantic journey. Nevertheless, unlike a week earlier when I had three alternatives on the table, at that moment I had no options left.

The day to set sail to the United States finally arrived. We left Marina de Vilamoura around 4:00 o'clock in an overcast afternoon. Standing on the dock waiting for Dan to clear customs procedures, I looked out at the open ocean with considerable preoccupation. The dark clouds hovering in the distance looked like the event horizon of a massive black hole I could no longer eschew. I had entered the point of no return. For better or for worse I had only one way to go: ahead. And even though the sea was moderately tranquil, I placed a scopolamine patch behind my ear as a precautionary measure to mollify my building anxiety.

Like most vessels crossing the Atlantic Ocean from Europe, the plan was to sail to the Canary Islands, which takes approximately 4 nights, rest for a couple of days before leaving for the roughly 20-day trip to the Caribbean. From the island of Antigua it'd take another 4 to 6 days to the Panama Canal, and then another 3,000 thousand nautical miles-plus sailing up north to Seattle. It's a very long trip. But as long as my propensity for motion sickness didn't kick in, both the time and the distance did not bother me.

The combination of favorable winds, calm sea, and the scopolamine patch working its wonders, I was enjoying myself the first two days onboard. Without seeing land for two days, all I knew is that to the portside of the vessel there was the West Coast of Africa somewhere. The weather had opened up and turned out to be a most pleasant sailing experience, especially at night during my night watch shift. I shall never forget the feeling of bewilderment I experienced beholding a starry night sky like I'd never seen before. It was as though the cosmos that hid behind the Sun light during the day came out at night to reveal the mysterious nature of its infinity. The only thing bothering me was Dan's tardiness to replace me from my night watch duty—a half hour-plus late two nights in a row. But that was just the sour appetizer in a smorgasbord of ill-omened moments to come.

"Keep an eye on that vessel," Dan said while placing a pair of binoculars next to me during my morning shift at the helm.

On the starboard side sailing perpendicular to us heading toward the West Coast of Africa, a full-size ship moved in our direction. It was early in the morning of a sunny day and I could see it through the binoculars clearly. It was a large fishing vessel with a number of crewmembers moving about onboard. Moments later Dan showed up again.

"Let me take a look," he said yanking the binoculars out of my hands noticeably agitated. The vessel was definitely navigating toward us; and the closer it got the more ill at ease he became. He kept the binoculars glued to his eyes for a long time before heading down to the cabin with a sense of urgency.

I couldn't figure out what the fuss was all about. To me, it was but an innocuous commercial fishing boat out at sea carrying on its business. Although it was obvious that the ship was about to cross paths with us, it didn't look like we were in an imminent collision course. But when Dan emerged from the cabin along with Patrick holding a large metal box, I felt edgy wondering what the hell was going on. He nervously opened the box and I was shocked to see its content: an arsenal of handguns, a shotgun, a scoped rifle, and plenty of ammunition. I realized I was about to participate in some sort of bizarre naval battle against fishermen.

"Do you know how to use this?" Dan asked after handing me a 9mm. pistol. I stared at the weapon in my hand without saying a word. "If not, you're gonna have to learn on the job."

I was befuddled and scared. All of a sudden, we were all armed and ready for war; Dan with a shotgun, his wife with a rifle, and Patrick and I with handguns. I was mystified about what was going on; but by the tense expression in Dan's face, I could tell this was some serious business.

As the big fishing vessel got close enough to the point we could count how many men were onboard, I heard the pumping of the shotgun and I feared what was about to happen next. I noticed the globs of sweat inundating Patrick's tense pale brow while feeling the moist in my own forehead. This was not a situation I could have ever anticipated. And to think that all I worried about was seasickness.

As the fishing vessel sailed by with the men on the deck waving friendly at us, an enormous sense of relief was almost palpable in the air. Dan sighed out loud while disabling the shotgun; his wife went back to the cabin to fix a double martini; Patrick started giggling as if amused to being still alive; and I stared at the firearm in my trembling hand wondering how in the world I ended up on the verge of a potential gun fight. As I watched the fishing vessel sail away toward Africa, I wondered what could have happened that I wasn't aware of.

"What the hell was this all about?" I asked utterly bamboozled and oozing out tension through my voice.

"Piracy," Dan replied. "It can happen anywhere in open sea. There have been many cases of yachts robberies and murders in high sea recently. It's not like you can dial 911 to get the cops to come to help you out. On a boat out at sea you're on your own."

I was flabbergasted. I had no idea piracy existed in modern times. In my mind, I'd always linked the concept to the early navigational times of discoveries; like buccaneers encroaching on Spanish galleons to take over their precious cargoes of wealth.

It took me awhile to recover from the unexpected naval battle drill I'd just experienced. Alas, as the day went on things got even hairier before sunset. With billowing gloomy clouds building in the horizon and the wind whistling a sinister tune, Dan received a message on the radio that strong gale winds and stormy weather lay ahead on our path to the Canary Islands. Hence, he decided to change course and sail to Morocco to avoid the tempest.

Later on when I was doing my night watch shift, there was no infinite cosmos for me to behold. The overcast sky seemed to reflect the extreme anxiety of the moment and the distress accumulated during the day. Alone at the helm on the deck, I dreaded the big waves swaying the boat up and down to ever higher zeniths. Out of an abundance of caution, I harnessed myself to a metal bar fearful of falling overboard and being lost at open sea in the darkness of the night. What a terrifying death that would be. Eager to go back inside and get some much needed rest, I looked at my watch and noticed Dan was way past half-hour late to replace me, again. Pissed off with his continuous lack of consideration, I started stomping on the deck right over his cabin to get his attention.

"What da fuck are you doing?" He burst out of the boat spewing out his anger at me with a disgruntled face.

"You're late again. I need to get some sleep," I said assertively and not intimidated by his outburst of unjustifiable rage.

After going on a diatribe emphasizing his owner/skipper status on the vessel, he climbed up and nudged me off abrasively. By the time I hit the sack, I knew this was not going well in any direction. My newly found awareness of modern day piracy, anxiety about seasickness, and unexpected storms of both weather and bad temper made for an inauspicious combination for smooth sailing across the vast Atlantic Ocean. I closed my eyes and while induced by moderate nausea, I fell asleep harnessed to my bunk bed on the bow of the ship that thumped loudly every time it hit the water.

On the way to the Canary Islands after two nights in the port town of Safi in Morocco, I'd already made up my mind to get off the boat. The titillating adventure of sailing across the Atlantic Ocean didn't feel as exciting anymore; to the contrary, it felt more like embarking on a nightmare on purpose. Although I was determined to disembark on the island of Gran Canaria without having a clue of what I'd do next, I wasn't by any means willing to forfeit the aspirations of my life. I would continue on without ever quitting again.

"Are you kidding me?" I exclaimed holding a $50-dollar bill in my hand after asking Dan for reimbursement of my $100 payment. "Why are you giving me only half of my money?"

"This is what you get back. Take it or leave it," he said turning his back to me and walking back inside the boat.

Although my clenched fists twitched with the temptation to smack him in the mouth, I opened them up instead to pick up my duffel bags and walk away. I'd been stiffed by an inconsiderate greedy geezer. But as I heard the footsteps sounds of my tennis shoes on the gravel, I suddenly realized that I had much more important matters to dedicate my attention to. I needed to know what I was going to do next and where I'd spend the night. I was back to square one of what I'd experienced many times in the past year. It was déjà vu all over again. As for the shorter cash in my pocket, I'd already overcome significantly more stringent deficit and I made it just fine. Emboldened by past successful experiences, I was determined to continue on the journey I'd intended to follow when I left Portugal: I was going to the United States of America; but this time would be unlike any other in the past.

I was beginning to feel convinced of the truth behind Hamlet's words to his good friend Horatio: "There are more things in heaven and earth, Horatio, than are dreamt of in your philosophy." It was becoming crystalline clear to me that there were invisible forces operating within my actions. It was as though the perennial philosophical quandary of determinism versus free will blended into one synthesis of reality. Every time I made my move and relinquished the need to control the outcome of my actions, mysterious guiding forces came to my aid showing me the way to go. Having missed the opportunity to sail across the Atlantic Ocean with David and his wife to L.A. might have been a blessing in disguise. Because they were young, amicable, and welcoming, the likelihood that I'd get off on the Canary Islands was nearly nil. And after having experienced seasickness even with the scopolamine patch behind my ear—and for only a few days out at sea—I wasn't sure how I'd handle a potential chronic case of seasickness for days in a row without standing on solid ground. But based on my experience in the Mediterranean Sea, I had no doubts that a similar situation in the middle of the Atlantic Ocean might have posed a veritable threat to my life.

Assured of what I wanted to do, I left my bags in the office of the local harbor and headed downtown to find the best deal on an airfare ticket to New York City. As I strolled along a small picturesque park, I heard distant sounds of soothing guitar playing accompanied by a melodious female singing voice. The music halted my steps on the spot. I stood there listening for quite some time as it calmed my revved up nerves. After identifying where the sound waves were coming from, I followed them to their source. As I got closer, I saw a beautiful young brunette girl sitting alone with her music on a bench under a Dragon Tree in an inconspicuous part of the park. My first inclination was to walk toward her, but I felt intrusively self-conscious of getting between a woman and her music in the serenity of her private space. Suddenly, she lifted her head and looked at me across the long patch of grass that separated us, physically. Then, she flashed the brightest light I'd seen in a long time. After what I'd gone through sailing from Portugal to the Canary Islands, her luminous smile felt like a lighthouse inviting me to a welcoming haven.

"Beautiful music," I said as I got closer to her looking into her eye thinking of her as the music I referred to.

"It takes a fine listener to appreciate it," she replied.

And from that moment onward we would be together and form an inexplicable strong bond in a very short timeframe. Ursula, the young German woman vacationing on Gran Canaria with her family, had a magnetic persona cloaked underneath her beautiful face and figure. When she smiled, her slightly slanted eyes squinted as two dimples formed on each side of her lambent cheeks. The more we talked, smiled, and casually touched each other, the more undeniable it became that she and I had a connection that transcended the common dimension of physical perception. I told her about my situation and she suggested hanging out with me until I left the island.

After shopping around and purchasing the best deal and soonest flight to NYC, Ursula took me to a secluded beach she knew about for an afternoon dip. When we got there it was obvious that bathing suit was optional. She smiled at me impishly before undressing to the last piece of clothing. I smiled back and followed her lead. Then, she held my hand and we ran to the ocean as if we were two innocent children playing in some Garden of Eden by the sea. In the evening, after she went home to get some blankets and let her family know she'd be out for the night, we went out for some fun time *à deux*. We dined at a local joint washing down our fresh fish meals with plenty of good Spanish wine, talked about intimate details of our lives, laughed over the silliest jokes, and enjoyed ourselves as if we'd known each other for a very long time. After dinner, we headed to *Playa del Inglés* where we spent the night in a secluded corner of the beach. Making passionate love with Ursula under the eyewitness of glittering stars was one of the most sublime sexual experiences of my life. Lying next to each other effusively satiated, I could feel genuine love flowing between us in the silence of the night where only the gentle waves breaking ashore could be heard.

Staring at the countless stars above, I wondered about the nature and function of time relative to relationships. How was it possible to feel in love with someone I met just hours ago and feel her love for me in return? Conversely, I knew of people who had been married for decades and never really loved each other. There was something powerfully mysterious about this energetic emotion we call love. But as I indulged in my musings, suddenly it dawned on me that by that same time later in the day I'd be on my way to the United States. I felt a deep stab of sadness pierce through my heart realizing that this genuine love I was experiencing would be very short-lived, which deepened my inquiry into the nature and function of time in significant life's events. Perhaps, time is more a qualitative measurement than a quantitative amount of its elapsed passing. Ten hours of quality time can be infinitely more valuable than 10 years of melancholy. I thought of Einstein's humorous analogy of his complex Theory of Relativity: "When you sit with a nice girl for two hours, it seems like two minutes. When you sit on a hot stove for two minutes it seems like two hours." Ultimately, the magic lies on letting time be eternal in the moment it lasts without thinking about its beginning or end.

In the morning, after having croissants and coffee at a quaint French-style bistro, we went to the secluded nude beach for a carefree day in the Sun. By mid-afternoon, we were both beginning to show signs of subtle anxiety with the approaching farewell moment. An off-comment from me, an awkward giggle from her, and the uncomfortable eye contact we shared now and then, all revealed the gradually growing pressure of the passing of time toward the culminating moment of separation. Inevitably, evening arrived along with the dreaded moment to say goodbye.

"Well...," she said in a barely audible voice at the bus station from where I was about to take the shuttle to the airport.

It was a poignantly awkward occasion. Although bidding farewell to dear ones at any time always felt painfully cumbersome to me, this time around was particularly disconcerting and heart-rending. Maybe my emotional struggles with goodbyes had deep roots in my childhood trauma of losing my mother at such a tender age; and in that instant, it felt like it was happening again in similar fashion: a short-lived love experience. Making an extraordinary effort to hold my emotions in check, I attempted to offset the budding discomfort.

"Please take this," I said handing her a beautiful hand woven blanket that had an enormous sentimental and utilitarian value to me throughout my adventurous journey thus far. I wanted to give her a keepsake that was meaningful and important to me, just as my crossing paths with her had been.

She took it from my hands without saying a word. Looking at the colorful blanket while rubbing her hand on it as if she caressed me, she seemed to be struggling with her own despondent experience of bidding farewell. When she finally raised her chin to look at me, her moist green eyes made me realize that I'd better hop on the bus to the airport right away or risk a last minute change of heart. With the bitter taste of departure overwhelming my soul's gustatory sense, I reached out to the sweetness of her lips and gently kissed her goodbye. Then, without looking back, I rushed onto the bus and waved from the window as Ursula stood there holding the blankie close to her bosom as if it were a comforting teddy bear in a child's arms. Not surprisingly, I caught myself dabbing my hand under my damp eyes.

On that bus ride to the airport, I reminisced over the extraordinary events in the past year. And being on a bus triggered a natural correlation between similar life-changing occasions. The bus ride from Lisbon to the Algarve region was preceded by 36 hours of agony, whereas that one to the Gran Canaria airport happened after an equivalent number of hours of sheer gratification. It was interesting to observe how a comparable allotment of time can be fraught with utmost delight or laden with agonizing distress. How cyclical the flow of joy and sorrow can unfold within similar timeframes. How a time of utter desolation can switch to another of great elation; be it in minutes, hours, days, months, or years. That sudden realization somehow eased my mind into surrendering to the perennial unknown, which another phase was about to begin. From South America to Europe and now to the United States, the concatenation of my continuous movement was steadily leading me toward my ultimate destiny.

I checked-in my duffel bags and sat down alone with my thoughts. Slouching on the uncomfortable hard plastic chair with my legs splayed, my mind wondered about what lay ahead in the next leg of my prophesized journey. In a couple of hours I'd be on my way to Madrid to get on my connecting flight to New

York; and then, well, I didn't know. Nevertheless, I was confident I'd find out in due time. The lessons and experiences of the past year had imbued me with unwavering confidence that I could face any challenge with resolve. Entering the dark tunnel of the unknown no longer ignited fear; instead, it fired up a fierce determination to get to the light at the end. I was already a changed man and I was not even half way done.

As I straightened up my slumped stiff body, I suddenly turned my head around and casually glanced at the airport lobby entry way in the distance. Stunned with unexpected joy, I stood up and started walking toward her with a grin from ear to ear.

"What are you doing here?" I asked hugging Ursula tighter to my chest than when I last saw her at the bus station.

"I had to bring you something," she said. "I figured since you gave me your blanket you might need this at some point."

Then, she handed me a mummy sleeping bag nicely folded in its own roundish bag that I held in my hands while looking into her eye.

"Oh yeah, and this, too," she said breaking the momentary silence while reaching inside her large handbag. She pulled out a brown paper bag with a turkey sandwich, an apple, and a small bar of dark chocolate inside. "You might get hungry later."

For the next half-hour she sat next to me nestled cozily on the comfort of my shoulder. We just held each other in a most sublime embrace without saying a single word, for none was needed. Soon the loudspeaker announced the boarding for my flight. Reluctantly, we disentangled our embracing arms and, without saying a word, we walked to the departure gate side by side. Unlike when we bid farewell at the bus station downtown, this time our loving bond seemed to have matured. Somehow we knew that our loving experience was supposed to have lasted the few hours we shared and not a minute longer. But as Einstein predicated, it's all relative. And using his witty explanation about his Theory of Relativity in reverse, the few hours I spent with Ursula might as well have been a blazing hot stove for it felt like many years.

"Best of luck to you," she said after kissing me on the lips.

I winked at her, caressed her suntanned cheek, and kissed her on the forehead before turning around to never see her again. The seemingly brief time we shared, however, that has remained with me to this day—and so has the sleeping bag she gave to me.

Unlike on the flight from Rio to Lisbon that I slept throughout, on the plane from Madrid to NYC I could not bat an eyelash. While the flight to Lisbon had burdened me with desperate anxiety, the one to New York got me bursting at the seams with excitement of new adventures to come. Now I was an experienced traveler—the kind the elder Greek tourist I guided in Rio told me about—who had overcome intermittent homelessness, continual unemployment, debilitating seasickness, and even the scare of potential piracy in open sea. I'd grown a lot in the short span of a year and felt emboldened with self-confidence.

Like a mighty sword hammered into shape under fire, I'd been forged by adversity into a self-reliant weapon for my own survival. I was ready to take on my next challenge in the United States of America; the country that would become my adopted motherland.

PART II

Having not dropped my eyelids over my eyeballs longer than a blink of an eye for hours straight, I should have been feeling exhausted. Instead, I felt invigorated and excited with the anticipation of what I thought to be my American adventure.

"We'll be landing at JFK International Airport shortly. Please observe the fasten seatbelt light," the captain announced as I peeked through the window and saw the expansive New York City lights below. I could feel my soul dancing to the exhilarating rhythm of my heart beating like drums in a carnival party. I was happy to be back to the United States; and this time it would be like no other. Somehow I felt as if I were a long gone son—albeit adopted—who had come back home at last.

"What are you doing here?" My sister exclaimed in the intercom of her apartment building when I rang the bell. "I just got your postcard from Portugal a couple of days ago saying you were going to sail across the Atlantic Ocean to the U.S."

She buzzed the gate open and I came in thinking about her observation. Only a few days ago I was aboard a yacht on my way to crossing the Atlantic Ocean by sea. Suddenly, like the gale winds that changed the weather that deviated the original sailing route to Morocco, my fate had once again taken an unexpected turn of events. I knew that either in the Caribbean or after crossing the Panama Canal, eventually I would have to make up my mind about what to do in the U.S. However, I didn't feel pressured to make any premature decisions because I still had some three weeks of sailing to mull over my options. Besides, I didn't know what or whom I might encounter along the way that could unwittingly determine my next step. But change happened so fast that I now had to adapt and contrive a what-to-do-next strategy in a hurry. I had no intention of crowding my sister's place for long;

and as exciting as New York City was, I had no intention of staying there either. The time to come up with a moving forward strategy arrived much quicker than I'd anticipated.

On my third day in NYC, I was already feeling antsy about not knowing what to do next. I decided to go for a long walk in Central Park to sort things out in my head. After a pleasant stroll late in the afternoon, I was still unable to concoct a plan of action for the near future. But as the dim light of dusk began fading in the early evening, its last glimmer illuminated my intuitive perception with a sudden epiphany that made absolute sense to me.

"That's it!" I spoke out loud to myself abruptly halting my steps. "I'm going to Los Angeles."

Since my first opportunity when I decided to leave Portugal was to go to L.A. on David's yacht, I figured it was an indication that it was where I was supposed to go to in the first place. If it weren't for the encumbering details that hindered my ability to join David and his wife, I'd likely have sailed across the Atlantic Ocean in what could have been one of the most exciting—and potentially most dangerous—adventures of my life. And yet, not having done so might have also saved my life from an agonizing seasickness death. Also, in all likelihood, I wouldn't have met Ursula either, which would have been a significant loss of a unique and meaningful love experience in my life. But now it was all coming full circle. The natural unfolding of events I could have neither controlled nor predicted was revealing the magic and the mystery of the true meaning of kismet. It was as though life guided my steps without my needing to know where I was heading. At the right time and under the right circumstances, the answers emerged from the depth of the unknown to the surface whenever they needed to be revealed. By the time I reached the corner of Fifth Avenue and 37th Street my mind was made up: I was going to Los Angeles.

The following morning I woke up enthused and resolute to purchase a one way airfare ticket to L.A. My enthusiasm was temporarily tampered when it dawned on me that, not only I'd never been to Los Angeles, I didn't know anybody there either. Although I felt emboldened by my recent successful experiences in Europe, going to a big city without any connections was a significantly more intrepid undertaking. Nevertheless, I was determined to follow through with my plans and I wasn't going to allow my trepidations to obstruct my will. That afternoon I shopped around until I ended up in a travel agency at the Rockefeller Center mall where I found the best deal. Bereft of any qualms whatsoever, I purchased the airfare ticket to L.A. to depart in three days. Alas, those three days would prove to be uncomfortably longer than the hours within them could pack. They ended up being very painful days—literally.

"Damn!" I blurted out in the middle of the night feeling my upper left molar tooth throbbing like a hard hit war drum. I spent the rest of the night awaken, moaning and worrying about the unexpected inauspicious happening. Holding my pulsating face as if my heart beat between a molar and a wisdom tooth, I dreadfully realized I was experiencing a toothache from hell—and maybe only severe vertigo can be worse than an acute toothache.

Unable to get any sleep at all, I rose before the Sun did. With a cold ice pack pressed against my face, I paced back and forth more troubled by the fact that I was supposed to leave in a couple of days than the excruciating toothache itself. Going to Los Angeles harboring an agonizing toothache was tantamount to getting on a boat for a transatlantic voyage already afflicted with debilitating vertigo. I couldn't possibly go to a big city I didn't know anybody handicapped by an incapacitating toothache. I had to see a dentist, but I could not afford the prohibitive cost of a dental office visit; and even less so treatment that would siphon my meager savings to oblivion. Furthermore, I'd already purchased the airfare ticket and didn't have time to spare either. All of a sudden, I was in a real bind with a major challenge to overcome.

The next two days I oscillated between panic and despair, both of which were accompanied by incisive oral pain. Torn between giving up my plan—and losing the money on my nonrefundable airfare ticket—and embarking on a daunting adventure magnified by an adverse physical handicap, I realized that the cause of my emotional terror and physical discomfort was rooted on wavering psychological disturbance. In spite of my swashbuckling attitude to conquer the next traveling adventure regardless of the circumstances, after removing the layers of my bravado, at the core I found a natural apprehensive human element that exposed my vulnerability to myself. Deep inside I knew that going to a big city without knowing anyone was no small assignment, and that was unwittingly giving me the heebie-jeebies. Yes, going back to Portugal from Brazil in similar circumstances and with less money in my pocket was a very difficult undertaking, though it was facilitated by a gargantuan desperation that I didn't feel about going to Los Angeles. My going to L.A. was motivated, not by fear or despondency, but by a conviction that my destiny was to be fulfilled by taking that next step in the grand tour journey of my life. Thus, I was not going to allow an awful toothache—or even a severe bout of vertigo for that matter—to become an impediment to my calling.

Valiantly, I packed my duffel bags and headed to the airport determined to go through with my plan. In an unexpectedly bizarre turn of events, by the time I entered the aircraft I started feeling lighter and more relaxed. After placing my carryon bag in the overhead compartment, I sat down at my window seat, buckled up the seatbelt, and exhaled while exuding a mixed monotone sound of anxiety and relief. As the plane headed to the runway for takeoff, a titillating anticipatory excitement took over me. Once I felt the landing gear lifted off the ground, I realized I'd forgotten about my toothache. I wasn't in pain anymore and I had not even noticed it. As mysteriously as it'd shown up, my toothache vanished in thin air—and I never experienced any other teeth-related issue again in nearly a decade.

The likely psychosomatic toothache served me very well. It gave me the opportunity to rise above my fears and doubts while solidifying my commitment to my goal. Although the anticipation of the challenges ahead still tickled my self-assurance, I felt more emboldened than ever before. I felt primed to embark on a new adventure; and who knows, maybe I'd earn a heavenly reward in the city of angels.

❧❖☙

As soon as the airplane approached Los Angeles airspace, I caught myself involuntarily cracking my knuckles. Peeking through the window from a few thousand feet above ground, I watched in dismay a sea of lights stretching through the horizon as if I flew over a luminous concrete jungle. Curious, I glanced at the window across the aisle and the lights didn't seem to end on that side either. Suddenly, I started nibbling on my lower lip feeling my anxiety level rise while the airplane descended. I'd just realized how huge and spread out of a city Los Angeles was. Although I was heartened by my previous experience in Europe, this time around the chips on my gambling table seemed stacked up against my odds. I knew right away that this leg of my journey would require summoning up all my survival skills and chutzpah I'd amassed in the last year, for I would need every ounce of it.

With a clear visual memory of the expansive light covering the horizon of the city etched in my mind, I thought I'd better spend the night at the airport before venturing into a big city I knew nobody and had no idea where to go. I ambled around LAX looking for some cozy and quiet spot I could doze off until sunrise. Once I located an inconspicuous ideal setting, I placed my duffel bags down on the floor and leaned against it to spend the night. As my mind wondered incessantly what I would do in the morning, I casually surveyed the crowd moving about. Parading before my eyes, there were blond and beautiful young tanned people; speedy businessmen swaying their briefcases in sync with their fast moving feet; talkative airlines flight attendants rolling their luggage along; subdued Mexican-looking cleaning crews minding their business; dressed to the nines goodie-two-shoes with their design name suitcases; and even a scary and rowdy group of young African Americans wearing red bandanas. Later I'd learn they were likely members of the "Bloods," the rival gang of the "Crips;" some of the various disreputable cadres of crooks in town. Eventually, I'd also find out that in the city of angels criminals and riffraff abounded in every segment of society. But at that moment, I had an inkling that the people of Los Angeles were afflicted with some sort of schizophrenic collective personality disorder.

When I woke up in the morning rubbing my eyes before releasing a lion's yawn, I reluctantly stood up, stretched my arms out, and took a deep breath contaminated with both air pollution particles and feelings of apprehension. There I was, alone in a ginormous city, with no idea where to go, and no connections to assist me. Although I was aware of the enormity of the challenge before me, I felt confident that I'd pull it off somehow. After all, I'd done it before—albeit in a much less intimidating and strenuous environment—and I trusted I'd do it again. But as it's often the case, the first step of a thousand mile journey is the most difficult to take.

With a Styrofoam cup of coffee in one hand and a local area map in the other, I scrutinized my surroundings on paper and realized that nearby Santa Monica looked like my best option to get started. Once I'd decided what to do, I tossed both the coffee stained map and the empty cup in a trashcan and walked out of LAX like a gladiator walking into the coliseum imbued with both excitement and fear. I hopped on a city bus and shortly thereafter I arrived at my first destination in Southern California. The game was on and I'd better be ready to play, otherwise I'd be trounced by the overwhelming adversity I was against.

On a strictly instinctive initiative, I got off the bus as soon as it drove past Pico Blvd. Unsure of which direction to go, I started walking toward the ocean and ended up at the Santa Monica Pier. As soon as I got there, I dropped my duffel bags on the ground and soaked in the loveliness of my surroundings. The offshore sea salt breeze flowing into my nostrils; the squawking of seagulls circumventing the fishermen on the pier; the sight of palm trees lining up Ocean Avenue; and the warmth of the shining Sun light on my body, all of it made me feel comfortably at home; except, of course, for the fact I didn't have one. Hence, my most pressing need was to find out where I'd spend the night.

After a long time basking in the pleasantry of the moment in a brief respite of positive indulgence, the rumbling in my stomach let me know it was time to move. I walked a couple of blocks inland to a fast-food restaurant where I ate and set up office to put together a plan of action. With the local newspaper in hand, I perused through every single advertisement searching for any information that might offer a hint to an opportunity. After a couple of hours circling ads and taking notes, I realized that I needed to get acquainted with the area before dusk. Thus, I removed a small backpack from one of my duffel bags and filled it with essential items, as well as the rolled up mummy sleeping bag Ursula gave to me. As for the large bags, I was wondering what to do with them when I looked across the street and had my answer.

"I can definitely keep them for you," a friendly young woman at the front desk of a modest hotel chain said when I asked if she could keep my bags overnight. Her affable demeanor reminded me of the young lady at the hotel in Portugal where I worked for a week. "We have a safe storage space for our guests' luggage. I'll keep yours there and you can come to pick them up any time tomorrow."

Free to explore the area, I walked around Santa Monica like a sleuth on an investigative mission. I identified addresses and locations in the newspaper ads I'd circled, familiarized with streets and neighborhoods, while at the same time keeping my eyes open to a potential sheltered place to spend the night. After a long circuitous exploratory walking, my growling tummy reminded me that it was time to go back to my fast-food restaurant office to work on my immediate needs: to eat and determine where I'd spend the night.

I don't know what time it was but the Sun had set for quite some time by the time I finished my insalubrious meal. At that point I'd already decided that I was going to sleep somewhere on the beach; probably under the Santa Monica Pier. I figured it would be a much more convenient place than it was under the smelly fishing boat that sheltered me on the beach in Portugal.

I was about to get up and head toward the pier when a freckled-faced young blondish man approached me.

"Are you done with the newspaper?" He asked walking in my direction as I gathered my belongings getting ready to leave.

"Other than the classified section, you can keep the rest if you want," I said.

"Cool. I appreciate it," he said before a long pause in which he frowned at me in an inquisitive way. "I noticed the accent. Where are you from?"

Usually, this is a question that I—and most foreigners and immigrants I know—resented when asked shortly after meeting me. Although I understand the curiosity factor, sometimes it is laden with bias that can lead to discrimination, which I'd experience many times in the future. But in that particular case it didn't bother me at all. I could tell the friendly young man was more interested in establishing a welcoming bridge than opening a chasm of prejudice between us.

"I'm Brazilian," I said hanging my backpack on my shoulder and getting ready to leave.

"No shit! Brazilian? You got to be kidding me?" He said sounding surprised and oddly excited with my answer.

I smiled awkwardly and nodded feeling as surprised with his unexpected reaction as he was with my response.

"Man, that's one of the coolest people I've ever met," he said unable to contain his excitement. "I spent some time in Rio and I loved it."

"That's my hometown," I said.

"No shit! What are you doing in Santa Monica, man?" He asked.

I paused not knowing what to say, until I decided to copycat his comment. "I'm spending some time in Southern California."

"That's so cool, man," he said. "I can show you around if you're interested. Where are you staying?"

His last question left me stumped. I hesitated until I stammered a one-word answer out of my mouth. "Nowhere."

"What do you mean nowhere?" He asked looking puzzled.

"I just got here today and I don't have a place to stay yet. I'm still finding my bearings," I said.

"Well, now you do," he said smiling broadly as if he were the one who'd just found much needed shelter. "If you don't mind crashing in the garage of my parents' house tonight you can come with me. Eventually, we can look for a more stable lodging for you. What do you say?"

There was nothing for me to say but thank you. I was stoked. All of a sudden, as I'd experienced many times before in my journey, my fate had taken an unexpected positive turn. As we walked on Santa Monica Blvd. toward 14th street where he lived, Clint shared with me that when he was in Rio someone he'd met on Arpoador Beach took him home and lodged and fed him. He was amazed with the hospitality bestowed upon him by a stranger and he felt this was his opportunity to pay it forward—and I was the beneficiary of a fellow Brazilian citizen's kindness.

Later that night after ensconcing myself in the sleeping bag Ursula gave to me, I wondered about the truth expressed in the words of Johann Wolfgang von Goethe's (1749–1832) famous quote: "Until one is committed, there is hesitancy, the chance to draw back. Concerning all acts of initiative (and creation), there is one elementary truth, the ignorance of which kills countless ideas and splendid plans: that the moment one definitely commits oneself, then Providence moves, too. All sorts of things occur to help one that would never otherwise have occurred. A whole stream of events issues from the decision, raising in one's favor all manner of unforeseen incidents and meetings and material assistance, which no man could have dreamed would have come his way. Whatever you can do, or dream you can do, begin it. Boldness has genius, power, and magic in it. Begin it now."

My life in Southern California had just begun.

Within a couple of weeks I was all settled in. Although Clint had gotten the approval of his parents for my sleeping in the garage for as long as I needed, I was determined to find a place of my own as soon as possible. Once I learned that the largest manmade harbor in North America—with more than 4,600 boat slips—was not far away, I headed to Marina Del Rey hoping to find a similar living situation I'd experienced in Marina de Vilamoura in southern Portugal. Although the odds of encountering an American version of Dr. Kazar Hamil were slim, I'd welcome any opportunity coming my way.

Hence, back to the proven erstwhile beaten path of hitting the pavement—or in this case knocking on boats' hatches—I went out to the marina on daily scouting missions. However, once I realized how huge the place was, I bought a $25 used bicycle in a garage sale so I'd have a set of wheels to move around. It didn't take me long to realize that in L.A. not having a vehicle—even if it's only a bicycle—is a serious transportation handicap tantamount to being crippled. Now able to be more freely in motion, I spent days in a row roaming through a marina that was as widespread as the city of Los Angeles itself. But on a bike, I was able to ride the whole circuit: Mindanao Way, Tahiti Way, Marquesas Way, Fiji Way, and all the adjacent lanes. I covered most of the area, but nary a fraction of the thousands of yachts moored at the upscale harbor. However, all I needed was one lucky encounter.

One late afternoon as I was about to ride back to Santa Monica after a fruitless day looking for housing and work, I saw a young man standing on the deck of a large sailboat packing his tools in a box. It was obvious that he'd been working on the boat. Although I didn't think he'd share information with potential competition, I decided I had nothing to lose and approached him with doubtful expectations. It ended up being an auspicious stop.

"Dude, there's so much work in this marina to keep the U.S. National Guard busy for a year," he said when I asked about prospective odd jobs.

"What about living onboard arrangements? Are they plentiful as well?" I asked assured that I had made the right connection.

"Those a little bit trickier to come by, but there are some out there," he said looking at me askance. "Are you looking for work or to live onboard?"

"Both," I said unhesitatingly.

"Well, maybe I can get you started with the work part," he said. "Right now I have a backed up list of customers that I can hook you up with in exchange for a percentage of your hourly rate. How much do you charge?"

"I...don't know. What's the going rate around here?" I asked.

He looked at me realizing that I was fresh off the boat so to speak. I was clearly not in the know and in need of work, which led him to make me what I thought to be a fair offer.

"Listen, I can set you up with some of my customers at twelve bucks an hour, you pay me two, and you make ten dollars an hour. How does it sound to you?" He asked.

"When do I begin?" I replied smiling with gratitude.

We shook hands and I helped him put his tools away while we chatted and got acquainted with each other. Marvin was a nice bloke—an Englishman, that is—who'd been working in the marina for a couple of years. He seemed to know the ins and outs of the business, the local community, and some of the movers and shakers in the area. When I emphasized my need to find a stable housing situation soon, he told me that he knew a couple that was renting a walk-in closet with a single mattress in it, plus the sharing of the bathroom and kitchen for a pittance to Santa Monica's standards. It would be a good way to get started until my situation improved. And just like that, I'd found work and a place to live in a one stop inquiry.

Within two weeks of arriving in the city of angels, I was settled in my own walk-in closet room on Bay Street, which was at a prime location a block away from the beach in Santa Monica. Although the apartment was in an old unkempt building, the place was clean and proper. More importantly, however, the young couple from whom I rented the space and I hit it off from the get-go. He was a tall good-looking Colombian man and she was a petite blond; a typical Southern California girl. I moved in hours after we met and we struck a good friendship that lasted through the duration of my time living with them, until their livelihood turned into an occupational hazard for me and I was compelled to move out. But in the meantime, I was thrilled about the favorable unfolding of my new adventure. I had work, a place to live, and I was beginning to make friends. Soon it would be summer and I couldn't wait to find out what the future would bring.

Summer arrived in full force and I came right along with it. A few months had passed since I arrived at LAX and now I was flying high. With a modest livelihood in place, I started upgrading my standard of living. I retired the bicycle as my principal means of transportation—though I never got rid of it—and bought a Honda 750cc as my new motorized vehicle. In addition to improving significantly my ability to move about, the motorcycle allowed me to explore one of the most beautiful coasts in the world. Riding my Honda on Pacific Coast Highway (PCH 1) from L.A. to San Francisco was an exhilarating experience of visual and kinetic pleasure.

As a surfer boy from Rio, of course I had to buy a surfboard, which I did long before I bought the motorcycle. At first I carried the board while riding my bicycle through the bike lane from the Santa Monica Pier to the Manhattan Beach Pier searching for waves to ride. Later, when I traded the motorcycle for a VW van, I surfed from Zuma Beach in Malibu to San Clemente in Orange County. Life was good. I was immersed in my California dreaming experience and I didn't want anyone to wake me up.

But not everything was so rosy in the city of angels; in fact, it was very white. Los Angeles in the 1980s was plagued with the cocaine consumption way of life. Although it is true the vicious culture was endemic in most metropolitan areas in the world, it seemed to me that it found its thriving environment in the city of make believe. Somehow the entertainment industry of Hollywood, along with the prevalent cultural obsession with appearances, youth, beauty, and wealth, all provided a perfect breeding ground for the nasty ego-boosting habit of cocaine abuse to proliferate. From doctors and judges to academics and high school students, it seemed that in every segment of society people were doing cocaine as if it were a casual item of consumption. Not by any chance an innocent observer of this cultural trend, soon I became acculturated in my new environment. But cocaine was just the tip of the iceberg in the frigid decadence of a society consumed by hedonistic pleasure. I was first introduced to the city's licentious way of life in informal and gullible fashion.

By late summer I had befriended a nice group of people I played beach volleyball with at the south side of the Santa Monica Pier. One of them was a beautiful Japanese girl who dated one of the local players. I had a tremendous crush on her; and since her boyfriend didn't seem to mind my subtle flirtatious interactions with her, I upped the ante and started making more audacious passes at her. Emboldened by his obvious indifference to my increasingly aggressive initiatives—I supposed they had some sort of open relationship—I began prying through the chinks of their cracked relationship determined to break in until I'd eventually be able to penetrate her. One day an opening occurred and I eagerly pounced on the chance to have a taste of that succulent geisha.

"My birthday is coming up and I'm throwing a party at Jessica's house this Friday. I'd love for you to come," she said with a salacious look in her slanted eyes and a naughty intonation emphasizing her last sentence.

"Of course I'm coming," I said replicating the inflection of her voice. There was not a modicum of doubt in my mind it was an invitation to have sex with her.

Friday evening arrived not a moment too soon. I showed up at the address she gave to me curiously excited about how we'd make it happen at her birthday party. As I walked in the crowded living room, she rushed to greet me and I was immediately smitten with her looks. Wearing a red traditional Japanese kimono, she looked like a tantalizingly sexy oriental goddess with her long black hair cascading down to her waistline.

"I'm so glad you made it," she said after kissing me on the cheek while holding my hand. "Go get yourself something to drink and I'll catch up with you again soon."

I estimated there were a little over a dozen people scattered through the festive environment. It was a fun-filled atmosphere with people drinking champagne, snorting coke, and chatting with a pleasant soft jazz music playing in the background. I meandered around talking with the few folks I knew from the Santa Monica Pier volleyball group while having my share of champagne and cocaine. I was feeling really good and excited with anticipation. In the meantime, I kept looking around wondering where I'd find a private *dojo* (a room to practice martial arts) where I could stick my *katana* (sword) in the *saya* (scabbard) located between the legs of the gorgeous geisha.

High and distracted by casual conversations, soon I noticed that almost everyone had moved to the backyard. I stayed put waiting for the birthday girl to come get me assuming she'd take me to one of the bedrooms for our own private celebration. I couldn't wait for her to blow my fiery manhood candle and make a sexual birthday wish I intended to fulfill. I was alone in the living room when she showed up.

"Come with me my sweet boy. Let's go have some fun," she said holding my hand leading me to the backyard.

"Wait!" I said halting my steps. "There's an empty bedroom right there to the left."

"I know," she said nonchalantly pulling me along to follow her toward the backyard. "That's not where the party is."

As soon as we stepped outside the kitchen, I could hear the cacophony of moaning sounds and naked men and women making out with one another in and around a large bubbling Jacuzzi. Startled, I stopped in disbelief while watching, for the first time, an uninhibited orgy taking place before my eyes. This was not by any stretch a traditional birthday party. It was an orgiastic festival of grandiose proportion. A girl handling three guys at the same time; another offering oral sexual pleasure enhancement to a copulating couple; women on women; men on men, including the hostess' boyfriend having sex with another guy, which made me understand why he never minded my advances onto his girlfriend. I was stunned. I'd never seen anything like it before.

"Come with me and let's have a party of our own inside the house," I said holding her hand as I moved away from that repulsive scene. I wanted to fuck her really bad, but only the two of us.

"You don't understand," she said pulling her hand away from my steady grip. "This is a hot tub party."

"I thought it was your birthday party and we were going to share a gift together," I said.

"That's true, but I'm not sharing the gift with you only," she said before turning around to join the other maenads in the Dionysian bacchanal.

I left the house feeling utterly frustrated and disappointed. Although I'd eventually have sex with her a few weeks later in my walk-in closet space, that night was a wake-up call to my awareness of one of the many sordid characteristics of the zeitgeist of Los Angeles in the 1980s. I ended up going to a couple of other seemingly casual gatherings that turned out to be wild orgies under the guise of laid-back parties. I even went to one with my roommates in which he left his woman behind "to let her have some fun" but he wasn't into orgies himself. I just couldn't wrap my mind around the idea of leaving a live-in girlfriend at an orgy knowing she'd be fucking god knows how many guys—and girls—overnight. Apparently, there was a complete indifference to monogamous relationships in L.A.; or perhaps, I was the old-fashioned South American who couldn't grasp the openness of a liberal carefree sexual lifestyle.

After awhile, it became obvious to me that the cultural scene in Los Angeles was infused with sex (predominantly orgies), drugs (mostly cocaine), and, as I'd soon find out, a predisposed demeanor for superficially biased social status appearances. In fact, had Shakespeare written *Hamlet* at that time in L.A., the main character would have questioned the quandary of his troubled existence not as "to be or not to be, that is the question;" but instead, he would have added a materialistic twist to what was important in that decadent urban culture: "to have or not to have, that is the question."

❧❖☙

After a few months in town, I'd already sensed how shallow the local culture was. From tanned body builders parading in Speedos through Venice Beach to convertible Porches zooming by Pacific Blvd., it was unambiguous that the zeitgeist of the city revolved around youthful good looks and flaunting affluence—the latter was either real or concocted for the purpose of appearance. I felt as though I participated in some sort of real life Hollywood production in which I had a cameo role of quasi-invisibility. What it took me awhile to find out was how deep the shallowness really was.

After having experienced a few turn downs by young women once they learned I didn't have money and lived in a walk-in closet in a rundown building, I became aware of my handicap on the L.A. dating scene. What usually started out as seductive flirtations, radiant smiles, and mischievous twinkles in the eye, often ended up with dismissive excuses, sour facial expressions, and shady looks, before my dating interests walked away unceremoniously. In very few occasions, I felt like I had a legitimate shot at having a steady girlfriend, which I wanted and pursued with determination. One of them was a beautiful brunette who was an anthropology graduate student at UCLA with whom I shared intellectual compatibility, mutual physical attraction, fun times, and stimulating conversations. But as usual, it was a matter of time and she, too, skedaddled as soon as my economic limitations became known. There was a time, however, that the rejection had more to do with my ethnic background than my financial status—and it was also the instance when the bond was the strongest.

Sarah and I met at *La Boulangerie*, a quaint French eatery on Bay Street in Santa Monica. I used to go there almost daily to have coffee and croissants and read for hours in the lovely outdoor patio. It was a perfect place to hang out with a book. After meeting Sarah, the coffee, the croissants, and a book were no longer necessary, though I always had them as well. We met there regularly and spent hours talking, laughing, touching, and looking into each other's eyes in silence with utmost intimacy of spirit. Then, I'd walk her to her red BMW where we made out with passionate abandon. We both knew it'd be a matter of time and we would consummate our affection with a no holds barred physical connection. And as the weeks went by, it was undeniable that we were developing earnest feelings for each other—and that's when she dropped the biased bomb of rejection on me.

"We must stop seeing each other," she said unexpectedly minutes after arriving.

"What?" I asked wondering whether she was pulling my leg.

“We can’t see each other ever again,” she said in a somber tone of voice and without looking at me.

“What are you talking about?” I asked beginning to realize the seriousness of her intent. “We’re clearly growing feelings for each other, Sarah. Our relationship is picking up steam.”

“That’s exactly why we must stop seeing each other,” she said still not looking at me.

“I don’t understand. This makes absolutely no sense to me,” I said unwilling to resign without a fight.

“You know I’m Jewish. What you don’t know is that I come from a very orthodox Jewish family background,” she said fidgeting her hands on the table.

“So?” I questioned monosyllabically flummoxed by what I perceived to be an irrelevant comment.

“Well, you are not Jewish. And my father would never accept anyone into the family who is not Jewish. And since our feelings are growing, we must stop it now before we get hurt,” she said now staring at the floor as she spoke.

“I can convert to Judaism; I can even get circumcised if required,” I said facetiously trying to assuage the tension of the conversation.

“My father would never accept anyone into the family who is not Jewish by birth. Our relationship doesn’t stand a chance, and for that reason I must leave now,” she said finally looking at me in the eye. “You’re a good man and I’m sure there’s a good woman out there for you.”

And just like that she stood up and walked away from me. I never saw or heard of Sarah again.

I wouldn’t say that I was heartbroken, but I was definitely disappointed and baffled by her unexpected reaction. I’d always thought of the Jewish people as the ones who were persecuted and ostracized by the ignorance of prejudice. Suddenly, I understood first-hand the discrimination they constantly bemoan about, though I still had no idea what they might have gone through during their trying days in the 1930s in Nazi Germany. What I never would have expected was that one day I'd be biased by one of them the same way they were by anti-Semitics; that is, with unjustifiable bigotry exclusively based on ethnic distinction. I couldn't comprehend how race, religion, or any other differentiation should be validated to poison promising human relationships.

The sting of losing Sarah to unforgiving dogma didn't last long. I quickly moved on opening myself to new romantic possibilities. However, I kept running into different kinds of prejudices, some of which would follow me along in the years ahead. Later, after becoming a step-citizen of the United States, both my country of origin and my distinct accent would become motives for discrimination. Since a large percentage of my natural born fellow citizens do not consider naturalized citizens as "real Americans"—just like my stepmother differentiated me from her "real sons"—I'd been primed to learn how to cope with this type of favoritism. As for my unique accent, it has worked as a double-edged sword. In some occasions, what has been often extolled as a charming accent has been a veritable boon. However, there have been many other situations when I've been negatively judged by it; mostly by prosaic-minded individuals.

Unfazed by prejudice and ignorance that I could not control, I was determined to continue pursuing romantic connections. With a different strategy in mind, I decided to start targeting older well-to-do women who already possessed what I did not. Therefore, my precarious financial situation should not be a hindrance to a potential rapport. With that in mind, soon I realized that supermarkets, especially the ones located in affluent neighborhoods, were one of the best hookup spots in town. The Marina Del Rey mini mall supermarket proved to be an ideal cougar hunting ground.

Wearing a black wife-beater covering my toned and tanned torso, yellow trunks, and flip-flops, I walked in the supermarket to buy peaches, which often I ate with gluttonous appetite while riding my bicycle around the marina. I was absent-mindedly filling in a plastic bag with the soft-skinned juicy fruit when she suddenly appeared right next to me out of nowhere. Delightfully surprised, I beheld that gorgeous middle-aged female specimen with coveting interest. The shapely blond with bright blue eyes wearing a short spaghetti-strap white dress hijacked my attention. Gawking at her, I accidentally dropped a peach on the floor missing the open plastic bag. She smiled at me and that was the only opening I needed.

"They're very juicy and delicious," I said holding a peach in my hand with an intentional impish look in the eye.

"I bet they are," she said reciprocating my sexual insinuation with a seductive intonation of her own.

The game was on. We started a long and engaging lighthearted conversation punctuated with mirthful laughter. We walked out to the parking lot like two naughty kids heading to the sandbox to have some not-so-innocent fun. By the time we got to her convertible MGM sports car, I was certain that I'd get her contact information and I was on my way to having a gorgeous cougar girlfriend. Suddenly, her unexpected curiosity question put the kibosh on my lofty aspiration.

"You have such a charming accent. What part of Europe are you from? I bet you're Italian, aren't you?"

"I'm actually from Brazil," I said naively thinking my answer would give me an edge over her European-origin assumption.

"Brazil," she repeated in an enthusiasm dwindling tone of voice that disclosed her disappointment.

"Rio de Janeiro is my hometown," I said trying to salvage any chance of bouncing back into favor with her. I hoped the reputation of Rio as a famous fun-filled city would rescue my unfavorable Latin American status in the eyes of a culturally and geographically judgmental woman.

Unfortunately, it did not work. To my chagrin, my attempt failed and I wondered what happened. Moments earlier she was openly flirtatious and welcoming, but from the minute that I told her my country of origin everything changed on a dime. It was a very bizarre and sudden change of heart that made me speculate several hypotheses to justify such an abrupt behavioral transformation. Perhaps she had a disappointing relationship with a Brazilian man in the past; or maybe she was just biased toward any people south of Tijuana. In either case, she got in her car and drove away in a hurry as if skedaddling from a street mugger. Watching her car disappearing in traffic, I realized my place of origin wouldn't bail me out all the time. When I first arrived in L.A., telling someone I was from Rio de Janeiro was a great boon that led me to a much needed shelter. Sadly, to the ears of that gorgeous woman, it sounded as though I'd uttered a curse that doomed my expectations.

I didn't make a big fuss out of it. I'd already gone through a couple of eye-opening experiences with the zeitgeist of L.A. Maybe my letting go favored the winds of good fortune, for shortly afterwards beneficial encounters breezed my way. A few days later, I met a divorced 47-year-old sexy mamma, Heloise—ironically, she was Jewish—who had a lot of money and with whom I had a fantastic time both in and outside her Marina Del Rey luxury condo. I also connected with Mr. Raymond, a Canadian financier who owned a classic 1938 schooner that he wanted me to work on refinishing the vessel's entire woodwork. Also, I befriended some young Brazilians who would bail me out when the roof of my walk-in closet bedroom figuratively caved in on me. But in the meantime, I was having a grand time driving Heloise's golden sport convertible Mercedes Benz to Malibu, eating out in ritzy restaurants, and having passionate Oedipus complex-driven sex. And during the day, I worked on Mr. Raymond's boat moored on Mindanao Way.

Once again, my life was on the upswing.

Eventually, my agreement with "The Bloke" came to an inevitable end. We parted ways in good terms. He understood that once I started establishing connections with yacht owners on my own, I'd set up my own gigs without needing to dole out a percentage of my earnings, which ended up being a good sum of money. And my first commissioned work was on Mr. Raymond's one-of-a-kind 1938 wooden schooner. She was beautiful but she was in desperate need of a makeover. The varnishing was old and peeling off throughout the entirety of her 44-foot length body. It was a big challenging job for one man's work, but I was enthused to take on the task for which I would be handsomely compensated. Furthermore, I really liked him and there was obvious reciprocity of affection on his part. I was committed to delivering my highest quality work and turn his classic sailboat into a rejuvenated 1980s version of her 1930s self.

Throughout the negotiation process when we talked about the work to be done, compensation, and timeframe for completion of the job, I was so excited that I was remiss to notice the vessel's two masts; particularly the tall main mast. In fact, it didn't dawn on me until I showed up to work in the morning for the first time. The main mast proved to be a most daunting challenge I was uncertain I'd be able to overcome for one simple reason: I suffered from an acute case of acrophobia. Besides debilitating seasickness, there was nothing that intimidated me more than being on the edge of heights. In fact, it was so bad that my worst recurring nightmares often involved sitting atop a branchless tree, walking on narrow pathway by a mountain side, or hanging on a rope outside the window of the last floor of a skyscraper. In order to do this job, it would be necessary to experience a similar real life situation of the latter nightmare version. With my anxiety level significantly elevated, I realized there was a lot at stake on this challenge: my commitment to Mr. Raymond, my livelihood, and, most of all, an opportunity to overcome another colossal trial.

Standing on the deck looking up at the imposing mast, I wondered how in the world I'd be able to sand and varnish several coats from the very tip of what it seemed to me an endlessly long pole. Just the thought of doing the work made me queasy. I could feel blobs of sweat running down both sides of my tense eyebrows. I knew what I was up against. I decided that the best thing for me to do was to get started on the ground level and leave the menacing main mast for last.

After working diligently on the deck, hatches, borders, and every nook of wood that needed sanding and a few strokes of brush, I was impressed with the masterpiece woodwork renovation I was creating. She was looking shiningly gorgeous and I felt a strong feeling of accomplishment; except that I was far from finished yet. Although I was able to block out the thought of the intimidating task ahead while working on the ground level, the anxiety bubbling inside of me spilled over like molten lava writhing out of an erupting volcano. It seemed that every hour in the past weeks I glanced up at the inevitable task with anticipated fear. Eventually, the day came when I had to reach to a higher level—in dual fashion.

In an effort to overcome my debilitating phobia, I decided to tackle the tallest mast first. Sitting on a harken bosun chair with a plastic bucket tied around my waist, I looked up the mast and I couldn't muster the courage to hoist myself up. I felt the fright creeping all the way up from my pin-needled feet, until my mind trembled with the foreboding task before me. My sweaty hands felt slippery and unable to hold on to the rope. For a long hesitating moment I stayed paralyzed unable to budge. Then, I'd look around to behold the beautiful work I'd already done realizing I had one final step to have it completed. I had no way out; in fact, the only way I had ahead of me was up and I had to buckle down.

With extraordinary effort, I managed to reach half of the way up to the lower crosstree. The only problem was that I clinched on to the vertical spar as if it were a floatation device against the gravitational force of nature. Eventually, I would have to make use of my hands to sand, clean, and varnish several times. But knotted around the mast as I was with my arms and legs, I wouldn't be even able to reach inside the bucket where all the tools were, much less get any work done. Not capable of achieving any substantial upward motion, it took me a couple of days to inch my way up to the crosstree, though I still held on to it so tight that my biceps hurt. However, applying the same perseverance born out of despair that I'd experienced in the past, I finally reached my breakthrough moment.

Gradually feeling more relaxed and comfortable with the high swinging of the boat, I began trusting that, like going to foreign countries without knowing anyone, I was safe and protected with no reason to fret. The awareness of confidence triggered an elevated sense of enjoyment that raised both my body and spirit to new heights. Soon, I found myself on the very top of the mast looking down at the panoramic view of the marina. Imbued with indescribable pride, joy, and gratitude, I realized that both the climbing of that mast and my venturing into unknown circumstances abroad had contributed to my reaching the zenith of my potential. Either overcoming my fear of the unknown or conquering my fright of heights, I had managed to reach a new stature of being. In both instances I felt free and liberated, and therefore became capable of completing what I intended to do.

After pulling myself up to the top of the mast several times—and even swirling around as if in an amusement park ride—I accomplished a fantastic woodwork job. And in the end, both masts turned out to be the most beautiful part of my work. I'd created a *magnum opus* built with courage and determination to achieve what at first seemed like an impossible task. It was gratifying to realize I had done the same with my life thus far, even though I still had a long way to go. As for my acrophobia, I had slain a psychological dragon that no longer scared me with the spitting fire of fear.

"Wow! She looks absolutely gorgeous!" Mr. Raymond exclaimed when he saw his boat's upgraded looks for the first time. "We've got to sail her to Catalina Island next weekend."

I accepted his invitation and on the following Saturday morning he showed up with his daughter. The three of us sailed to the renowned island southwest of Los Angeles and anchored at a bay for an overnight stay. It was obvious to me that Mr. Raymond was playing matchmaker trying to hook me up with his daughter. I was stunned that a successful businessman would cull me, a young Latin American man with no financial or social status, to be a suitor to his only child. He must have seeing something in me that was worthy of his trust and I was flattered by his judgment. Although she was pleasant and pretty, we just didn't quite get on to dating level, which was a pity since I'd very much welcome the chance of potentially becoming Mr. Raymond's son-in-law. Unfortunately—or perhaps not—it wasn't meant to be.

Having made a good chunk of change with that long big project, I decided to take some time off and go on a driving "surfari" in my VW van along the California coast to Big Sur. However, when my housemates told me they were going to be out of town for a week on vacation to Mexico, I embraced the opportunity to have the place for myself and postponed my trip.

It was a good thing I stayed put, for I had to move out of my walk-in closet bedroom without any notice. Once I realized my welfare—and perhaps even my life—was in jeopardy, I had to bail out of the place in a hurry.

❖

I was having a grand time. After having worked really hard for the past few weeks, I finally had some fun-filled relaxing time at my disposal. I started out my days at my favorite hangout spot: *La Boulangerie* on Bay Street in Santa Monica. A cup of dark Sumatra coffee, a couple of sourdough rolls with strawberry jam and Swiss cheese, and a good book in hand, I spent my mornings with utmost leisurely pleasure. Then, I walked to the beach to chat with the new Brazilian friends I made, especially Tina, the smoking hot girl from Rio I had a crush on. By mid-afternoon, I drove to Topanga Beach to surf before returning to *La Boulangerie* for a late afternoon snack along with some more reading to feed my mind. Then, to close a perfect fulfilling day, I headed back to the beach to behold the stunning California sunset. Life was good and I loved it. And as an extra perk, I came home to have the place all for myself while my housemates were gone. As I was having the time of my life, all of a sudden things changed in frightening dramatic fashion.

On a Friday evening before the weekend my housemates were supposed to come back, the phone rang when I had just stepped out of the apartment. Since I'd been taking messages for them, I felt compelled by consideration to come back in to answer the call. As I walked by the kitchen, I picked up the notepad affixed to the refrigerator's door where I'd been jotting down their messages. Oddly, the pen I kept on the counter was nowhere to be seen. Opening the drawers looking for a writing utensil while the phone rang with uninterrupted demand, I quit searching and just rushed to the living room to answer it. It was a phone call from hell—and the devil was enraged.

"Get that mother-fucker Tony on the phone right now," a raspy irritated male voice barked in my ears like a rabid pit bull ready to bite my head off as soon as I said hello. I could feel an undeniable sense of urgency in his rigid demand.

"He's not here," I replied tersely tense. "May I take a message?"

"Put his bitch on the phone then," he said and the crescendo exasperation in his voice made me feel uneasy.

"She's not here either," I said beginning to regret having come back to answer the phone.

"You better not be fucking with me, you shithead. If I come over and find out you're trying to cover up for them, I'm gonna blow your fucking brains out," he yelled at me as I felt the telephone receiver slipping off my sweaty trembling hand.

"No…, they're…not here, but they should be back from Mexico tomorrow," I said impulsively before realizing I might have given out more information than I intended. Choking on my parched throat with my voice subdued by terror, the stringent threat of my interlocutor was deadly intimidating. I was scared shitless.

There was a brief pause. I could hear the man's heavy breathing crisscrossing the phone line straight into my brain; the brain he threatened to blow out. Then, all of a sudden, he blurted out a furious warning that it felt like a 6-plus Richter scale magnitude earthquake had just struck the San Andreas Fault.

"Listen to me, you shithead. You tell those fuckers that if I don't get my one hundred grand and the kilo of snow they owe me by Monday, I'm gonna come over and raise some serious mother-fucker hell. I'm gonna blow all of your fucking heads off. Do you hear me?"

"Y...e...s…," I stammered the three letter word out.

Then he slammed the phone in my face without saying anything else. I stood immobile holding the telephone receiver, until the loud busy signal made me realize I was in a state of stupor. As I gradually recovered from the startling outburst of fury, I began understanding how Tony and Suzy lived a carefree lifestyle without working. It was safe to surmise that their "vacation" trip to Mexico was more likely a business trip. Still in shock, I walked out of the apartment wandering through the streets of Santa Monica without knowing what I was going to do.

I decided to head to the popular restaurant on Ocean Ave. where a couple of my Brazilian beach buddies worked. I could use a glass of wine or two, and some casual chatting would do me good, too. I needed to turn my mind off from the recent experience that temporarily stunned me. After a couple of glasses of wine, I began to self-disclose my dilemma to Marta, one of the Brazilian girls who waited tables in the joint. At closing time when chairs were already placed upside down on top of tables, she sat down next to me and threw me a lifeline.

"It sounds pretty scary and serious," she said after hearing my story. "I can talk to my housemates tonight and see if they're agreeable to squeeze you in our apartment. Give me a call tomorrow morning and I'll let you know."

First thing in the morning I gave her a holler. Her housemates—all six of them—agreed to add a seventh to the mix. Relieved and stoked, I immediately packed my duffel bags, wrote a lame excuse farewell note to Tony and Suzy without mentioning the threatening phone call, for I figured they already knew what it was all about anyway. Placing the apartment key on the kitchen counter atop the note, I locked the place from the inside and ran for safety in my newly found Brazilian sanctuary.

My new abode was in a three-bedroom and two baths apartment on McLaughlin Street south of Venice Boulevard. There were three girls in one bedroom, a couple in the other, and Marta and her roommate in the third. They agreed to let me sleep on the floor of their bedroom on a temporary basis until I found other living arrangements. I got along so well with the girls and the other housemates that I ended up staying for many months. It worked out to be an ideal situation, for it was cheap, friendly, and fun.

Now I understood why Clint, the Californian young man who let me crash in his house's garage, was so impressed by the hospitality he received from strangers in Brazil. For the first time abroad, I experienced firsthand the kindness of the Brazilian people. I felt both good and proud to have cultural roots among such fun-loving people. And boy, did we ever party!

Cocaine was everywhere in the city of angels; and my newly found milieu was no exception. Since there were lots of people dropping in our place on a regular basis, I had no idea who was the main provider of the coke that lined up on the living room glass-top coffee table in the evenings. With everyone pitching in to the "coke money jar," we had a regular supply of snow to last an entire winter. Soon, acid lysergic diethylamide became a regular presence in the party scene, too. The only thing that was more pervasively abundant than drugs was sex; another ubiquitous L.A. party feature, though orgies were not something I ever witnessed among the Brazilian crowd. We all liked to fuck—a lot!—but with a girl at a time and in the privacy of our bedrooms.

Sharing a bedroom with two girls got everyone outside our apartment thinking there was some serious *ménage à trois* happening, which was not true. Actually, I was having an affair with one of the girls from the other bedroom. Although there were occasional embarrassing moments of getting caught in the middle of the act when somebody barged in the bedroom, we manage to be diplomatic about it, and in the end we all got along very well. We were free loving people, not sexual degenerates engaged in untamed bacchanalia.

As time went by, I gradually moved on from my marina gigs. Not only was I getting tired of sanding and varnishing wood, but there was also an unexpected lull in the number of jobs coming up. Thus, when an opportunity to work at a bookstore in Santa Monica showed up, I embraced it with the enthusiasm of the bona fide bibliophile I've always been. However, being used to making much more money with my boat gigs, the minimum wage I earned did not make up for the pleasure of working among books. It was a matter of time and I reluctantly quit the job. It was around that time that a familiar unpleasant feeling started creeping up into me once again.

Like the time in the south of Portugal when I had a seemingly perfect living situation, and yet felt dissatisfied and in need of change, I was beginning to feel unfulfilled with my life in L.A. It was time to shake things up and embark on new adventures elsewhere, though I had no idea where to go or what I wanted to do with my life. At first I considered living in my VW van while moving about the California Coast in a temporary carefree lifestyle. But in order to live the life of a bon vivant vagabond, I needed money to sustain my months-long surfing safari. With a gradually dwindling bank account balance, I needed to reevaluate my options. Feeling stuck in a hut of uncertainty once again, I needed to take some time off to think things over.

I decided to go to New York City for a couple of weeks to take inventory of my life. Caught in the excitement of the city that never sleeps, I thought about moving to NYC and create a new adventure there. However, the prospect of moving backwards—geographically or otherwise—was frightening to me. I'd been traumatized for life when I moved in the opposite direction of my intention. And because I'd resolutely committed to never quitting again, going backwards was not a viable option at any level. I knew that moving forward was the only way to go. Besides, the hope of fulfilling Lucia's pythonic promises for my life had been burning inside of me ever since my 36-hour ordeal.

Unsure of how to proceed, I decided to explore my possibilities via an unorthodox way. I felt like I needed to dive deep into the muddy waters of my mind to spearfish a catch of insight.

Hence, I dropped acid that I brought with me from L.A. and went for a long stroll in Central Park with my sister in tow.

Having lost the sense of time, we meandered around the park while I searched, fruitlessly, for some sort of clarification to my uncertainties. Every time I thought about my quandaries and questioned what would be the best way to go, all I came up with was the conviction that no matter what direction I followed I would be alright. I suppose that the recollection of my past experiences under the influence of a powerful mind-altering substance exacerbated my already solid self-confidence. Thus, as my mind wandered along with my feet, I felt I had absolutely nothing to be concerned about. In quintessential Taoist fashion, I knew that all I had to do was to flow with the unfolding of the events and everything would work out fine in its own timing. However, as much as I embraced the Taoist principle of *wu wei* (action through non-action), I knew that I would have to make the first move to trigger the kinetic energy in order to activate the principle of *wu wei*; but what the first move should be remained unknown.

Walking in the park near 72nd Street and Central Park West, I was about to commit a major and potentially dangerous blunder. Still feeling the effects of the acid lysergic diethylamide running through my system unabated, suddenly I was glad I'd brought my sister along. If it weren't for her intervention, I'd probably have been brought back to sobriety in some aggressive manner unaware of my mistake.

"Look! It's Yoko Ono!" I exclaimed watching my idol's widow walking surrounded by two sizeable bodyguards. "I have to go ask her many things I've always wanted to know about John Lennon."

"Are you out of your mind?" My sister said holding my arm as I was already moving toward the party of three. "Well, of course you are out of your mind, which is the reason you've got to control yourself. This famous woman's husband was assassinated just a few years ago; that's why she's walking with bodyguards. You get within 10 feet of her and your nose will be flying off your face 10 yards away."

And that's how my trip in Central Park ended: without answers to my questions; neither from Yoko Ono nor the ones I had about what I should do next. Soon, my two weeks sojourn in NYC came to an end and I went back to Los Angeles as uncertain as I was before.

଒❖ഩ

After spending almost two years in L.A., I had had enough of the ostentation and debauchery of the local culture and decided it was time to move out of town. The problem was that I had no idea where to go next. Determined not to move backwards, I began considering to continue moving west across the Pacific Ocean. I thought of going to Australia or New Zealand, though sailing was always a scary option to entertain, even in the seemingly mellow Pacific Ocean. Then, when I least expected, a new possibility emerged serendipitously while I was surfing at Zuma Beach in Malibu. Sitting on the surfboard waiting for the next set of waves to come, I chatted with a South African man who casually shared with me how he made an easy living in Los Angeles.

"It sounds like a great gig," I said when he told me that he was a caretaker of a house in Beverly Hills.

"It couldn't be better bro," he said. "Good pay, room and board, and plenty of spare time to surf. What's there not to like?"

In between surf rides, I picked his brain and found out that there were several agencies in town that specialized in connecting house caretakers with well-to-do clients throughout Southern California. Wanting to leave L.A., the prospect of moving farther south appealed to me. I needed to buy some more time to figure out what I wanted to do in the long run; and mulling it over in a different town seemed like an ideal situation.

Without wasting any time, the next day I worked on an embellished résumé, bought a used jacket at a thrifty store, and contacted a few selected agencies in person. To my pleasant surprise, within a week I landed my first interview with an elderly couple in Laguna Beach, a lovely artsy town some 50 miles south of L.A. in Orange County. As luck would once again brighten up my way, the interview with the late septuagenarian retired medical doctor and his wife went very well and I became a front runner for the job. A couple of days later the agency contacted me to let me know I'd been hired.

The following week I moved into the cottage by the swimming pool of their picturesque property on the hills of Laguna Beach with a beautiful partial view of the ocean. In addition to room and board, they paid me a decent salary for what turned out to be a very easy job. Other than shopping for groceries, cooking meals, some minor yard work, and sporadic odd tasks—they even had a housekeeper who took care of the house cleaning—I had plenty of free time at my disposal. And since they needed me only in the afternoons and early evenings, I spent every morning surfing at the renowned Huntington Beach Pier. Sometimes on the weekends, I'd drive my VW van down to San Diego and slept in my cozy wheeled motel. Life was grand again; at least for the time being, for deep inside an insidious dissatisfaction lingered on unabated.

Indeed, by all measurable standards of living for a young surfer boy from Rio, I had landed the ultimate job situation. And yet, like my laidback lifestyle living onboard *Lady Promise* at Marina de Vilamoura, the discontent I experienced seemed to grow inside of me with every passing day. There was something missing that the seemingly auspicious circumstances of my life were not delivering. Perhaps, I was maturing and yearning for more than just fun in the Sun.

Three months into what seemed like an ideal state of affairs, the reality was that I had reached my limit. Despite, the daily surfing, pleasant jaunts down the Southern California Coast, comfortable living conditions, and dating a beautiful girl I'd met in San Clemente, I was feeling discomfortingly bothered. Although it made no sense to me to feel even remotely unfulfilled, I could not deny the strong craving for more; not more of the same, but something uniquely new, though I had no idea what that might be. I was frustrated that regardless of the beneficial circumstances of my life I felt irretrievably glum. Something had to change.

On Christmas Eve my girlfriend and I had dinner at The Queen Mary, the iconic 1936 ocean liner permanently moored at Long Beach harbor. It was a lovely romantic evening followed by passionate lovemaking in which I broke my record of sexual endurance by simultaneously climaxing five times with her—that record would be broken in my early 50s with the most compatible sexual partner of my life. I woke up in the morning with her head nestled on my chest and my right hand firmly holding her roundish buttocks. Although she was sound asleep, I noticed the delineating smile in her face subtly disclosing her silent satisfaction and innermost emotions. She resembled the fairytale character, Snow White, awaiting the magical kiss of her adoring prince who would awaken her into being. She looked happy, whereas I, in spite of my inflated male ego sexual prowess pride, felt perturbed without knowing why.

After showering and having some coffee in the hotel room, we went to a quaint coffee shop to have breakfast. Talkative and exuding undeniable happiness, she placed her elbows on the table with her chin gently touching her interlaced hands. Then, she gazed at me with loving eyes for an uncomfortably long time. I felt uneasy deciphering the silent message she conveyed, which was similar to the smile I'd noticed when she was asleep on my torso earlier in the morning. Suddenly she spoke and I quivered.

"I think I'm in love with you," she said allowing her words to convey what her eyes were already saying loud and clear.

I didn't know what to say. I looked out the window to avoid the uncomfortable eye contact while feeling an urge to dash off in a hurry. At the same time, I felt guilty and at fault to have led her on unwittingly. I was already in inner crisis mode and had plenty of sorting out to do. The last thing I wanted at that time was to get in a serious romantic relationship with her—or anyone else for that matter. I knew I needed change, but not of that kind.

Suddenly, I lost my appetite and our conversation became more of her soliloquy than our dialogue. Between her hints of moving in together and other innuendos involving serious relationship ties, I nodded disingenuously, half-smiled in two-faced fashion, and occasionally said something just to pretend I was harking her words. But my mind had already run away and started demanding my body to follow. Soon, it reached a point that I could not pretend any longer and I had to leave right away. I came up with some lame last minute excuse of some work I had to do. She looked disappointed but was supportive and understanding of my fabricated needs. Then, I dropped her off and drove away carrying a heavy burden of guilt. It so happened that as the events of the following weeks unfolded, that Christmas morning was the last time she heard from me again. With a great deal of shame and self-reproach I ghosted on her.

Driving without purpose or direction on highway 405, I felt dishonest, disheartened, discouraged, and ashamed of myself for the unintended outcome of my affair with her. She was a nice girl and the thought of hurting her feelings made me feel sick to my stomach. The more I indulged on my mental self-torture, the more miserable I felt succumbing deeper into negative emotions. The unpleasant experience is all Santa got as a Christmas gift for a naughty boy who was now feeling wretchedly self-conscious.

As I approached the outskirts of Los Angeles from the south, I decided to drop by my former Brazilian housemates' new home (they had moved into a house by the time I'd moved to Laguna Beach). I knew that if there was somewhere my spirit could be lifted up that was the place to go. Alas, my mood was much worse off than I thought, for even though there was an animated Christmas party going on inside the house, I chose to stay in the backyard by myself ensconced in a red hammock alone with my blues.

"What're you doing here, man?" One of the Brazilian guys said as he walked outside and spotted me by chance. "You missed the memo, bro. There's a party happening inside."

"I guess I'm in need of some solitude," I said succinctly and the forlorn tone of my voice must have drifted across, for he came over to talk with me to cheer me up.

We chatted briefly and he told me about the great time he had in his recent vacation to Hawaii. His excitement about his experience reached the zenith when he talked about Maui, which he referred to as his favorite island of the three he'd visited. After the conversation was over, he started walking away until he suddenly halted his steps. Then, in an uncanny manner that I interpreted as a message sent to me through him, he turned around to have one final unexpected thing to say. His words had an enormous impact on me and determined the trajectory of my next move.

"I don't know bro, but I get a feeling that you'd really like Maui," he said in an eerie tone of voice while looking at me with hazy eyes. "I think you should consider checking it out."

"That's it!" I blurted it out loud to myself as I watched his disappearing in the distance. "I'm going to Hawaii."

The very next day I gave notice to my Laguna Beach employers. Two weeks later I was standing on the departure gate at LAX on my way to Maui with a short stay on the island of Oahu.

The change I desperately needed was about to begin.

❧❖☙

At first my own excitement prevented me from noticing how keyed up everyone around me seemed to be.

"Oh my God, this is so cool!" A young pretty woman blurted out loud unable to contain her child-like enthusiasm as we lined up to board the aircraft. Holding on to her boyfriend's arm with an ear-to-ear grin, she looked and sounded like a little girl about to enter Disneyland for the first time. By sheer chance, I would see her again at a later date under much different circumstances.

In my turn, I was exuberant in silent joy and imbued with anticipation to be going to the equivalent of a surfer's Disneyland. However, to me this was not meant to be a pleasant vacation of temporary enjoyment. I was on a mission; a scouting mission in the pursuit of my promised destiny. I had both short and long-term plans—and even an alternative option in case the long-term plan didn't pan out. The short-term plan was the easiest and most fun: I was going to go straight to the world's renowned Mecca of surfing on Oahu's North Shore to surf Banzai Pipeline, Sunset Beach, and maybe even Waimea Bay, if it was not terribly huge. I would spend a few days there sleeping in a rental car before hopping on a Mid-Pac flight (the small propeller inter-islands airplanes available at the time) to Maui to work on my long-term plan: to come up with a situation that would allow me to be on the Valley Isle for a longer stay. But if for whatever reasons it didn't work out, then I'd consider heading for Australia or New Zealand. In fact, once I found out that sailing the Pacific Ocean is supposed to be much less intimidating than the Atlantic Ocean, I thought I might even be able to handle my propensity for seasickness and willing to take the risk of sailing from Honolulu harbor to Oceania. But that was my backburner option. There was one thing I was determined not to do: to go back to the U.S. mainland, except to pick up the rest of my belongings, sell my car, and return to Maui for what I hoped it would be a long sojourn.

Like oxygen circulating in the atmosphere, Brazilians seemed to be everywhere; and the North Shore of Oahu was no exception. In fact, because of the widespread surf culture in a country with 4,600 miles of coastline, I expected to find Brazilian surfers in Hawaii, but not in such large numbers. Sometimes it seemed to me that Portuguese was the official second language on the North Shore beaches. Of course, it was a matter of time for me to befriend some of my compatriots; and once again, as usual, their open friendliness came through for me.

"How da fuck you manage to get any sleep in this tiny little car, bro?" The Brazilian surfer I met in the parking lot at Sunset Beach asked me while passing me a fat Hawaiian pakalolo joint.

"I have to choose between stretching my legs or stretching my dollars if I want to go the distance," I said handing the doobie back to him. "It's only for a couple of days anyway."

"Well, if you want to come crash on the living room floor with four other dudes in our place you're welcome to," he said after exhaling a cloud of THC infused smoke in the air.

And so I did.

The two bedroom apartment they rented not far from Sunset Beach was filled to capacity. Since people were always coming in and out of the place, it was hard to keep count of how many people were actually staying there. I estimated around a dozen surfers spent the night on a regular basis. Soon, I also suspected that surfing was just one of the activities that drew those young men to the North Shore. When I overheard a conversation involving delivery of cocaine, I realized that the popular L.A. drug was ubiquitous even among young athletes in Hawaii. And like Tony and Suzy, my housemates in Santa Monica, I could tell that at least some of those guys had found a way of funding their surfaris to paradise. It was none of my business, and I figured that for a couple of days I'd be alright hanging out with them before leaving for Maui—until something happened that scared the daylights out of me.

"Fuck no way, man, it's your fucking turn," one dude yelled at another in a feisty discussion about whose turn was it to wash the dishes.

"Are you fucking kidding me? Me and Tico did it last night, bro. It's you guys turn tonight," the other bawled so loud it hurt my ears.

Soon pandemonium broke loose. Everyone was shouting at one another claiming the right not to do the dishes. There was no violent behavior of any kind, but the decibels reached such a high pitch that a crystal glass could shatter into smithereens. As the intense raucous verbal fracas continued going on for quite some time, a few moments later there was an even louder noise outside the apartment's door that totally freaked me out.

"This is the police. Open the door right now or we'll knock it down."

My first thought was to jump out through the window, until I realized I was on the third floor. Still traumatized by my experience at Tony and Suzy's place in Santa Monica, I was sure the police had come over to bust a cocaine ring and I, an innocent bystander, would be arrested for something I had nothing to do with. I thought my adventures, my dreams, and my life's aspirations were all over in an untoward circumstance I didn't bargain for. I started regretting having accepted the generosity of the Brazilian surfer to crash at their place for a couple of nights. I'd have been much safer sleeping in the uncomfortable economy-size rental car on the beach. Now it was too late and it was all over.

"We got an emergency call that a potential deadly fight was happening here," the cop said as soon as one of the guys opened the door. "Is anybody hurt?"

Once the cops found out that it'd been nothing but a harmless argument among rowdy Brazilians trying to determine whose turn it was to wash the dishes, they cracked up and left the place laughing out loud as if they were exiting a stand-up comedy show. Still trembling with the anxiety of being arrested for a crime I never committed, I sneaked out of the place and skedaddled with a strong sense of urgency. That night I slept deeply and comfortably in the narrow back seat of the undersized rental car as if it were a king size bed in a luxurious five-star hotel room.

After a couple of days surfing the North Shore of Oahu, I headed to Honolulu airport to go to my ultimate destination. Imbued with unbridled excitement, titillating anticipation, and boundless hope, I boarded the bouncy inter-island propeller aircraft to the Valley Isle of Maui where my life would eventually change forever.

ଓ❖ຣ

Unbeknownst to me at the time, I was just about to land on the island where I'd build the foundation of my future. Beholding the turquoise water below adorned by the green lush Haleakala in the distance, I rejoiced in the enjoyment of the magnificent aerial view as the plane descended toward the runway. The thrill of coming to such a paradisiacal island filled me with ineffable joy and anticipation. The middle-aged man sitting next to me likely felt the drift of my transparent excitement.

"Is it your first trip to Maui? He asked as I looked out the window.

"Yes," I replied monosyllabically uninterested to converse.

"Well, if you're going to be anything like me it won't be the last either," he said disclosing some excitement of his own. "It's an awesome place to kick back and relax. The best investment I've ever made was getting a timeshare in a Kaanapali Beach condominium. What part of the island are you staying?"

"I don't know where I'm staying," I replied curtly not interested in engaging in small talk.

"You don't know? How can you come to Maui and not know where you're staying?" He asked frowning with intrusive curiosity that began bothering me.

"I'll figure it out when I get there," I said dismissively.

"Goodness, you're a hardcore young man. You come to a place for the first time not knowing anyone and you'll figure it out as you go. That's impressive," he remarked shortly before the airplane landing gear hit hard on the runway.

With my eyes closed I smiled internally thinking of the triviality of his comment. After all I'd been through in the past years, going to a place like Maui without knowing anyone was a cinch. There was nothing hardcore about it; much to the contrary, it was going to be as gentle as the breeze blowing from the open Pacific Ocean.

Once on the ground, my first impression of my surroundings surprised me. Considering Maui's growing reputation as a vacation destination, I was amazed at how small and unassuming the airport was. A large barn-like main building, a couple of runways, and four truncated luggage conveyer belts running outside the building, Kahului Airport bore absolutely no resemblance to its current twenty-first century modern expanded version. In spite of the conveniences of up-to-date facilities, the quaint charm of the small town airport I landed on for the first time in the mid 1980s remains in my memory as a relic of my deep bond with the island that would come to call "Mamma Maui;" the island that would give birth to my new life.

After picking up my duffel bag and surfboard, I headed to the car rental area where a sign of an underrated competitor in the industry stood inconspicuously on the corner. It read: "El Cheapo, the best car rental deal on Maui." That's where I got an old beat up Toyota Corolla rental car for a bargain price—or Maui cruisers, as the locals called those worn out vehicles circulating on the island. I had long term plans to carry out and managing my limited budget was *sine qua non.*

After a couple of days getting acquainted with the island's surroundings and taking the time to have some fun, I turned on the all-business mode mentality and started searching for connections and situations that could facilitate the unfolding of my long-term plans. First, I explored the different locales of the island. Although upcountry Maui was the place I liked the best, it didn't seem like the most suitable location for a newcomer, since both housing and jobs were hard to come by. The districts of Kahului and Wailuku were even less favorable for a newly arrived *haole* (foreigner) to settle down among mostly locals. Then, I decided to try the bustling artsy town of Lahaina on the west side where more opportunities seemed available. However, it didn't take me long to realize that it was an expensive area and I should continue looking for other alternatives. After checking out all my options, I ended up selecting the Kihei-Wailea area in the south side as the most promising region to make something happen. There were plenty of shared rentals—albeit none could be deemed affordable—and jobs in hotels, restaurants, and tourist stores abounded, even though the low pay rate would require some serious overtime just to make ends meet. Hence, I set camp with my El Cheapo rental car at the Kamaole Beach Park III parking lot and from there my exploratory endeavor began.

Through *The Bulletin*, a free local publication that listed all sorts of advertisements ranging from dating hook-ups to chicken eggs for sale, I connected with two older Filipino ladies who rented rooms in their house in the hills of Kihei. The two amiable sisters who took genuine liking of me had one room available for rent, which they'd already granted to someone else by the time I contacted them. However, since they had not received any payment yet, they rescinded the offer to the other prospect and made the room available to me instead. I paid the first month's rent and left my surfboard and duffel bag with them before going back to Los Angeles to sell my car and pick up the rest of my belongings. I had set up the grounds for what would be a decade-long stay in the bosom of Mamma Maui; the place where I'd be reborn to my new exciting life.

Although I had no means of making a living yet, having secured housing in a welcoming environment was a great first step in the right direction. With the remaining savings I had plus the cash the sale of my car would bring in, I'd be able to stay afloat for a few months; a reasonable timeframe for me to make something happen. And in the unlikely case I'd not be able to land a job somewhere, the option of going to Honolulu harbor and finding a boat to sail to Oceania was still on the table, though I dreaded even thinking about it, for I was growing tired of living the *bon vivant* vagabond lifestyle. What I would not do under any circumstances was to move backwards. I had learned my lesson the hard way, and henceforth I would never quit again until I realized the promises of my destiny that had been prophesized to me.

With my scouting mission to Maui successfully accomplished, I flew back to Los Angeles to make the final arrangements for my permanent move to Hawaii. As soon as I got off the plane, I went searching for a pay phone to call one of my Brazilian friends to pick me up at the airport. To my astonishment, I saw the young woman who was übber excited on the flight to Honolulu. She must have been on the same flight back to L.A. but I had not noticed her until then. This time, however, she displayed the opposite disposition she had just two weeks earlier. She looked morose and taciturn when I talked with her while her boyfriend spoke on the pay phone while I waited for my turn.

"How did you like Hawaii?" I asked dubiously.

"It was O.K.," she mumbled in blatant contrast with the demeanor she exhibited when she left.

"Oh, I loved it! In fact, I liked it so much that I'm coming back to live there for awhile," I said trying to animate the dispirited casual conversation.

"Really? You're moving to Hawaii?" She asked showing some vague signs of interest. "That's what I told Mike we should do, but he chose to blow a whole lot of cash staying in fancy hotels in Waikiki and eating out every night. Now we're broke."

I didn't know what to say. I remained quiet waiting for him to be done with the telephone so I could make my call. Suddenly, I noticed her looking at me with longing eyes as if she wished she were with me instead. She gave me a flirtatious smile and a subtle wink in the eye that I ignored. I wondered if she'd learned that I spent my nights in rental cars—one was a legit El Cheapo model—would she still be yearning for my attention. I doubted it. After all, she was an L.A. girl.

"Fuck! I can't believe my brother is not willing to come pick us up. What an asshole!" Her boyfriend erupted in frustration after banging the telephone receiver. "Let's go get a taxi."

"Get a taxi? We don't have any money left," she protested.

"We'll figure it out," he said picking up his luggage and walking away as she followed him while arguing nonstop on the way out of LAX.

At that moment, I felt fortunate to be on my own and in charge of my destiny. What I didn't expect was to feel even more grateful as soon as my phone call to my friend went through.

"Of course I'm coming to pick you up. I'll be there in thirty minutes max," my friend said with genuine enthusiasm. "And I'm bringing a bomb of a joint that I got from a Jamaican dude in downtown L.A. Stay put, bro, I'll be there shortly."

That night I realized that having a brother has nothing to do with biological relations. The true DNA of brotherhood lies in authentic friendship.

Selling my car proved to be more difficult than I anticipated. Because I had to be back to Maui within a week, I didn't have the luxury of time to advertise it properly. Ideally, I would love to have had my VW van in Maui, for it was a mobile home that would have saved me a great deal of money in rent. However, the shipping cost was prohibitively out of the reach of my budget. The second best option would be to sell it to an individual buyer who'd pay a more seller-favorable price. Since neither alternative was possible, I was compelled to hawk my beloved VW van to a used car dealership, which I sold for much less than it was worth it. I took solace in the lessons of the past: compared to the money I lost in the airfare ticket I purchased from Lisbon to Rio de Janeiro years back, this was not a significant percentage deficit—and not as impactful under the circumstances.

With only a bicycle to move about in my last day in L.A.—a full circle of how everything started—I couldn't help but reminisce over my earlier days when this was my only means of transportation. It'd been almost two years since I arrived in the city of angels. Riding along the promenade from the Santa Monica Pier where I played beach volleyball to Marina Del Rey where I overcame my acrophobia while making a living, I mulled over the experiences and lessons I'd accumulated in my sojourn in Southern California. I had many pleasant recollections, like riding my motorcycle along Pacific Coast Highway and experiencing the haptic joy of having the ocean breeze blowing against my tanned shirtless chest on a sunny day. But I also had quite a few unpleasant memories, like the threatening phone call that scared me out of my wits and propelled me to move out of my walk-in closet bedroom. And then there were the incidental events; like meaningless entertainment sex; unbridled cocaine indulgence; invitations to birthday party orgies; and everything in between. But all things considered, my time in Los Angeles had greatly contributed to my personal development.

On the way back from Marina Del Rey, I stopped at Venice Beach to bid farewell to the uniquely famous spot in Southern California where I passed by numerous times on my way to and from work. Nothing seemed to have changed: the street artists performing for chump change; the vendors hawking their wares to tourists; the gatherings of the homeless—many of whom were Vietnam War vets—and the disoriented druggies roaming aimlessly through the crowds. Everything looked exactly the same to me. The only thing that I noticed to have changed significantly was me. I was not the same as when I observed that environment for the first time. I'd grown into the maturity of the latter years of my youth and I was ready for the next stage of my life.

As the beautiful scarlet sunset formed in the horizon, I walked toward the ocean and sat down on the white sand to watch that amazing spectacle of nature. Hearing the gentle sounds of waves breaking on the shore as their foam swirled below the mark of the ebbing tide, I became introspective recapitulating my daring journey hitherto. Long before my time in Los Angeles, I had embarked on an adventurous tour de force that led me to that very moment I revisited the past years of my life. From the life-changing day when I, out of utter desperation, mustered the chutzpah to go back to Portugal feeling scared, with little money, and without knowing anyone in the foreign country I had just left less than 36 hours earlier, I had grown a great deal. I realized I'd become a bona fide full-fledged man who was about to set off on a brand new phase of my life. This time, however, I had even more ambitious aspirations.

Now approaching the last year of my twenties, I looked forward to the years ahead with a different perspective. Although I was immensely appreciative of my gallivanting time in Europe and most recently in California, I was maturing and beginning to yearn for a more stable living situation. In fact, the alternative option I had reserved in case things didn't go well for me in Maui lost its luster to the vision of my future. The idea of getting on a sailboat and cross the Pacific Ocean to Australia or New Zealand triggered a great deal of anxiety and distress in my being—not to mention a legitimate concern about my propensity for seasickness. I realized I was getting tired of living like an international vagabond traveling from country to country over land and sea. Also, I started longing to resume my academic studies and incorporate into it the extraordinary empirical knowledge I'd accumulated through my travels over the years.

After the Sun had long ensconced behind the now shadowy horizon, I got to my feet and walked back to the promenade to ride my bicycle to my friend's place where I was staying. Pedaling slowly on the dark bike lane, I wondered if, perhaps, I should have remained with my girlfriend who had professed her love for me on Christmas Day. Eventually, we would have gotten married and I'd officially become an immigrant to the United States of America. I'd settle down and build a domesticated family life in my new adopted motherland. But right then it was a moot point, therefore I dismissed the thought as quickly as it passed through my mind. Besides, if it were about formalizing my immigration status, I could have asked my sister to apply in my behalf. In any case, the truth was that the gallivant lifestyle no longer appealed to me as it once did. I was weary of moving from place to place with no specific destination and no sense of stability.

Tired from both the bike pedaling and my fruitless musings, I decided to stay in the moment and take it one day at a time. All I needed to know right then was that I was going to Maui to start a whole new adventure; a new chapter in the book of my life that I'd been writing with masterful dexterity. I couldn't wait to see how the story would unfold toward its destined conclusion. But in order to find out, I had to take each day as if it were a blank page that needed to be filled with meaningful content until the denouement arrived effortlessly.

The next day I was at LAX to fly back to Maui. The writing of the most consequential chapter of the book of my life was about to get written.

❖

When I landed the second time at the Kahului Airport, as soon as I got off the plane and my feet touched the ground, I could feel the ʻĀina (land) welcoming me like a mother embracing a returning son. I felt as though Mamma Maui was whispering in my ears: "Aloha ʻoe i ko Maui" (welcome to Maui).

After settling in my bedroom in the Filipino ladies' house, the sense of urgency to find work was exacerbated after the engine starter of the Maui cruiser I bought malfunctioned just days after purchasing it. Trying to keep my spirit up in the face of unanticipated adversity, I resorted to good humor to deal with it the best I could. Because I had to push and jump in my beat up Nissan station wagon to get it started, I dubbed it my "Fred Mobile" in reference to Fred Flintstone, the popular T.V. cartoon show of my childhood in the 1960s (he used his legs to get his car started, too). Although it didn't solve the car problem, it perked up my attitude about the circumstance I could not afford to change at the time. However, it did not alleviate the pressure to come up with an income stream to deal with the issue.

After hitting the pavement in Kihei determined to make something happen, my efforts, word of mouth, and some luck, all contributed to my connecting with a nice young couple who ran a side gig cleaning tourist rentals in the area. I worked with them for a couple of weeks until I learned about a job opening at the Pacific Whale Foundation. The organization owned a 58-foot power boat that took tourists on snorkeling tours to Molokini, the submersed volcano crater off the south shore of Maui. I loved the gig; except that I ran into the same problem I had working on the big game fishing boat in the Algarve region of Portugal: I got seasick. Once we anchored in Molokini, the swaying of the boat and the smell of the food we served to the tourists did a number on me and I had to quit after only three days on the job. Now I knew for sure that my last resort plan of sailing to Australia or New Zealand was off the table for good. At that point, there was no way I'd take a chance to sail across the Pacific Ocean, in spite of its favorable reputation. In the meantime, the financial pressure was mounting with every passing day. I had to take whatever job came my way; and that ended up being an assistant cook position at the well-known IHOP restaurant chain.

"Do you feel good about it? Are you ready to hit the ground running?" The manager who trained me for almost two hours asked me after showing me the last instructional video.

"Sure," I replied unhesitatingly out of necessity to work.

"Good. Let's get started," he said leading the way to the restaurant's kitchen.

He perfunctorily introduced me to the kitchen personnel, most of whom were so busy they didn't even notice I arrived, and left in a hurry to attend to his duties.

"God damn it! I fucking burned myself again," an over-the-top stressed out cook yelled while dropping a frying pan on the greasy sticky floor.

"Two over easy eggs, blueberry pancakes, no butter, and jelly on the side," a hassled waitress shouted as she placed the written order on the counter and vanished as quickly as she showed up.

"Is it always like this?" I asked one of the cooks while watching another waitress dexterously place several plates on a tray before dashing off to the jam-packed restaurant.

"Every day it's real busy in the morning hours," he replied while turning bacon strips on a hotplate without looking at me. "It's less crazy in the afternoon."

Agape, I observed the operation in awe wondering how long I'd be able to withstand the frenzied working pace. This was not what I'd envisioned as the living in paradise lifestyle.

"Are you gonna be standing there all day or are you gonna give me a helping hand over here?" The clearly pissed off cook addressed me while wrapping up his burned hand with a dirty white wet towel.

Without saying a word, I removed the apron, turned around, and walked away under the reprimanding eyes of the manager who'd spent a couple of hours to train an employee that didn't last 15 minutes on the job. I'd just broken my record for the shortest job I've ever had. My 5-day streak at the industrial laundry facility in Switzerland and the hotel in Portugal—both not related to seasickness—suddenly felt like commendable tenures.

Frustrated, disappointed, and concerned about the growing demand to make some money soon, I budgeted the numbers of my savings with the precision of a Swiss train schedule. I went on a ramen noodle soup diet that I fortified with hard boiled eggs, bread, and whatever cheap veggies I could get my hands on. That's all I ate until I had a source of income. Then, one evening when I'm having my undiversified dinner at home, an employment opportunity happened haphazardly.

"I'll be going back to Indiana in a couple of weeks," the fellow who rented the other room in the Filipino ladies' house said. "If you're looking for a job, you should go talk with the manager of the restaurant where I work because they'll sure need to fill in the vacancy. The place is always mobbed."

The next day I showed up at the posh golf course in Wailea where the restaurant was located to apply for the soon to be vacant busboy position. I suppose I made a positive impression on the owner/manager, for he hired me on the spot. The Japanese-American man and I got along very well for the month I stayed on the job. He seemed to hold a not-so-subtle bias against *haoles* (although the Hawaiian word means foreigner, it is most often used to refer to the white race). Because I was Latin American and golden brown tanned, he categorized me differently from the rest of his floor staff, who were mostly *haoles.* Sometimes he invited me to sit down at his table during my breaks to talk about the large Japanese-descendent population in Brazil, which is the largest in the world. Although I liked him and I didn't mind doing the job—unlike other menial jobs I held, in this one at least I moved around a lot—I realized that I could make much more money as a waiter. The tourists tended to tip very well and even the job itself seemed somewhat better than busing tables. After I hinted to him my aspirations and he didn't respond as I expected, I started looking for waiter jobs at other restaurants. In my very first interview I hit it out of the park with my bat corked with bullshit.

"You seem to have the qualification to take the job," the interviewer said after I unloaded my concocted bullshit story about working at fancy restaurants in Santa Monica before moving to Maui. I gambled telling him I was currently employed at the Wailea Fairway restaurant without mentioning in what capacity. In addition, I gave him a reference from a supposed restaurant manager in Santa Monica, which was a friend of mine who'd agreed to participate in my shenanigan, but he fell for my trumped-up spiel and didn't bother contacting anyone. Evidently, I had a successful interview that felt like an audition in which I delivered a fantastic bullshitting acting job. Although I'd never worked as a waiter in my life, I didn't have a scintilla of a doubt that I'd excel at it. I had good people skills, excellent memory, and tons of stamina. How hard waiting on tables could be?

It worked out even better than I anticipated—and I actually enjoyed the work. The restaurant was located in a beautiful setting by the sea with a panoramic view of Kaho'olawe Island, which made it to a pleasant working experience. And because the restaurant functioned in what in the industry lingo was called "burn and turn" style, the shift went by quickly and I had a pocket full of cash at the end of the night. Committed in earnest to the "keep the customers moving" policy in order to maximize my tips, I worked with expeditious efficiency, which raised bizarre suspicions among some of my peers.

"Hey man, where can I get some?" A fellow waiter whispered in my ear as I'm picking up my order at the kitchen counter.

"Get some what?" I replied unclearly with a ticket order between my teeth.

"Some coke, man. Where can I get some?" He said softly while leaning toward me.

I put the plates back on the counter to pick up the ticket that fell out of my mouth as I looked at him utterly puzzled.

"What makes you think I know where you can get some cocaine?" I asked feeling suspiciously apprehensive about his unexpected request. I'd been traumatized in Los Angeles, scared shitless in the north shore of Oahu, and therefore I became paranoid that he might be an undercover cop, even though I had nothing to feel guilty about.

"C'mon man, I've been in this business for a long time. Nobody works this fast unless they're primed," he said with a frown as if he had suspicions of his own.

"I am not on drugs and neither do I know where you can get them," I said looking at him in the eye with subtle defiance before taking my orders to my customers' table.

He never believed me and became unsympathetic to me for the duration of my short-lived tenure at that restaurant. I can see why he suspected I was on the high-powered white energizer, for I'd consumed plenty of it many times in the past and I knew exactly how it felt and what the behavior looked like. But at that time, the only stimulant I was under the influence—besides lots of the black stuff; coffee that is—was my commitment to abide by the burn and turn policy so I could make more money. And since the manager seemed very satisfied with my "experienced waiter" performance, I gave my coworker the cold shoulder and kept busy at work minding my own business. Things were going well for me and I didn't want to jeopardize my job in any way. Unfortunately, for reasons beyond my control, I fell out of favor with the restaurant manager.

A woman I'd barely made acquaintance with days earlier unwittingly put a dent on my good gig. The cute Vietnamese worked in the restaurant next door, which was part of the itinerary of the flower girl who worked in the area's bars and restaurants. One evening at the end of my shift, the flower girl approached me while I chatted with the manager.

"Are you Sebastian?" She asked me.

"Yes," I replied inquisitively.

"Binh asked me to give this to you," the flower girl said handing me a beautiful red rose.

The manager's eyes abruptly widened and he looked at me as though I'd committed an unforgivable violation. It so happened that he had a major crush on the Vietnamese woman I'd been casually flirting with during the day on the beach. Unaware of his romantic interest, there I stood with a gifted rose in my hand from the woman he was after. The damage had been done irreparably. By the time I found out he had the hots for her it was too late. Thus, the day after having complimented my outstanding professional performance, he fired me unceremoniously without verbalizing a reason for my dismissal.

It ended up not being so bad after all. Having had that interaction with the flower girl was going to be a life-changing event.

❧❖☙

When the Filipino ladies found out I'd lost my job, they mobilized to assist me in the most unusual way.

"We want you to meet our niece," one of them said smiling as if they knew of an even better job opportunity. "She is very pretty and she's an American citizen."

"You know, if you marry an American citizen you can get a good job; and she'd be a very good wife, too," the other said giggling with unconcealed excitement.

A few days later they introduced me to their niece. As they said, the girl was quite pretty and young; I'd say around 20-years-old. At first look, I was favorably impressed with her dark long hair cascading down to her curvaceous slim figure, her glittering vivacious brown eyes, and a pearly smile that prompted lovely dimples under her high cheek bones. But that was it. Once we started talking, I realized we couldn't converse even at a rudimentary level. I couldn't imagine being able to spend much time with her outside the bedroom. Actually, the thought of getting her laid excited me a great deal, but I immediately expurgated it knowing it would generate negative repercussions with my hospitable landladies. As for getting hooked with her because of her citizenship status, I had other opportunities in the past that I passed without regrets. Besides, I still held the trump card of asking my sister to apply in my behalf. Hitherto, all I had wanted was to live an exciting adventurous life. Although the thrill of my gallivant lifestyle was wearing off, I was taking one day at a time to see how my kismet would play out.

Now with bona fide experience as a waiter, it didn't take me long to find another job—and life was on the upswing again. I liked working in the evenings, for it freed up my day time to spend on the beach. And once I found out about the daily volleyball action happening at Kamaole Beach Park I in Kihei, I became a regular member of the group. As the clichéd phrase stamped on T-shirts sold in shops catering to tourists proclaimed, "Life is a Beach"—and I loved it!

Soon I became a popular figure at the park, both for my beach volleyball skills and being the only guy who played in a Speedo. The guys looked at me askance, but the girls who gathered around the court seemed to enjoy both my presence and bathing suit. Every now and then when I dove for a point-saving dig or jumped high above the net for a crushing spike, I'd hear some sighing sounds from the girls watching the game. If they enjoyed watching me as much as I enjoyed having them there, they were having a lot of fun.

One day I noticed someone familiar among the girls. It was the flower girl whose delivery of a red rose also delivered the *coup de grace* to my job. I almost didn't recognize her in her bathing suit, for I'd been used to seeing her fully clothed, well-coiffed, and with make-up on. I thought she looked as pretty during the day as I'd seen her at night. After playing a volleyball match, I sat next to her to introduce myself.

"I'm so sorry to hear you got fired because of it," she said when I shared the ticklish situation she unwittingly put me into.

"It actually worked out in my favor," I said trying to allay her subtle pang of guilt. "I got an even better job at the Wailea Steak House where the customer base is of higher tipping quality; and I don't even have to burn and turn to make it a good night."

We continued chatting for a long while and I enjoyed the time I spent with her. We went for a dip in the ocean and swam together to a vacant sailboat anchored offshore, which was always there as a permanent feature enhancing the tropical environment.

That very same night when I was busy at work, another waiter told me that the restaurant hostess wanted to see me.

"The flower girl asked me to hand this to you in privacy so you wouldn't get in trouble again. She made a point that this one is from her," the hostess said holding a red rose in her hand.

I was touched and I looked forward to seeing her again.

The next morning I went to Kamaole Beach Park more interested in seeing her again than playing volleyball. When I arrived she was there as if awaiting me with equal anticipation. We went for a swim to the sailboat again, but this time we made out while holding on to the vessel's anchor rope. From that day onward we started dating and seeing each other daily. I was spending more time at her place than mine, until we decided that it would make sense for us to move in together. She volunteered to come over to help me move my stuff; and even though I didn't have much to need help with, I accepted her offer as a goodwill gesture of co-operation in our budding life together. We'd become a couple.

When I told my Filipino landladies that I was going to move out, they were visibly disappointed, which in a bizarre sort of way made me feel good. But when B.L. showed up to help me, they could not masquerade their discontent.

"I think my niece looks much better than this *haole*," one of them said frowning while staring at B.L. who stood far away oblivious to the ladies uncontained chagrin.

"She does," I said gently touching her shoulder. "Unfortunately, I don't think I'm the right guy for your beautiful niece."

I gave them both a hug and expressed my gratitude for their welcoming kindness. Meanwhile, B.L. walked by carrying one of my duffel bags and a small cassette tape player I'd brought with me from L.A.; my only source of indispensable music. They both looked disdainfully at B.L. as she passed by toward the door. Inside, I couldn't help but smile in appreciation for their caring for me and wanting to set me up with their beloved niece. Years after moving out, I'd occasionally drop by to pay a visit to my Filipino ladies friends, especially after the oldest one passed away.

Sharing B.L.'s one-bedroom apartment on Walaka Street in Kihei was definitely an upgrade from the small bedroom I rented—and a real luxury compared to my walk-in closet bedroom in Santa Monica. Besides, not having to share a bathroom, kitchen, and refrigerator space with three other people proved to be a welcoming convenience. Even the sloped street made it much easier for me to get my Fred Mobile started without having to push it with the driver's door open and jumping in at acceleration. But as our relationship progressed at a much faster pace than we'd anticipated, we thought that eventually we should get a new place to start our new life together. Although I lamented having to let go of the ease of getting my car started without having to push it every time I left home, it was a very small perk to relinquish in comparison to moving into a nicer place in the near future. Suddenly, life-changing events kept coming my way.

In a dazzling full-moon early summer evening, B.L. and I went for a night walk on the beach. Strolling barefooted on the sparkly white sand and holding hands in silence, I looked at the reflection of the moonlight on the ocean and it felt like a pathway connecting directly to the moon. The more I gazed at it, the more it resembled a sort of nighttime white rainbow mirroring the Sun light on the surface of the ocean. Perhaps, I mused, there was an equivalent of a pot of gold at the end of the shiny white bridge connecting the shore where I stood and the open ocean. I halted my steps wondering whether there was something in it for me. Then, I turned to embrace my walking companion and we kissed with seething passion.

Not long afterwards, we were back in the apartment making love with uninhibited abandon. Even in the high heat of sexual fervor, my mind seemed to be oddly fixated on the image of the majestic white light reflected on the ocean. And as I approached climax, I saw and felt myself running across that white pathway with uncontained anticipation, until I exploded in a boisterous expression of ineffable sexual pleasure. Then, the unexplainable ensued.

"Something has just happened," I said lying next to her staring at the ceiling with my eyes wide open.

"Oh boy, you could say that again," she replied while twirling the hair on my chest with her fingers. "This one was for the records book."

"Seriously, something meaningful has just happened," I said again feeling puzzled by the peculiar awareness that an unusual event had just taken place; something far beyond an extraordinary love-making act.

All of a sudden, I got up and started pacing back and forth in the living room. I was flummoxed by the uncanny post-orgasmic experience; something I'd never felt before. Then, I noticed how the full moon light pierced through the half-open curtain in the window faintly shining on my feet; like the pathway of light I imagined when I was walking on the beach. I stood there immovable and perplexed.

"Are you feeling O.K?" B.L. asked coming out of the bedroom looking preoccupied.

"Yes…yes, I'm fine," I mumbled as I continued trying to make sense of an experience I could not comprehend.

A few weeks later, I learned what had occurred in that magic night when I felt like I'd walked on a shiny pathway of light over the ocean.

"I am pregnant," B.L. told me after returning from a visit to the gynecologist office.

❖

The pregnancy was the catalyst to our decision to get married. At that point, we'd been living together for a couple of months and our relationship was thriving. Not only our feelings for each other were growing at a steady pace, but now with a child on the way the logical thing to do was to formalize our union in matrimony. And considering how everything was unfolding effortlessly, I realized the time had come for me to take the next step in my life. Now with fatherhood looming in the horizon, I accepted the fact that it was time to domesticate the *bon vivant* vagabond and turn him into a legitimate family man. Hence, in the courtroom of Judge Komo in Wailuku, Maui, we got married and my life changed completely ever since.

I wasted no time to begin planning for the next phase of my family life. First and foremost, I wanted to resume my academic studies; something I knew I would do sooner or later. I thought it would be a much better course toward a good paying job than marrying the Filipino ladies' niece as they had suggested. In the meantime, there were immediate financial needs that had to be addressed, especially with a child arriving in the months ahead. Although B.L. had managed to keep a money-making flower selling gig on her own, it was time for us to turn it into a bona fide business that we could expand, both in the scope of operation and profitability. Thus, I took the helm of the business ship determined to sail it toward a better quality living in paradise.

By the end of the year and a couple of months before our child's birth, we had a thriving legitimate business entity we called Hearts & Flowers—with the corny tagline "beauty is our business." I developed business cards, flyers, brochures, and other marketing materials that I spread all over the south and west side of the island. You'd be hard-pressed to walk into a hotel, condominium, shopping center, or even look at a bulletin board in a supermarket and not see a Hearts & Flowers marketing material. The effort paid off handsomely with several orders for flower arrangements and flower leis, many of which turned into regular business accounts. At the same time, we expanded our restaurant clientele base and even hired flower girls to meet the growing demand. Business was booming.

As far as my long-term personal goals were concerned, I was thrilled to have resumed my traditional schooling. I enrolled at the local community college and started amassing the required prerequisite credit courses for my baccalaureate degree at the University of Hawaii. At the same time, I initiated the process of transferring all the acceptable credits I'd earned at the Federal University of Rio de Janeiro, which significantly expedited my graduation timetable while saving me plenty of tuition money. Having qualified for student loans, which I repaid within a few years after graduating, I was on my way to achieving my academic aspirations. Everything was going well in all aspects of my life. But like sailing in open sea, you can never tell when you'll come across stormy weather.

Since the flower girl gig we offered was a small supplemental source of income to most girls who took the job, it became a revolving door that required constant recruiting. And by the time B.L. was late in her pregnancy, she wasn't able to go out as often and we needed more help than usual. It was at one particular interview that I intuitively knew we were about to sail some rough seas ahead.

"You've got to be kidding me? Do you really want to hire this woman to work for us?" I asked B.L. with a great deal of misgivings about the woman who'd just left our apartment. "She gave me the heebie-jeebies from the moment she walked into our place. I have a strong visceral feeling this is not going to pan out well. For God sake, couldn't you feel the bad juju she exuded?"

Unfortunately, B.L. was as adamant about her choice as I was about my intuition—and I was right. The witch-looking bitch cunningly worked her shenanigans behind the scenes while working for us. After learning from B.L. all she needed to know about the business, she eventually set up her own independent gig and even managed to snatch away some of our restaurant accounts. Soon, she became our main competitor in our area of operation. Like the gale winds on the sailing to the Canary Islands that forced us to go to Morocco to avoid the storm, now at the helm of our small business I was compelled to alter our course in order to adjust to change. But since this only affected the restaurant stake of our business, I perceived the untoward circumstance as the right time and opportunity to make the move to upcountry Maui—the place on the island I always wanted to live—and explore other possibilities in a different region. However, we had to remain patient, for it would not be practical to relocate when our child was about to be born.

And so we waited for the indescribable elation that the birth of our child generated, albeit it was also fraught with the most nerve-racking fright I've ever experienced in my life.

☙❖❧

It was almost 2:00 o'clock in the afternoon when the water broke. It happened a few weeks before the due date. Standing naked in the living room over a small puddle, my wife looked at me in disbelief as I took a snapshot of the exciting moment.

"Guess who's going to be a dad soon?" I said jokingly trying to alleviate the tension expressed in her taut facial muscles.

Having prepared for the occasion from the early days of conception, we'd already made the necessary arrangements with an experienced midwife who had been involved throughout the entire pregnancy. A licensed nurse and very well regarded in the island community as the best in the business, we felt comfortable having her in our corner. B.L was doggedly adamant about having a water birth at home, and this midwife was reputed to be an expert in this type of birth delivery. At first I was reluctant to go along with the idea, but B.L. was unwaveringly determined to give birth this way and I wasn't going to object it. My role was to support her at such an important and physically challenging experience. Eventually, after researching about the safety and the extraordinary benefits of water birth for both the mother and child, I actually became enthused about this approach. At the time, there were longitudinal studies coming out of the former Soviet Union evincing how children born underwater were more susceptible to developing superior qualities ranging from higher intelligence to more subtle salubrious advantages. It made sense that after going through the traumatic experience of squeezing through the birth canal, the buoyant liquid milieu the infant had been familiar with for nine months was the best suited environment for coming out into the world.

After calling the midwife to let her know what was happening, I followed her instructions on how to sterilize the bathtub and prepare everything for one of the greatest moments of my life. The birth of my child would prove to be even more meaningful than I could possibly have imagined—and one of the most frightening experiences as well.

By early evening the midwife arrived with her assistant, an oxygen cylinder, and a small medical luggage with the gadgets of her trade. After a brief moment of casual conversation while eating the spaghetti dinner I'd fixed for all of us, the rest of the evening into the wee hours of the morning was all about focusing on the most important event of my wife's life and mine.

"Push, push," the midwife repeatedly encouraged my moaning wife who contorted and gasped with intense physical discomfort. In my turn, I gently caressed her face trying to be supportive while witnessing a ballsy feminine act of bravery. With my camera nearby and on standby mode to photograph the historical event, I kept waiting for the grand soirée when my child, whose gender was unknown, would come out into the foremost element of life to be born into a brave new world.

"Push, push," the midwife repeated as I noticed the head spurting out of the vagina like a blossoming bud of a magnificent flower. I looked at the clock that I had set to the precise time and grabbed my camera. Then, at 2:23 a.m., gushing out in the midst of a colored cloud of blood and bodily fluids, I could barely see the newborn underwater. It resembled images I'd seen of supernovas exploding in the Cosmos giving birth to new stars. But this was my special star; the most amazing gift I'd ever received was now in the hands of the midwife.

"It's a girl," the midwife said.

I was awestruck watching my daughter with her eyes wide open underwater beholding us as if she knew exactly what was going on. Snapping out of momentary distraction, I started shooting photographs of that miraculous spectacle of nature. She stayed underwater for quite some time seemingly content to be breathing through the connected umbilical cord that I'd soon cut asunder, which I did in silent ritualistic fashion welcoming her into an independent life of her own. With a pair of surgical scissors in hand, I felt like King Arthur releasing the mighty Excalibur sword from the stone it'd been attached to for so long. It was the most significant symbolic act I've ever performed.

"Why don't you get in the tub to hold her and rub the mucous on her skin while we go to the bedroom to deliver the placenta," the midwife suggested as I unhesitatingly got in the blood smeared bathtub water without any qualms. Blissfully blessed, I held my minutes old daughter as if she were a delicate precious stone that I gently polished with nature's balm. Enveloping her in my arms while gently rubbing her soft skin, both she and I were silently serene. For a moment, I felt as though time had come to a standstill, until she suddenly started bawling as if she intuited what was happening to her mother in the bedroom.

"Call the hospital right away," I overheard the midwife's tense voice instructing her assistant.

I immediately jumped out of the bathtub holding my newborn in my arms and rushed into the bedroom.

"What's the matter?" I asked with my voice oozing apprehension.

The midwife didn't even have to respond. The consternation in her eyes and the bloody mess on the bed delivered an unvoiced disquieting message. Looking at my wife lying in a pool of blood prompted me to take immediate action without any further ado.

I handed my baby child to the midwife's assistant, grabbed the wheeled desk chair, placed my exhausted-looking wife clad in a nightgown on it, and rolled her out the door toward the parking lot leaving a trail of blood drops along the way. The midwife followed me frantically through the hallway while the assistant stayed behind with my infant daughter. With B.L. buckled up on the passenger's seat, I headed to Maui Memorial Hospital like a bat out of hell driving way above the speed limit in the wee hours of the morning. The midwife followed me driving her own car.

As I'd eventually find out, it was a case of retained placenta; a condition in which all or part of the placenta remains attached to the wall of the uterus after delivering the newborn. Complications of this condition include heavy bleeding, potential infection, uterine scarring, and often requires blood transfusion; and in some cases even a hysterectomy. If not treated quickly, these complications can lead to death.

I barged into the hospital pushing my semi-conscious wife on a wheelchair. I noticed the clock on the wall showing 3:35 am.

"We've already called the doctor. She's aware of your wife's condition and has told us what to do," the nurse on duty said. "The doctor will be here soon. In the meantime, let's get your wife properly situated in a bedroom."

Looking at my wife's mortally pallid expression with IV tubes hooked up to both arms, I wept quietly wondering whether I'd have to raise an infant daughter on my own. Somehow the experience of having lost my mother when I was just 4-months-old surfaced like an erupting volcano with fiery lava flowing emotions. I dreaded that just like my birth preceded my mother's death, now my child's birth could do the same to my wife. If that happened to be the unfortunate case, I vowed to myself at that moment that I'd never do to my daughter what my father did to me; to the contrary, I would love, protect, and shelter her from all harm and danger for as I long as I lived. Unlike what happened to me, never would I associate her birth with any untoward outcome she was not responsible for.

"We'll need to get a blood transfusion started right away," the nurse said addressing me and the midwife whose face looked almost as colorless as my wife's.

"I do not want a blood transfusion," my wife mumbled almost inaudibly. It was the first verbalized response she'd uttered since we left our apartment. I was surprised with her unexpected resolute reaction when she already looked half-dead. Torn between doing what I thought to be the best for her wellbeing and respecting her adamant determination, I gave in to my intuition that there were other undetectable parties involved in this decision-making process. My presentiment—or more likely it was her own ESP that was the determining factor—proved to be a potentially lifesaving decision. Since it was the early years of the AIDS epidemic, later on we would learn that the blood supply of Maui Memorial Hospital at the time was tainted with the human immunodeficiency virus. Our future could have taken an ill-fated twisted turn had B.L. not voiced her objection to the blood transfusion.

Noticing how uncomfortable and unhelpful the midwife was standing there fidgety, I suggested her returning to the apartment to check on my baby girl. She didn't hesitate to accept my suggestion and dashed out of the hospital almost as quickly as I had barged in. Not having her around somehow placated my fretfulness. Alone with my semi-unconscious wife in a hospital room, I immersed in my turbulent emotions in which my hopes and concerns mingled in distress. I was legitimately worried that not only I'd be a single father from day one, but also that I was about to experience the loss of a mother again. I was sad and terrified.

Suddenly, I heard footsteps in the hallway fast approaching the door.

"Let's see what we got here," the petite Japanese-American medical doctor said walking her somnolent-looking self into the room.

Then, in very blasé fashion, she stuck her latex gloved hand inside my wife's vagina and started yanking out smithereens of placenta tissues while talking with me causally as if we were at a tea party.

"Your wife lost a lot of blood; and since she refused to have a blood transfusion, I want to keep her here under observation," she said before instructing the nurse to keep B.L. very hydrated.

"And you'll need to bring your baby, too," the doctor continued. "Since according to our records your wife has negative blood type and yours is positive, we need to determine the Rh factor of the infant and evaluate her overall health as well."

The Sun had already risen when I drove on Mokulele Road back to Kihei to pick up my infant daughter; and shining bright on my way back to the hospital in Wailuku. With the midwife's assistant on the passenger seat holding my child, I did the double roundtrip feeling emotionally and physically exhausted. By the time I was alone in the apartment, I passed out on the living room floor where I slept for nine hours straight.

When I awoke up feeling somewhat revitalized, I thought of calling my father to let him know I'd made a grandfather out of him for the third time. When I told him the exciting news, he was disturbingly quiet on the phone for the longest time without saying a word. It was an eerie silence followed by an even more spine-chilling moment.

"You do remember what day is today, don't you?" He finally spoke and his voice was clearly choked up with emotions.

All of a sudden, I realized that in the midst of the exhilaration and extreme stress of the day, I'd been remiss remembering the significance of the date. A chain reaction of goose bumps flooded through my skin as if a dam had broken loose inside of me. I felt inundated in a torrent of awe, joy, and gratefulness.

It was the day of my mother's birthday. I felt as though someone who had been taken away from me had returned at last.

☙❖❧

What at first seems to be a drawback is often a leap forward in disguise. When our flower business took a hit from betrayal, unforeseen possibilities began blossoming.

Shortly after our daughter was born, we moved to upcountry Maui; by far my favorite place to live on the island. After deciding to branch out our flower business to the central and north side of the island, relocating was the best option for the new direction we were taking. In addition to establishing positive connections with restaurants in the region, we began diversifying our business by targeting a novel category of clientele we had not considered before. Ironically, we ended up exploring a new market in the south shore we'd just moved from.

I don't recall how the idea came about, but in hindsight it baffles me why it took us so long to realize that selling flowers at luaus was a promising possibility. Although there was no bypassing the competition already in place, I thought that coming up with novel ideas to deliver goods and services could give us an edge and put us in the pole position in the competition race. After researching the Maui luau market, I learned that the Lahaina-Kaanapali west side luaus were dominated by large businesses and nearly impossible to penetrate. However, in the south side of Kihei-Wailea area, there were chinks in the competition wall through which I could infiltrate with the use of some creativity. Thus, by offering to sell the flower leis while stringing them on site as a tourist attraction, I managed to secure four major accounts with the most popular luaus in the area. This new venture ended up being one of the best gigs I'd ever had; tantamount to my well-remunerated laid-back job on Dr. Hamil's yacht in the Southern Portugal region of Algarve. Suddenly, my life was on the upswing again: I'd become a father, resumed my college studies, had a new exciting business gig, and I'd moved to the place I always wanted to live since I first came to the island. It was my *maikai ke ola* (life is good) time again.

Living in Makawao, the historic *paniolo* (cowboy) town in upcountry Maui, was in itself a welcoming life-changing event. We lucked out to rent a reasonably priced old plantation house in a 5-acre open field with a glorious view of Haleakala, Maui's dormant volcano. Although the dwelling was in the last years of its existence in structural precarious condition—when we moved out six years later the landlords tore it down—the surroundings made up for its outdated deficiencies many times fold. The open fields with cows grazing freely; the three gardenia bushes around the house that infused our living space with delightful fragrance; the steeple of Makawao St. Joseph's Church visible from the distance—and the soothing sounds of its bells on Sunday mornings—among other visual, olfactory, and auditory sensorial enhancements that contributed to a quaint bucolic environment that greatly nurtured my spirit. The place was so idyllic that, in spite of its fairly derelict condition, I dubbed it "The Love Shack;" the place where our family love was nurtured every day. To this day it still remains as one of the most memorable homes I've ever lived, not to mention that it was an ideal place to raise my child.

By the time we moved upcountry my life was in ascending route. In addition to having our flower business in reset mode, I was completing my studies at the local community college with well-planned aspirations. My goal was to earn a bachelor's degree from the University of Hawaii, and then continue on to graduate studies all the way to a doctoral degree, just as I had intended in the earlier years of my youth. But with a business to run and a family to raise, I had to take it in strides and pace my progress accordingly. And in the midst of all my obligations and responsibilities, I still managed to carve plenty of time to go surfing at least a few times a week. Indeed, I was having a paradisiacal experience in a tropical heaven on Earth. It was one of the happiest times of my life.

As far as the flower business was concerned, B.L. and I worked out a perfect operational scheme: she handled the restaurants while I took charge of working the luaus. During the day, we sat down on the small living room floor of "The Love Shack" to get the preliminary part of our work done. Beholding the majestic Haleakala summit through the window, we listened to Hawaiian music while stringing beautiful leis of all types of flowers: plumerias, tuberoses, pikakes, orchids, gardenias, carnations, tea-leaves, among combinations of flowers we concocted to create fragrant floral works of art. Once they were done, we placed them in the refrigerator we had in the outhouse where we kept all our flowers. Then, by late afternoon I headed out to the luaus and she to the restaurants in the early evening.

Among the luaus I worked at, including the ritzy oceanfront hotels in the upscale Wailea area, my favorite, most profitable, and by far the one I had more fun than any other place I've ever worked, was located in an unsophisticated inland grounds on South Kihei Road. It was at this venue that I earned a new persona and even a new name that I've cherished and honored through the years hitherto. As a good-looking golden tanned Latin American young man who resembled a Hawaiian to unsuspecting *malihinis* (tourists), soon I became an integral feature of the luau as a sort of an external appendage of the show. It all began when the master of ceremony and the star of the luau approached me to make it official and christen me with my new Hawaiian identity.

"Sebastian is a very *haole* name," said Jesse Nakooka, one of the few pure Hawaiian blooded men in the archipelago and the best entertainer on the island of Maui bar none.

I smiled awkwardly watching him as he sized me up with a broad smile of his own.

"When I look at you I don't see Sebastian; I see Kilakila Haleakala," he said with utmost conviction. "That's it. Now I know who you are. We'll talk again later, Kila."

That evening when he stepped on the stage he made an announcement encouraging the crowd to go see "Kila's beautiful flower leis." From that day onward no one ever called me Sebastian again. I'd been unofficially baptized with my new Hawaiian name—and I absolutely loved it. In fact, to this day I still use it when I'm requested to leave my name in informal settings when my actual name is not required. In my heart, I am and always will be as much Kila as I am Sebastian. And when I found out the meaning of the name, I became even more warmhearted about it. I deemed the combination of Kilakila and Haleakala to be perfectly suited as a proper name for me. Whereas the latter means "House of the Sun," the former means "majestic, having poise that commands admiration." Since Sebastian is a name of Greek origin meaning venerable, Kilakila bore significant similarity to the concept of venerability. Indeed, Kilakila and Sebastian are synonymic names with meaningful etymological roots.

I sold my flower leis at Jesse's Luau Polynesia for many years. Never have I had again as nearly as good and fun gig as I had at Jesse's luau. I never got tired of watching the show over and over again; or eating *kalua* pig hot out of the *imu* with *poi*; or downing mai tai cocktails while making money; and, notwithstanding, the uninhibited flirtatious attention some of the hula girls gave me. It was the ultimate enjoyment in the workplace a young man could ever have. While many people who came to Hawaii had to scramble on shitty jobs to enjoy a couple of days off in the Sun, I cruised through a fun-filled carefree lifestyle that allowed me to have plenty of time to enjoy the island I called home. But as my daughter grew before my eyes, so did my sense of responsibility and the desire to create a more stable professional future. Perhaps, it was time to expand my business.

Although Makawao was a sleepy hamlet in upcountry Maui, there was a great deal of tourist foot traffic from folks coming down the drive from Haleakala National Park. Once I noticed how many tourists passed through town on a daily basis, I realized the potential to start a new business venture. It didn't even take much mulling over the idea before jumping on the opportunity to take a chance at something new. It started out when I spotted a small dilapidated empty storefront on Baldwin Avenue, the main street in town. Without wasting any time, I contacted the landlord to negotiate a proposal I had in mind. In exchange for dirt-cheap rent, I would renovate the place and turn it into a pleasant-looking store, which would benefit not only the landlord, but also all the other merchants in the area. It was an easy sell that didn't require much convincing, for there was nothing for the property owners to lose and a lot to gain. After all, the place was unused, unattractive, and unprofitable. Hence, I embarked on a new business venture of starting a retail store selling imported goods from Brazil.

With nearly nary capital and a surplus of creativity, I was able to pull off what many merchants and business advisers had told me would be an impossible undertaking: to open a retail store in Maui with a few thousand dollars. The most optimistic estimates I received from the so-called experts were north of 70 thousand dollars, which included lease, furnishing, insurance, initial inventory, signage, marketing materials, among other necessary supplies. I managed to be able to open my store single-handedly in three months with less than five thousand—and according to countless feedback I received from customers and walk-in browsers, it looked adorably charming. Using straw mats from Thailand to cover the decrepit walls; decorative hand-weaved baskets from the Philippines; secondhand carpet from the Salvation Army—in good condition, albeit with a few stains—and doing all the labor myself, my efforts paid off handsomely. As for the merchandise, with a strong dollar against the Brazilian currency at the time, I was able to stock up the shelves with enough clothing, leather goods, some semi-precious jewelry, and the celebrated Brazilian bathing suit—the store's best selling item—to get the business off the ground. Alas, it didn't fly high enough and not for long.

Some six months after starting the new business, I realized opening a retail store was not a good move after all. Unable to afford to hire help, managing an already busy flower business, and going to school proved to be too much work that compromised, not only the efficiency of all my committed activities, but also the quality of my life in Hawaii I had enjoyed till then. Even though we made a decent profit out of the venture, we decided to close the store down before the one year anniversary. There was no point in going after the fallacious concept of the pursuit of profit—or the misleading euphemistic term happiness—when genuine happiness that already existed was sacrificed. Nevertheless, the experience and personal satisfaction of pulling off a retail business in Maui on a shoestring was rewarding and worthwhile. It proved that I was capable of doing what the experts called an impossible task; and more importantly, it showed me that there are no limits to ingenuity fueled by determination.

The closing of the retail store coincided with the closing of another chapter of my life that was just around the corner. At that point, I'd already learned that life unfolds in cycles of death and rebirth of phases comprising of continuous transformations. As a moment, a day, a week, a month, a year all lead to the next, so do the experiences intrinsically connected to the passing of time; like the chapters of a book leading to the denouement of a story. What I didn't expect was to be on the verge of getting acquainted with death; once as an eyewitness and twice in empirical fashion.

I was driving down Kauhikoa Road to Hana Highway on my way to Ho'okipa to go surfing without a concern in my mind. Suddenly, as I approached Franz's property in Haiku, I felt a strong inclination to stop by to see him and his wife whom I'd befriended through an advertisement in *The Bulletin* about free-ranging chicken eggs for sale many years back. The late sexagenarian German couple lived in a sprawling bucolic property where dozens of chickens roamed freely in the large acreage field with a gurgling creek running year round. Since I had not seen them in awhile, I thought of stopping by for a quick visit. On the other hand, I was on my way to the beach and that was definitely an inopportune time. As I got closer to the dirt road entrance of their property, a peculiar tug of war between my purpose and intuition took place inside of me: one foot stepping on the throttle and the other wanting to hit the brake pedal. Oddly confused about what to do, I pulled over their driveway almost instinctively at the very last minute. As soon as I walked into their house, I knew why I'd been intuitively directed to stop by.

Puzzled by the loud playing of Buddhist monk chants recording that obstructed the sound of the doorbell, I walked in gingerly toward the living room and I was perplexed with what I saw.

"Oh my God, what's going on here?" I asked a foolish impulsive question in the face of the obvious. Franz was dying. Lying on the couch in a fetus position with wide open unblinking bulging eyes and barely breathing, I could tell that he recognized my arrival right away. With his wife kneeling next to him holding his hand with a desolate expression in her eyes, I was stunned as to how and why I'd been "called" to their place at that particular moment when Franz treaded the razor thin edge separating life and death.

"What can I do?" I asked almost inaudibly through the loud and disturbingly quasi-macabre sound of guttural chanting. His wife looked at me without saying a word; and yet, I could hear exactly what her eyes were asking of me in silence.

There was a fourth person in the room. A younger woman from the Buddhist temple Franz frequented who was blatantly aroused by the sight and experience of death. Her facial expression, mannerisms, and not-so-subtle display of excitement, all revealed her bizarre exhilaration in the face of death. She was the one who had decided to play the deafening chants that was having a negative emotional impact on the grieving wife, and perhaps even on the dying man.

"Please turn the tape off," I asked politely but in a commanding tone of voice with unwavering determination.

"Oh no, you don't understand. The monks' chanting facilitates the passing," she replied without budging. "It enhances the ritual of death as he crosses over to nirvana."

I utterly disregarded her woo-woo hokum and walked to the stereo and turned it off myself. It was obvious to me that she was the only one getting enhanced by the morbid ritual of death she seemed to be enjoying in a ghoulish way. As she paced back and forth speaking nonstop about the significance of the moment, I lost my cool and vociferously yelled at her to shut up. She cowed away to the kitchen and some sense of serenity suddenly returned to the living room. Franz' wife looked at me and I could feel the relief and gratitude in her eyes.

I approached my dying friend whose staccato breathing faded away piecemeal and observed, with inquisitive curiosity, the last moment of a human being's life. Gazing at the old man in a final fetus position, I recalled the time I witnessed the birth of my child. Now, I'd witnessed both the first and last moment of a human being's lifetime, and I marveled at the similarities of seemingly divergent transitions. As a moment, a day, a week, a month, and a year, life, too, moves on with the passing of time toward a mysteriously unknown experience that maybe can only be comprehended when reaching the epilogue of the book of life.

Immobile with unblinking wide open fisheyes, only his faltering breathing signaled that he was still alive. However, I could clearly sense that he was aware of what was happening in his surroundings. With his wife holding his hand while caressing his moribund face, I took a step forward, closed my eyes, and quietly sent out energetic-infused thoughts of peaceful wellness toward him. Then, to my astonishment, as soon as I opened my eyes to look at him, he emitted two gentle puffing sounds and his breathing stopped altogether.

"He's gone," his wife whispered while gently placing his hand down on his now dead body.

I helped her to get up and walked her to the yard outside for some fresh air of life. As we passed through the kitchen, the eccentric death worshipper rushed into the living room to behold the dead man. I stayed for awhile and after assisting the widow with the necessary phone calls, I went back home wondering about the serendipity that turned what would have been a joyful surfing day into a mournful death experience.

A few weeks later, I'd be driving the same route to Ho'okipa to go surfing. This time, however, I was about to encounter my own experience of death.

It had been weeks since I went surfing. I'd come down with a nasty flu that forced me to rest and sidetracked me from surfing against my will. Craving to get back in the water, as soon as I felt moderately well, I headed to my *de facto* Maui playground: Ho'okipa Beach Park.

Filled with anticipatory joy while blasting Pink Floyd's *Dark Side of the Moon* in my pick-up truck cassette player, I was excited to go surfing again late afternoon after such a long time. Perhaps because of the time of the day, I unexpectedly recalled the scare I had in the water the last time I went surfing at Ho'okipa . With the parking lot lights already on, dusk had been replaced by early nighttime and only two other surfers and I remained in the water. Suddenly, one of them sounded the alarm to imminent danger.

"Holy shit! Look at da fucking shark," the fellow bellowed as his voice echoed the sounds of panic in the darkness.

The three of us wasted no time to start paddling frantically to shore. Scared out of my wits, I paddled my surfboard faster than I'd ever done before. Fueled by an overflow of adrenaline in my blood system, I kept my eyes on the pavilions at the parking lot feeling the urgency of the moment and a desperate impulse to reach it as quickly as possible. Still far away from my target destination, all of a sudden I gasped when I saw the sea creature that was terrifying us emerge to the surface a few feet away from me.

I started laughing nervously when I realized that was not the day I was going to die at sea.

"It's a fucking turtle," I yelled out to the other guys noticing the large shell buoying harmlessly nearby me.

Because it was dark, the time sharks come close to shore to hunt for their dinner, it was reasonable to mistake an emerging turtle shell for the fin of a shark from the distance. I smiled recalling the incident as I approached Ho'okipa lookout area. When I pulled over and got out of my pick-up truck, I looked down at the swell rolling in with a mix of excitement and trepidation. It was huge; something between 18 to 20 feet tall waves coming in continual sets. Since I had not surfed in awhile and still had some remnants of gunk in my lungs from the flu, I couldn't help feeling unease about the unexpected size of the swell. However, I was already there and longing to get in the water. I was not going to allow myself to be intimidated by apprehension. Besides, there were a lot of guys out surfing and I longed to join the fun.

Since Middles (the moniker for the middle surfing spot at Ho'okipa Beach Park) was fairly crowded and where the biggest waves were breaking, I decided I'd be better off surfing Pavilions (the most easterly surfing spot at Ho'okipa) where there were only a few guys riding. I strapped my leash around my left ankle, got on my board, and paddled out ducking through a series of breaking waves and strong foamy bodies of water until I reached the lineup where some dozen other surfers waited for the next best set to come in. Sitting peacefully on my board beholding the stunning Maui north shore scenery, I was taken by surprise when someone shouted to alert the rest of us.

"Outside, outside," the voice reverberated a thrilling and yet uneasy tone to the anaphoric call. By the time I turned around to look, everyone was paddling out on the double as a colossal set of waves moved in rapidly from the open ocean bulging up as it approached the shallow shore. Without hesitating, I started paddling as fast as I could while watching the mammoth wall of water building up before my startled eyes. As the tip of my board barely overcame the first high elevation obstacle, there were several other lofty waves marching on undeterred. Coughing and spitting out some green gunk, I tried to paddle faster when I realized I was getting tired when I needed my energy the most. I had to make it over a few ginormous waves before I could be in a safety zone. However, the more I paddled the more depleted of energy I became, which was a compromising physical state if I didn't make it over the mountains of water. Feeling like David facing the Goliath of the sea, I pushed on forth to get over one more giant wave, but alas the outcome of my story was not as promising as the biblical account. In my case, Goliath prevailed.

As the crest of the wave began crushing down on me before I could reach its passing point, my surfboard slipped off from under me and twirled up in the air before hitting me in the head. Woozy and discombobulated, I felt as though I was being swallowed up by an unforgiving Leviathan whose overwhelming water pressure snapped the leash attaching me to my surfboard. Underwater chaos ensued. Tossed around within the churning water like a ragdoll inside a fast cycle washing machine, I desperately tried to get to the surface before the limited amount of oxygen in my lungs expired. Without my surfboard to hold on to as a floating device decreased the odds of my chance for survival. In an unprecedented situation, I realized I was in a fight for my life.

Barely able to get my head above water, I started huffing and puffing while desperately attempting to swim sideways to get away from the wrathful path of the merciless swell. But it was a fool's errand, for a powerful current kept pulling me back to the epicenter where the massive waves were crashing in sequence. I took another one in the head and back to the high-powered spin cycle that hurled me about in chaotic underwater motion. By the time I managed to get my head above water again I was beginning to fade away. And as the current kept dragging me back to the center point where the waves were breaking, I realized I wouldn't be able to last much longer. Then, another huge volume of water trampled on me as I submerged in what I felt it was going to be my burial site.

When finally I was able to get to the surface again in what seemed for the last time, I looked around but my ability to see was severely compromised by a fuzzy haze. I couldn't tell if I was facing the open ocean, the shore, or the sky. My fainting vision was blurry; my breathing, like Franz' in his deathbed, was in staccato mode, and my arms and legs felt limp and useless. I knew I was dying. And having always believed that I would live a long life, I felt disappointed with my kismet, though I didn't see the point of resisting the inevitable. At that moment, I consciously bid farewell to my life and my loved ones whom I hoped would be able to retrieve my body for the purpose of cognitive closure. I surrendered to my death while waiting for the next wave to wrap up the final moment of my earthly existence.

Floating in the water unable to distinguish the tenuous light before my eyes, I wondered if I had already passed. Suddenly, I realized I was facing the sky and there were no famished waves coming to gobble me up. The set had passed and not I. Thus, I mustered a modicum of emergency energy to swim slowly to the side where the current was not pulling me out to the open sea. Taking several floating rests along the way, I was able to start swimming back to the shore to be born again.

As soon as stumbled out of the water onto the beach, I was stunned to see my wife and daughter there waiting for me. They'd never come to the beach when I went surfing by myself; neither before nor after that day.

"What are you doing here?" I asked bewildered and still struggling with my heavy breathing.

"I don't know," my wife replied nonchalantly. "I just had a strong urge to come see you; a strange feeling that if I didn't come here I would not see you again."

I never knew what to make of that bizarre incident. Since I was absolutely convinced that I was going to die that day, I wondered whether my wife and daughter showing up on the beach played any role in my second chance to life. I suppose I'll never know. What I do know is that the next time I had a brush with death, I was the one who was going to have the prescience to spare them from tragedy.

ꕥ

The small Honda CRX's trunk was packed with the two large coolers I transported the flower leis to my favorite luau gig. On the back seat in a protective cardboard box, I carried the decorative flower arrangement I placed on the table where I showcased my leis to attract interest from potential customers. On the passenger's seat there was a permanent equipment feature: a child car seat. As my daughter grew into an adorable 3-year-old, she became a most valuable helper to the family business. After taking her with me for the first time, I realized that having her stringing flower leis on a straw mat next to me was a magnet of attention that significantly increased sales. It was a no brainer to have her as my regular companion, especially because she loved going to the luau with me. However, that day after loading the car, I stared at the child car seat for a long time and then, inexplicably, made an impetuous last minute decision.

"I think I should keep her with you today," I said to my wife right after turning the car on.

"Why?" B.L. asked frowning at me suspiciously.

"I'm not sure," I replied as vaguely as she probably felt. "Maybe I just need to spend some time with myself."

Under my daughter's whimpering objection, I drove away with a sour taste in my visceral glands that left a tart feeling in my heart. Every now and then I looked at the empty car seat next to me and wondered why I made such an unfounded decision. My daughter had become both a pleasant companion as well as an increasing-sales asset. I didn't have any rational explanation to validate my impulsive last minute decision to leave her behind. And as for the lame fabricated excuse of needing to be alone, I was actually missing her companionship.

"Where's that cute little daughter of yours?" One of the hula girls asked me as I was setting up my display table.

I'd been asking that question to myself since I left home without a legitimate answer to satisfy the inquiry. But answering the hula girl's question, I made up an excuse that she wasn't feeling well when in reality I was the one who wasn't.

It was one of the strangest luaus I'd ever experienced; and it had nothing to do with what was happening in the periphery of my internal discomfort. Not many tourists approached my table; and the few who did, I engaged with them perfunctorily without my usual uplifting tempo. I was off my game. Sales were under par at best. I didn't eat from the lavish buffet as much as I often did; and the strangest of all, I didn't enjoy the show either. Something was not right and I didn't have the slightest clue what that might have been.

Feeling somewhat morose, I packed my excessive flower leis surplus along with the almost bare cash box and left much earlier than usual. As I crossed the quaint little bridge over the koi pond leading to the entryway of the luau grounds, I experienced an eerie sensation of having crossed some sort of threshold separating two distinct phases of my life. Unbeknownst to me at that moment, it was the last time I would walk on that bridge again. The best gig I'd ever had finally came to an unexpected end. It was my last luau.

I drove back home absent-mindedly and at a slower speed than usual. With the radio on playing classical music, I tried to relax and disengage from my own vacant thoughts as if to provide relief to my uneasiness of spirit. Soon, I was driving uphill on Haleakala Highway approaching my shortcut left turn to Makawao via Hali'imaile Road; the narrow and dark two-lane road through the pineapple fields. Suddenly, a pair of bright headlights showed up from around the corner at high speed, slid off the road, and came straight in my direction. In a reflexive split second move, I pulled the steering wheel away from the incoming blinding light but I could not avoid getting hit almost head on. It was the moment my life changed dramatically with long-term repercussions.

As the swerving bright lights headed toward me in an unavoidable collision course, my heart raced faster than the oncoming vehicle. In a state of awe triggered by the anticipatory high speed crash, I unwittingly entered some paranormal twilight-like zone where my experience of time was perpetuated in a nanosecond. For what felt like an eternity, I was spinning inside an enormous rapidly rotating black and white spiraling vortex where time seemed to have come to a standstill. At the center of the bizarre geometric sphere resembling a rotating time tunnel, I saw myself disappearing as if I'd been pulled inside a powerful black hole. Then, when I regained a modicum sense of mundane reality, I was on my knees on the inside roof of my upside down vehicle in the middle of the dark pineapple field.

My first intuitive reaction was to check the child car seat just to feel immensely relieved realizing I was alone. After struggling in pitch-black darkness to find my way out of the turned over car, I managed to crawl out feeling excruciating neck pain. With soreness, cuts, and bruises all over my body, I attempted to stand up and walk out of the pineapple field toward the side of the road. But as soon as I got to my feet, the ground began spinning faster than the spiraling black and white vortex I'd experienced moments earlier. It was the worst vertigo episode I'd ever had and I was unable to endure it. My legs gave in as my body succumbed to gravity and I fell down vomiting uninterruptedly until I passed out. The next thing I remember was lying on a stretcher inside an ambulance whose loud siren pierced through my ears aggravating my vertigo further, which made me black out again before arriving at Maui Memorial Hospital. The place where I once dreaded facing my wife's death was the same where now I faced the prospect of my own demise. Fortunately, like the first time around, I made out of Maui Memorial Hospital without any significant loss. Other than cuts, bruises, soreness, excruciating neck pain and unbearable vertigo, I'd survived another close encounter with death. After that evening my life would never be the same again.

One disturbingly mysterious aspect of the accident came to light the following day. Lying in bed with a neck brace unable to make the slightest move, B.L. was the one who went to check the wrecked car in the junkyard to retrieve the coolers and other belongings, which were all there untouched. As soon as she came back home, she walked into the bedroom with a curious expression in her face.

"Why did you buckle up the driver's seatbelt after crawling out of the car? She asked.

"What are you talking about?" I asked sounding as puzzled as she was.

"The driver's seatbelt was buckled up. Why did you bother doing it?" She continued.

"I didn't. Why would I?" I replied befuddled with her observation.

"Well, everything inside the car was an untouched mess. It's obvious that nobody got even close to it. Why was the driver's seatbelt buckled up?" She insisted with a valid inquiry to which I had no answer.

By the time she finished speaking, I thoroughly recalled the sequence of events of the accident. Since the experience of spinning inside a black and white vortex when the car was flipping over, the immediate recollection I had afterwards was being on my knees on the inside roof of the car. In hindsight, I should have been upside down with the seatbelt securely wrapped around my waist and shoulder. And yet, to my utter bewilderment, she was telling me the driver's seatbelt was buckled up. How could it possibly be? It would make no sense for anyone to do it on purpose after the accident. But even more incomprehensible was the fact that I ended up on my knees on the inside roof of the car without having released the device. And yet, the first moment of awareness I had after the vortex spinning experience, I was already on my knees without having to make any effort to disentangle myself from the seatbelt. To this day I wonder why I was not upside down on the driver's seat after the car crash; and why the seatbelt was still buckled up in the wrecked car in the junkyard.

Inscrutability of incidents aside, the accident wrecked my life as much as it did the car. In addition to developing a chronic case of periodic bouts of debilitating vertigo—my most terrifying experience that the neck injury perpetuated—I was unable to work for a long time, which eventually led to the demise of my luau flower business accounts. And to add insult to injury (the clichéd expression is referred here literally), the legal battle against my own car insurance company dragged on for a long time. Since the drunk driver who hit me was uninsured, I had to hire an attorney who secured almost half of my compensation working on my case. I had to endure a frustrating and disappointing legal process, which culminated with my learning that the drunk driver ended up only paying a fine for not having mandatory car insurance. Had he killed me instead of only ruining my life, he'd be prosecuted for involuntary manslaughter; but since I survived, all he got was a punitive dollar amount slap in the wallet. In my turn, it took me months to recover physically, emotionally, and financially from the car crash that turned my life upside down.

Eventually, I had to start over from the bottom again. Having lost my business and with my health compromised by regular bouts of vertigo, I was limited in my ability to pursue good quality work. Hence, I ended up getting a shitty desk job with a slave-wage in a place where the cost of living is stratospheric. I would not be able—financially or otherwise—to carry on my new untoward condition for too much longer. Something had to give.

The challenging consequences of the car accident turned out to motivate me to make some fundamental changes in my life. As Friedrich Nietzsche's (1844–1900) popular aphorism goes, "what does not kill me makes me stronger."

From working in a lovely fun-filled environment to toiling away in a sedentary office desk job was not an easy transition. Desperate to get some work, I applied for all sorts of employment; and that was the one I landed: an assistant, secretary, receptionist, among other incidental functions at the Maui AIDS Foundation. It was the early years of the deadly epidemic and having a firsthand experience of that health calamity was humbling. The devastating effects of the disease; the wide-range of people getting infected with the virus; the prejudicial scourge of AIDS in society; all of it made me aware of the many dangers lurking in the microscopic world. If HIV were a virus as easily transmissible as COVID-19, the AIDS crisis likely would have become the worst and most deadly pandemic in human history; the black plague of the late twentieth century.

Although the job itself was aggravatingly tedious, I learned to appreciate my fortunes. Firstly and foremost, I was thankful for my wife's refusal to get a blood transfusion at the time of the birth of my daughter. Had she not been so adamant about it, both B.L. and I could have been clients of the organization that I worked for, since there were people who had contracted the virus via blood transfusion at the local hospital at the time. However, it was the day when the beautiful flower-girl who used to work for us came in to register for services that I realized the broad scope of everyone's vulnerability to deadly diseases; be it AIDS, cancer, or any other malignancy skulking in the biological world. In her case, the HIV virus was transmitted to her through her bisexual boyfriend. I was saddened to witness first hand a beautiful young woman deteriorating piecemeal until the illness claimed her life leaving her child son orphan.

Despite my gratitude for what could have been a negative outcome that never happened, the dreary routine of the job was killing me in a different way. Already in my early 30s and without a professional foundation upon which to build my life, I was growing steadily uncomfortable with the passing of time. I felt stuck in a hut and not making any significant career progress or improving the prospect of a better livelihood. Notwithstanding, my paycheck was dismal. I knew the time had come for taking action to create a better future. Furthering my academic studies became paramount—and so did quitting the loathsome desk job.

At that time I'd already completed my Associate of Arts degree determined to climb up to the very last rung of the academic ladder. Thus, I applied for another round of student loans to continue my studies aiming at a Bachelor of Arts degree at the University of Hawaii, which had just begun offering an outreach program on the island of Maui. Another couple of years and I would graduate with honors and invited to join two academic honor societies. I was right on track to accomplishing my educational goals and very proud to put myself through college without anybody's help. I was an immigrant working hard to become the best productive citizen I could be. I was the head of my family and dedicated to providing for them to the best of my ability. Indeed, I was unwaveringly committed to take charge of my destiny, and I was far from done yet. I would not be satisfied until I reached the final step of my academic journey in which three solitary letters would add prestige to my name. With a lifelong passion for learning and a wealth of life experience, I was resolute about becoming a professional educator, which I believed to be my ontological vocation. Although I was running behind the traditional schooling age schedule, I would not allow the timing disadvantage to hamper my long-term goals.

As soon as my undergraduate studies at the University of Hawaii were underway, I started looking for work in the professional field I intended to pursue. My first opportunity came as a part-time P.E. and language arts teacher at Haleakala Waldorf School. It was a fortuitous event in manifold ways. In addition to landing a descent job in a lovely educational environment, my child got to attend a first-class private school tuition free. Also, I learned about a remarkable approach to education and the work of the extraordinary man behind it, Rudolf Steiner (1861–1925). Encouraged and undeterred, I continued searching for more opportunities to expand my credentials, which led me to earning a professional teaching certificate from the State of Hawaii Department of Education. Soon, I started teaching at the state's school for adults, as well as other regular gigs at adult education settings. Holding various part-time jobs in education and with a baccalaureate degree under my belt, I was right on track to accomplishing what I had set up to do. However, there was another very important goal of mine that I wanted to achieve as soon as I became eligible to apply for.

"Congratulations! You are now officially American citizens," the presiding judge proclaimed at the end of the ceremony where a couple of dozen exuberant participants crowded the small courtroom in Wailuku.

Gawking at the naturalization certificate in my hand, I smiled with ecstatic satisfaction and proud to have become a citizen of the United States of America. I knew that the 14th Amendment of the Constitution of my new adopted motherland granted me the same rights and privilege as any natural-born American citizen, even though some of my fellow citizens didn't always perceive me as legitimate. In fact, I remember reading a survey disclosing that among conservative Americans, 46% of them defined being "truly American" only those who were born in the United States. However, this birthright does not always prove to be true or guarantees acceptance and security—the example of internment of born American citizens of Japanese descent during World War II is a glaring illustration. Also, I've befriended a number of U.S. born citizens of Asian descent that some white Americans did not consider them to be legit citizens, though all the instances occurred on the U.S. mainland only and never in Hawaii where there are large numbers of Asian Americans. Rather than a country of origin issue, this pseudo-preconception of what constitutes a bona fide American citizen is clearly rooted in racial prejudice and other forms of ignorance harbored by prosaic-minded people.

Like my childhood situation in which my stepmother made preferential distinctions between her own blood children and me, now as a step-citizen the discrimination came, not from my adopted motherland, but from some of my native fellow citizens. Several times I've been singled out as not being a "real American" because I was not born in the United States and spoke English with an accent. This biased categorization opened up old childhood wounds that I promised myself I'd heal by being an exemplary step-citizen; just as I had tried to be an excellent stepson. This time around, however, I was determined to prove that being a genuine citizen was not intrinsically related to geographical determinants, linguistic foundation, or ethnic background, but to eminence in the embodiment of high standard citizenry.

As I walked out the courthouse, I recalled my journey up to that moment of my new citizenship. It was never something I'd intended to do when I left my country of birth. At that time, all I wanted was to get away from a family situation that had become unbearable. Becoming an American citizen was not a preconceived plan I had in mind when I left for Switzerland, Portugal, or even Los Angeles. All my exploits and misadventures that led to that moment were natural unfolding processes that culminated to a situation I had not envisioned from the outset. But as I gradually rebuilt my life in the United States, I felt a tremendous sense of belonging, pride, accomplishment, and gratitude for the country that offered me opportunities to develop my potential. I was determined to prove my fealty to both my adopted motherland and fellow citizens, in spite of the many prejudicial encounters I would face along the way.

Ironically, a unique characteristic that has served me well has also worked against me in many biased incidents: my accent. In addition to countless accolades referring to my “charming accent,” I’ve benefited a great deal from my personal linguistic charisma. My accent has contributed to my getting jobs, dates, attention, favors, among other positive outcomes in many situations. Conversely, my accent has been also stripped of its congenial appeal and turned into a prejudicial detriment in different occasions. However, I’ve found solace in my dealings with insensitive interactions based on one single observation: most of the time those who biased me because of my accent were often the parochial, uneducated, and uncouth individuals. Not wanting to emulate them by being intolerant of their ignorance, I’ve chosen to overlook their ill-mannered remarks with subtle smug. In the end, I know that my accent, like those of all immigrants—or New Yorkers, Bostonians, and, for Pete’s sake, Alabamians—is a linguistic characteristic woven in the fabric of American society. I would not get rid of my accent—and I couldn’t even if I wanted to—just as I would not let go of the significance of the naturalization certificate I proudly held in my hand at the time.

Now I was an American citizen. I was getting ready to start my college graduate studies. I held jobs in the field of work I wanted to pursue. I had a lovely family and I lived in a paradisiacal island in the middle of the Pacific Ocean. What else could a man want?

Change!

It was summer and I was taking a well deserved break to celebrate my accomplishments. In the past two years since I graduated from the University of Hawaii, I'd been accepted to a Master of Arts program at California State University. Ahead of me I had one final term before writing my thesis to earn my degree. I was gradually paying off my student loans without burdening my family budget. I felt like a tennis pro holding a handful of match points in a grand slam final—and I was acing my service game, literally.

A tennis aficionado and member of the United States Tennis Association, I participated in many regional recreational tournaments sponsored by the organization. When a fellow team member told me about an upcoming tournament independent from the USTA sponsored tourneys we played, he caught my attention and interest in what would likely be an exciting experience. It was the Maui County Tennis Championship happening during the weekend in July at the Royal Lahaina Resort. I didn't hesitate registering for the tournament and making reservations to stay over the weekend at the resort. It was family vacation time and I was revved up to kick some tennis butt in the process.

In my particular division (4.0 in the USTA ratings), there were five matches for the advancing players toward the final. To my pleasant surprise, I ended up being one of the final two to play for the trophy and the bragging rights on the island tennis community. At 37-years-old with a swollen surgically repaired right knee supported by a brace and an overdose of ibuprofen, my chances of beating the 16-year-old top tennis dog in the Maui high school scene were close to nil; and yet, close happened to have superseded nil. When my match point serve hit the inside T-bone service box line with an ace, I was ecstatic as if I'd won the U.S. Open. Like my young opponent, I felt like a high school kid, too. I was now the Maui County tennis champ in my division, and I was effusively elated about it. Except for beating my friend in the quarter-final match—and he was the one who had told me about the tournament—I had great fun throughout the competition. The rest of the day I dubbed as my "Victorious Sunday," I spent relaxing in the resort's swimming pool playing with my daughter, until I had an urge to have some me time.

It was already late afternoon when I decided to go for a walk along the stretch of Kaanapali Beach. With the Sun ensconcing behind the horizon in kaleidoscopic fashion, I immersed in my thoughts as the lukewarm water flowed over my bare feet before ebbing out back to the turquoise sea. Impulsively, I turned around to take a peek at my footprints on the wet sand in time to see them disappearing with another flow of ocean foam rolling in. At that moment, I realized that either literally or in symbolic manner, steps already trodden vanish with the next motion; be it of water or time. Also, I observed that I couldn't even see my footprints as my feet shaped them on the sand, for by the time they were imprinted I was already creating another one in my forward movement. In what seemed to happen in a nanosecond, I recalled my life's journey hitherto; all the steps that I'd taken leading to that moment of bliss walking on the beach at sunset in Maui on my

"Victorious Sunday." Then, breathing in the sea-scented air, I wondered where my current life steps would lead into the future.

Unexpectedly, my emotions transitioned from sheer joy to bleak sadness. I sat down on the white sand trying to make sense of a senseless feeling that simply did not fit in that special moment. The more I tried to rationalize the unpleasant sentiment, the more distraught I felt. All of a sudden, the truth washed over me like a tsunami generated by an earth shattering realization: it was time to leave Hawaii; the place I held in the highest esteem of all other geographical regions in the world. Although Rio de Janeiro is my original birthplace and will have always a special place in my heart, it is my "Mamma Maui" who gave birth to my new life; to the man I'd become as I headed toward the future. I love Maui dearly and more than any other place I've ever lived. The thought of leaving her triggered a negative emotional chain reaction. Perhaps, it tickled my orphan bone as I relieved the experience of losing my mother again, albeit of a different kind. It felt like a Shakespearean tragedy; like Juliet's self-inflicted dagger in the bosom when she learned about the loss of her lover Romeo.

As I sat there absent-mindedly gazing at the island of Lanai in the distance, the emotional discomfort could only be assuaged by the practical reasoning of my situation. I was a 37-year-old man with a family and a rapidly growing child. I was about to earn a graduate degree, but with limited prospects for more promising professional opportunities. I lived in a splendid place on Earth, but the cost of living in a privileged paradisiacal setting was exorbitantly high. As it was, I wondered, what would the footprints of my future steps look like if I didn't make a change? I had to take another plunge into the unknown. Besides, like the island of Lanai sitting there solitarily small in the middle of the Pacific Ocean, after living in Hawaii for almost 10 years, I began developing a nagging case of what the locals called "rock fever;" the feeling of isolation on an island.

I got to my feet and resumed walking back to the resort. With speedy steps, I moved forward propelled by the unyielding conviction that the time to leave Maui had come. As difficult and distressing the decision was, I had absolutely no doubt it was time to move to the mainland. The question was where would I go?

☙❖❧

Compromising is arguably the most important and challenging aspect of a harmonious relationship. Often it leads to mutually agreeable decisions, but sometimes it can have devastating effects on one or even both parties involved in the compromising process. Although we'd already talked and mutually decided that moving to the mainland was the right thing to do, the destination remained undetermined.

"How did you come up with Oregon?" My wife asked me with a furled brow as we sat at the kitchen table talking about moving to the mainland.

"Gut feeling," I blurted out as quickly as I had intuited it was the right place to go. "I just get a strong feeling that I'm really going to like Oregon and that it'll be good for us."

"But you've never been there, so you don't know," she said almost defiantly as I noticed her objection rising.

"As I said, it's a gut feeling; but of the very strong kind," I replied before taking a gulp of cold water that temporarily chilled my enthusiasm. "Do you have any suggestions?"

She paused for a long time without looking at me. It was obvious that she had ideas of her own. I waited for her turn to verbalize her thoughts. She picked up her coffee mug and looking at me from above the brim, she let me know what she had in mind.

"What about New Mexico?" She suggested.

"New Mexico! Are you kidding me? Do you want to move from lush Hawaii to live in the barren desert?" Both my reaction and the tone of my voice evoked my opposition to her suggestion.

"Why not? It's just as much an option as Oregon. I like the desert climate, and it's better than getting drenched all year long," she spoke defensively and the argumentative direction of the conversation started bothering me.

"Let's table the topic for now. We'll rehash it again later," I said standing up to walk outside to breathe some fresh air and gaze at Haleakala summit for inspiration.

If the thought of leaving Maui was not distressing enough, moving to a barren landscape was not something I had in mind. I couldn't picture myself living in a place where trees and large bodies of water are not abundantly around. Sure, there was the Rio Grande and its tributaries, but it was not like being surrounded by the Pacific Ocean and nearby waterfalls. While Oregon elicited images of meandering rivers, gorgeous lakes, majestically tall trees, and a stunning coast, my mental imagery of New Mexico was fuzzy and made me squint as if I had desert dust in my eyes. This was going to be the mother of all compromising. Somehow we'd have to find a common ground.

Contrasting to my wife's enthusiastic desire to move to New Mexico, I had absolutely no interest in relocating to the desert. It was an environment completely alien and unappealing to me. If I were to make such a dramatic change, I would need to come up with legitimate motivating reasons to convince myself that it might not be as bad a move as I expected it to be.

One afternoon while working on my master's thesis draft, it dawned on that I could apply for my doctoral degree at the University of New Mexico. Since I was gung-ho about pursuing a terminal academic degree, the possibility of continuing my studies at UNM was an ideal motivation to relocate to the area. Having earned most of my graduate studies credits in my Master of Arts in Humanities degree in history and philosophy—two subject matters I'm absolutely passionate about—I initiated contact with the university's history department and received a very welcoming response. It was the encouragement I needed to go after my professional goal of becoming a college professor, as well as a justifiable reason to move to New Mexico. Thus, I began making arrangements to pay a visit to campus; and while there, I'd scout the area in preparation for moving over. I would have to find a suitable place to live, a good school for my child, and a job. However, since I had not been accepted to the university yet, I was aware I was gambling on a positive outcome. But as Helen Keller (1880–1968) wrote, "life is either a daring adventure or nothing at all."

Firstly, I had to establish the groundwork within to prepare myself psychologically to what would prove to be one of the most difficult changes I'd ever gone through. Once I reluctantly surrendered to the idea of leaving Hawaii to move to New Mexico, I started grappling with the fact that I was going to transition from tropical islands to the dry deserts of the southwest. Departing from the geographical location I referred to as "Mamma Maui" felt like a miscarriage in reverse. In some dark chilly cavern of my mind where an infant mourned the death of his mother, the adult in me seemed to relive the unfortunate incident of my early childhood in a most bizarre parallel way. I began developing all sorts of physical symptoms, including more frequent and intense bouts of vertigo that knocked me out of my senses. One evening it got so bad—the most frightening health emergence I've ever experienced to date—that I was on the verge of asking B.L. to call 911. I felt as though my soul was abandoning my body as if the latter were a condemned dwelling that was about to collapse. I was physically, mentally, and emotionally in turbulent distress.

Approximately three months before our planned departure from the island I adored, I went to Albuquerque to scout the area. Staying at the University of New Mexico visitors lodging (La Posada), I engaged in a tandem effort to pave the way for my new academic life while preparing the grounds to move my family to the mainland. However, the uncertainty regarding my education ambitions kept me unease. At the time of my visit, I had not even submitted my official application yet; therefore I did not know whether I'd be accepted to the program. It was a risk I had to take in order to validate moving to New Mexico. My goal was to solidify my connections with the university's department of history during my visit, and then enroll in classes to prove my scholarly worth. But in the end, there were no guarantees that I'd be accepted. And considering that at that point I had not even gathered the required academic letters of recommendation for the application packet, I was playing crapshoot with my education future. But since I was partly using my schooling goals as a motivation to uphold a move I was extremely antsy to make, the ambiguity of the outcome of my efforts didn't really matter in the face of the only dreadful certainty ahead: I was going to move away from Mamma Maui.

From the moment I arrived at Albuquerque airport, I was immediately affected by the environment that ignited a culture shock. The billboards and advertisements plastered on the terminal's walls displayed a southwest flavor that didn't agree with my

Hawaiian palate. And once I stepped outside, the chilling dry early April air brushed against my face eliciting a distant haptic memory of what winter feels like. However, in spite of my first reaction to winter-like conditions, I must admit that when I woke up to an unexpected white morning, I was delighted to see snow steadily falling down and blanketing the arid desert soil. Despite the ephemeral winter weather thrill, what ensued didn't bode well to my expectations of the future.

Two days later, with wads of maps and information about housing scattered on the passenger's seat of my rental car, I drove around Albuquerque in awe of its utter lack of urban charm. Aside from the slightly scenic Sandia Mountain—a far cry from the majestic Haleakala Summit—there was nothing remotely picturesque about Albuquerque; to the contrary, it was a distastefully unattractive metropolitan area. Situated in the desert smack in the middle of two major interstate highways, it seemed to me that every street I drove by looked exactly the same. In fact, if it weren't for their respective names and perpendicular directions, I would have thought I was driving in circles. Everywhere I drove was but one strip mall after another with similar crossing thoroughfares. The city's streets were nothing like Baldwin Avenue leading to the quaint *paniolo* town of Makawao where I'd lived happily for many years; and this was where I was about to call home soon.

Although I was already afflicted with umpteen malaises long before arriving in New Mexico for my scouting mission, the psychological pressure significantly exacerbated my symptoms after my first drive around town. My lower back, which had been bothering me for weeks, all of a sudden stiffened like an iron board forged in the heat of distress. It was as though my back was functioning as a barometer of my mind exposing the enormous pressure inside the core of my being. It got to be so bad that I had to sleep on the cold floor every single night I stayed at *La Posada*. One night when I decided to go watch a show at the university's theatre to distract my preoccupied mind, I stood up at intermission and immediately fell to my knees unable to get up. It was an embarrassing moment that reminded me of how terribly tensed up I was. Years later when I learned about Tension Myositis Syndrome (TMS), Dr. John E. Sarno's (1923–2017) pioneer work about the mind-body connection indentifying stress as the fundamental trigger of TMS, I realized that I'd empirically validated his premise that lower back pain is a symptom of excessive stress.

At the end of what it felt like a very long week, I had accomplished what I came to New Mexico for. Except for a job, I made progress with everything else. I found a reputable school for my child, secured housing in a nice condominium with several amenities (swimming pool, Jacuzzi, tennis courts, clubhouse, etc.)—and for much less than I paid rent in Maui. Also, I felt confident to have made a positive impression in the Department of History at the University of New Mexico where I intended to pursue my doctoral degree. I had paved the groundwork to make a smooth and stable transition; at least in regards to its physical aspect. On the psychological front, however, the anticipation of moving to New Mexico felt as disorienting as the spiraling vortex I got caught in when my car flipped over onto the pineapple field.

❖

The last two months in Maui were the worst time of my 10-year residence on the island. Packing our belongings in sturdy cardboard boxes to ship them to New Mexico was a heartbreaking undertaking. Worse yet, watching them pile up piecemeal against the walls in our vacant "Love Shack" made me choke up with sadness. Even the stunning view of Haleakala summit from the living room window elicited an edgy feeling of melancholy. Once everything was packed, I started making arrangements with the shipping company to get the boxes out of sight. Lastly, I purchased three one-way airfare tickets to our new life on the mainland. What I considered to be the best 10 years of my life was coming to an end. However, in spite of the anguish brought about by the anticipation of departing from the place I adored, I didn't have a scintilla of a doubt that moving to the mainland was the right thing to do—like when I got on a plane from Rio to Lisbon after the 36-hour ordeal that changed my life. It was moving to New Mexico, a compromised option that I didn't partake my wife's enthusiasm that aggravated my mood. But now it was a moot point. It was a done deal.

After the boxes were shipped away, both the spatial and emotional emptiness became even more accentuated. The last step was to ship my pick-up truck that would drive us from Los Angeles to Albuquerque. With my wife's car already arranged to be sold on our last day in Maui, I had transportation for another week but no desire to go anywhere. I was mourning a loss as I'd done before in my life, but this time it was a place instead of an individual or situation. In the midst of my geographical bereavement, I realized that it was not only a location I was leaving behind, but a dual tandem of space and time; that is, Maui from the mid-1980s to mid-1990s. In no other space-time frame would my experience ever be duplicated, which proved to be true when I visited the island years later when it felt oddly different to me because the space-time connection no longer existed.

Indeed, any place—or person for that matter—reencountered at a different time when the first connection was established will not exhibit the same original familiarity, for neither time nor space can be replicated in the same way it once happened. There's constant change and transformation in everything. It's like a quantum mechanics investigation in which the position of a subatomic particle can be observed but not at the same time its velocity is measured, because both can only happen at a singular moment that cannot be observed simultaneously—this is Nobel laureate German quantum physicist Werner Heisenberg's (1901–1976) Uncertainty Principle. Despite my intellectualization effort to understand and accept my transformative situation, the experience of separation was poignantly keen.

Passing faster than I'd ever noticed before, time zoomed by and soon reached my last weekend on the bosom of Mamma Maui. I'd been in nostalgia mode long before that weekend arrived. I recalled ambling on the soft white sand of Kaanapali Beach and realizing it was time to move. It was at that entwined space and time singular moment of decision-making that the going away began, and now it had reached its culminating point. Thenceforth, leaving Maui became a matter of sheer physical formality.

On the Sunday of the last weekend, we went out to have brunch at one of the posh hotels in Wailea where I'd worked in my early days on the island. Sitting there on the lanai beholding the open sea scenery, I felt a wave of wistful thoughts wash over me. Munching on coconut pudding and drinking Kona coffee, I was sorely aware that I was experiencing my last moments on the beautiful island I'd called home for the best and most transformative decade of my life. As on the day when I won the Maui County Tennis Championship I dubbed "Victorious Sunday," that forlorn day I called "farewell Sunday."

Imbued to the core with a longing for what already had passed, I reminisced vividly one hot summer on a full moon night in my study in The Love Shack in Makawao. It was a sensorial memory of uttermost joy and complexity that happened in the eternal split second of space-time. I was writing while listening to *Smooch*—a most beautiful piece of music by Charles Mingus (1922–1979) and Miles Davis (1926–1991)—when a gentle breath of nature blew into my room carrying along with it the exhilarating fragrance of the gardenia bush that resided outside my window. As the sweet whiff drifted in, I could feel the molecules of the aroma blending in with the musical notes as if dancing in the air. As they waltzed around the room, their dance created an atmosphere of absolute ecstasy in an ephemeral singular moment; an instant in space-time that would become a part of my being forever. It was a Maui moment like no other; indoors, at night, and alone. That night I understood empirically the meaning of what I'd learned theoretically from the mystic English poet William Blake (1757–1827): "To see a world in a grain of sand; and a heaven in a wild flower. Hold infinity in the palm of your hands; and eternity in an hour."

After having brunch in Wailea, we went to spend the afternoon on the north shore of the island where I ached doing part with Ho'okipa Beach Park; the place I'd spent so many fun times surfing—and once almost died. At night, we had dinner at the restaurant where B.L. sold flowers for so many years to close the weekend in full circle. The farewell rituals had been performed and it was now time to leave Hawaii, for good.

The next day, I was mingling with sunburned tourists at Kahului Airport bound to the mainland; and like them, heading home; a new home I wasn't even acquainted with yet. With my daughter and wife hastily rolling their luggage trying to catch up with me, I moved toward the departure area as though heading to a Dantean gate leading to an inferno where I didn't know what to expect. By the time I heard the clicking of my seatbelt buckle, I was immediately transported to the untoward evening at Lisbon International Airport on my way to Rio when I endured a living nightmare that lasted some 36 hours. Fretfully, I wondered whether it was a sign of things to come; a similar arduous and soul-draining experience that pummeled me into an emotional pulp. However, as I fidgeted my fingers while hearing the wheezing of the engines on the runway, it dawned on me that trip to my homeland and back to Portugal had drastically changed the course of my life in unpredictable ways. Perhaps, this one would have similar transformative implications.

As soon as I felt the wheels disengage from the ground, my stomach grumbled with a peculiar kind of heartburn. I looked down through the window as the plane gained altitude and I sighed out loud feeling the moisture in my eyes. Watching the traffic flowing on Hana Highway through Spreckelsville, Baldwin Beach Park and beyond, I quietly bid farewell to Mamma Maui in gratitude for having nurtured me into the man I'd become, and for the wonderful years I spent on her lush bosom. I had evolved and made significant progress in my life since I first landed on the outmoded airstrip and barn-like building Kahului Airport in the mid 1980s used to be. And as I left from the updated modern terminal, I couldn't help but create an analogy between the airport and myself in different space-time. Both the airport and I had changed a great deal with similar noticeable improvements.

The 4-hour plus flight to Los Angeles was long and tiring. I took turns in my head between reminiscing over the past and projecting into the future that I didn't particularly look forward to. In spite of my trying to trick myself into creating a motivational factor to build excitement—the pursuit of a doctoral degree—I didn't feel my shenanigan worked as well as I wished. In fact, throughout my travels when I moved from one place to another, never had I felt this discouraged about going somewhere as I was moving to New Mexico. But based on my past experiences, by then I was aware that this was just another leg of the grand journey of my life; another milepost; a crossroad; a threshold I had to pass through to get to an unknown other side where new possibilities awaited. At least this is what I hoped for. In the meantime, a whole new set of challenges was all I could see in my future.

❖

Landing on LAX this time around was a strange experience. Although I was staying in the city of angels for only three days before driving to New Mexico, being back in L.A. elicited odd feelings about the time I lived there. I'd always considered the two years I spent in Los Angeles bitter-sweet; a mixture that I described as "entertaining consternation." Perhaps, because I was glad to be gone when I left for Hawaii, coming back, even if just in passing, was not a celebratory occurrence by any stretch.

To make matters slightly more awkward, my family and I stayed at my former older lover and her current husband's Marina Del Rey condo. In fact, they came to pick us up at the airport and were very welcoming in their home. Of course, I told my wife about the long gone affair I had with our hostess and she was, as I expected, indifferent to the information. But according to my former lover, she did not let her husband know that the friend and his family they were hosting was her erstwhile lover. I respected her perspective. However, the truth was that we'd established a solid friendship in the very early years of our love affair that had endured the passing of time.

Aware that my daughter was also going through the unavoidable stress of such a dramatic move—she was leaving friends and everything she'd ever known behind—I did my utmost to lessen both her physical and emotional disturbance triggered by the change. Being in L.A., taking her to Disneyland was a paternal responsibility I would not neglect. And responsibility would not be the right word to describe my recollection of the last time I went to the amusement park alone. It happened in the last month of my housekeeping job in Laguna Beach. On my day off, I decided to go to Disneyland by myself with a "yellow sunshine" in my pocket. I got to the park as the gates were opening, dropped acid shortly after getting in, and left at closing after riding the Pirates of the Caribbean multiple times in a row dangerously tempted to get off on one of the ride's turns. Flying high on yellow sunshine, I was smitten with a blond female mannequin I wanted to have sex with convinced she was flirting with me. Thankfully, the awareness of my compromised state of mind prevailed over my hallucinogenic temptation. But this time around, watching my daughter enjoying the same ride high on childhood innocence, I experienced vicariously a sense of redemption for my past adult mischief.

Taking sometime for myself in need to decompress, I wondered around town visiting places that held value in my memory bank. Strolling on the Venice Beach promenade all the way to Santa Monica Pier was an eye-opening experience regarding the current stage of my journey. It seemed that with every step forward, I realized more deeply the progress I'd made since I walked that same path for the first time more than a decade earlier. From the first boat gigs at Marina Del Rey to the short-lived housekeeper job in Laguna Beach, I'd come a long way since then. As I ambled along the familiar path some 12 years later, much had changed in my life. Now I was a married man with a family, had earned a graduate degree, and was in the pursuit of my highest academic aspiration. Infused with positive thoughts of accomplishments and motivated by my educational goal, by the time I reached the Santa Monica Pier I was smiling about the excitement of change and looking forward to the next leg of my life's adventures. Suddenly, moving to New Mexico no longer felt like a taxing endeavor, but more like an opportunity in the making; or at least it was the attitude I was trying very hard to anchor.

The next day Heloise drove me to Long Beach harbor so I could pick up my truck. I spent the afternoon preparing the vehicle for the following morning departure; checking tire pressure, engine oil level, filling the gas tank, among other safety measures. Then, it was all about turning the camper-covered bed of my truck into a dorm space for the alternating drivers and the child passenger. Stocked with water, snacks, and a great deal of determination to move forth, I felt confident we were ready to reach our new destination; both the geographical location as well as the unknown we could not plan for.

Up early in the morning and I was gun-ho about hitting the road. It was a hot summer day and I was ready to face the heat of my life's next adventure. After a long drive through the unattractive inland counties of California and the barren regions of Northern Arizona, eventually we reached our own desert when I wished for an oasis. At the border separating a desolate desert land from the other, my first impression was definitely not heartening, for I felt bamboozled by a message that lacked visual credibility.

"Welcome to the Land of Enchantment," read the large colorful billboard with a reddish barren background that extended for miles before my strained dry eyes. I got off the truck to stretch my arms and move my inactive fatigued legs. As I stood there in the middle of a sterile territory looking at a greeting sign suggesting that I was about to enter an enchanted land, I thought something was not right with that picture. I was either being lied to or my concept of enchantment was misconstrued. In any case, this was going to be my new home state, so I'd better come up with some enchanting reasons to make it work out somehow.

Soon we reached the small and ostensibly poverty-stricken Native American town of Gallup. It seemed to me that the farther I drove into the state, the more disappointed I became with its misleading highfalutin moniker. My perception of a Land of Enchantment was colored with a vision of places like Hawaii, Tahiti, and the South Pacific region at large. New Mexico, however, felt like the antithesis of anything even remotely enchanting. And Gallup exemplified my experience thus far. It was hot, humid, dry, barren, and populated with downtrodden-looking Native Americans, which exacerbated my sympathy for their historical plight. Having seeing Albuquerque, I knew I was heading to the upscale modern dominant culture's version of Gallup. After all the beautiful places I'd lived in my life, I was still incredulous that Albuquerque was going to be my new hometown.

Moving from the lush Hawaii to the harsh desert had a similar negative effect on me as when I took a tedious desk job at the Maui AIDS Foundation after having worked for years at the festive luaus; except that moving to New Mexico felt much worse. With the job I knew it was meant to be transitory, whereas I had no idea about the longevity of my sojourn in my new home state; a place that didn't resonate with my environmental predilection.

A few more extra hours on the road and we arrived at our new residence. The place we'd call home, in spite of the extra space and many amenities in the condominium complex, it was no Love Shack. But as I originally intended, having the conveniences we never had before made the transition slightly more palatable to the bitter taste of the move. For better or for worse we had to make it happen; and the first step was for both of us to find work.

After weeks scavenging through the employment section of the Albuquerque Journal, I submitted several job applications but received not a single response. Beginning to grow apprehensive with the delay in finding a job, one day I woke up with an intuitive feeling of going through the yellow pages book to find out what kind of businesses were around my area. There, in an inconspicuous listing among all others was the name of a new prep school located a couple of blocks away from my home. But it was already August and the beginning of the school year was a couple of weeks away. The chance of landing a teaching job with this timing in place was an unrealistic expectation; but maybe I could be a substitute teacher. In any case, having absolutely nothing to lose, I thought I should stop by to introduce myself, instead of mailing an impersonal résumé. Again, as it'd happened many times in my life, lady luck smiled at me with her ever loving eyes.

"The Social Studies teaching position was filled last month," the principal of the first year brand new school said as we conversed in our introductory meeting. "The last and only vacancy I have to fill in for this first academic year is a Spanish language teacher. Would you be interested?"

"Yes, I surely am," I said without hesitating. I supposed he assumed that because I was from Latin America it automatically qualified me for the position. But immediately after saying yes to his offer, it dawned on me that my knowledge of Spanish was remedial at best. Despite the similarities with Portuguese, my native tongue, Spanish is a different language with its own sets of grammatical rules, pronunciation, and other characteristics that differ from one Romance language to another. But how hard could it be teaching Spanish to middle-school kids? Besides, I'd always learned best with my self-didactic methods than in any other way. Compelled by the demands of my life's urgency, I was determined to expand my knowledge of *Español* on the double.

And just like that, from an inconspicuous listing in the yellow pages, all of a sudden I had a job; a teaching job that I got two weeks before the school year started. I beat the odds again. In spite of the unlikelihood of it happening at that time in the calendar year, getting hired made me feel confident about the circumstances turning in my favor. Besides, I was excited with the challenge of having to learn the subject matter on the fly, and thrilled that the school was conveniently located three blocks away from home. However, what was really keeping the fire burning in my belly was the pursuit of my highest academic achievement. Perhaps more than anything else, I wanted to prove to myself that I was worthy of a doctoral degree.

In the meantime, B.L. landed a job as a sales rep for an insurance company; a good fit for someone who had both the knowledge and experience in sales. In fact, she did so well that she earned many accolades within the company and quickly became one of their top agents. A year and a half into the job, she was acknowledged as one of the principal achievers and rewarded with an all-paid expenses cruise to The Bahamas for both of us.

In my turn, I became a popular teacher with both students and colleagues, which encouraged me to request the headmaster to invest in my professional development at the end of the first school year. Unhesitatingly, he obliged and I was awarded grant money for airfare, accommodations, and tuition cost to study in

Mexico for three weeks in an intensive study program at an internationally renowned Spanish language school in Cuernavaca, the historic capital of Mexico's Morelos State.

By the end of my first year in New Mexico, everything seemed to be going much better than I'd originally anticipated: we were settled in and making new friends; both my wife and I had decent employment; our daughter was doing well at her new school; and I was taking three graduate courses at the University of New Mexico for the Ph.D. program, even though I had not been accepted yet—but that was part of my strategy to get in. It felt like the trade winds were blowing straight into the main sail of my forward-moving vessel in the direction of my destination. But as any experienced sailor knows, the weather can change on a dime; and when it does, it's imperative to adjust the course according to the unexpected navigational conditions.

It so happened that both international trips were like lighthouses ashore pointing to a new direction. Within the six months between my coming back from Mexico and going to The Bahamas, unforeseen circumstances drastically altered the compass reading of my life's course.

❧❖☙

Traveling to Mexico was an exciting and necessary change of surroundings. Even though all was going well at the time, I still felt the need to get away from Albuquerque by myself to take stock of my life. The truth was that in spite of the positive flow of events, I was still dissatisfied living in a place that did not resonate with my geographical predilection. In the past year since we moved over from Hawaii, we took regular family trips to Santa Fe, to the beautiful mountainous region of Taos, and even venture into the small historic town of Las Vegas, which was a main post of the old Santa Fe Trail. New Mexico was a fine place to visit but not a region I felt at home. My quiet silent discontent lingered like a headache I couldn't get rid of. Going to Mexico was the equivalent of taking an aspirin to alleviate the discomfort.

As soon as I stepped out of the airport to take the bus to Cuernavaca, Mexico City immediately reminded me of Los Angeles; not because of surrounding similarities, but for its awful air pollution. Puzzled to be feeling nauseated when I had no trouble during the flight, I realized that the carbon monoxide and other toxic impurities infused in the air were the culprits for my sickness. I wondered how a city of 20-plus million people, most of whom living in precarious socioeconomic conditions, could withstand the ongoing barrage of pollutants released in the atmosphere while continue growing unremittingly. And yet, it was a ubiquitous urban dilemma everywhere in the world, which I've always struggled to comprehend. Sooner or later the levy of sustainability is going to give in and an ensuing flood of insurmountable environmental problems will likely inundate modern civilization. But instead of mulling over the world's ecological problems, at that moment my sole priority was to get the hell out of the unhygienic atmosphere as quickly as possible.

Located some 40 miles south of Mexico City, Cuernavaca was a much more amenable town. Known as the City of Eternal Spring because of its temperate climate and the profusion of flowers in its parks and gardens, the small town ambiance appealed to me as a place conducive to study, learn, and practice the Spanish language in the community. Being fond of both the Mexican people and food, it didn't take me long to spot some good eateries where I could enjoy a tasty meal while hanging out with the locals. I was stunned to notice that in the short span of weeks my Spanish had improved exponentially. Emboldened by my developing linguistic skills, at the end of three weeks when I finished my studies, I decided to reward myself for my accomplishments and do some traveling around.

As one of the main tourist attractions of all Mexico, I had to visit the intriguing Aztec city of *Teotihuacan*; the Mesoamerican city estimated to have been first settled in 400 B.C.E. Then, I wanted to explore the fascinating and mysterious pre-Columbian archeological site of *Xochicalco* in the western region of the State of Morelos. Finally, saving the best for last, it was all about heading south to Acapulco to spend a few days swimming in the Pacific Ocean again. I was having a grand time; and yet, there was something happening inside of me that contradicted my enthusiasm.

Standing at *La Quebrada* outlook area; the famous Acapulco spot where the *clavadistas* (divers) leap into a small cove in the Pacific Ocean from 135 feet high cliff, I marveled at their intrepid act and superb diving skills. I likened their dare-devil deed with the courage of jumping from the edge of the abyss into the unknown from which you cannot turn back. Figuratively speaking, I'd stood on a likewise rim a few times in my life; and like the *clavadistas de La Quebrada*, I dove into narrow and shallow inlets of opportunities with equal determination and gallantry. As I watched them perform their audacious act with a great deal of admiration, I realized I held similar sentiments regarding my own acts of bravery, even the ones that were propelled by utter desperation.

But while my eyes focused on their superb athletic performance, my mind was prematurely preoccupied with the ensuing weeks when I'd be back in Albuquerque. Soon the school year would resume and I was not as excited about it as I was when I first got the job. Teaching a foreign language to rambunctious middle-school students was not something I was willing to do for a long time. To me it was a temporary way of eking out a living; just another survival job. Although education was the field of work I wanted to pursue, teaching Spanish at middle or secondary level was far off the track of my long-term professional goals. I had higher aspirations. I wanted to engage intellectually with young critical thinking adults in college environments.

Since a terminal degree is the unofficial licensure for teaching at most universities' departments, I knew that earning a doctoral degree was imperative. Hence, the anticipation of finding out the status of my application at the University of New Mexico lingered on the back of my mind. However, the emotions associated with my expectations proved to be a double whammy. On the positive side, I was optimistically excited to be accepted into the Ph.D. program; after all, I did very well in the three courses I completed, and I seemed to have impressed my professors with my academic acumen. But on the other hand, I was aware my acceptance would entail having to stay in Albuquerque at least another two years, which was longer than I wished to endure. Like the industrial laundry job in Switzerland and the doorman post at the posh hotel in Portugal, I was afraid I wouldn't be able to stick around the required time.

Meanwhile, I tried to be mindful of the moment and enjoy the fun in the Sun like I hadn't in a long time. Swimming in the Pacific Ocean again was sheer bliss that I enjoyed profusely. However, the more time I spent in Acapulco the more I realized how much I didn't like living in the desert; a dislike that had remained unabated from day one. Every time I thought of having to live in Albuquerque for much longer, the butterflies started fluttering their wings of anxiety in my congested chest. The only motivation I desperately clung to was my desire and commitment to continue my academic studies to the highest level. But there were other problems, too.

Perhaps, I unwittingly harbored resentment to compromising. Residing in a place that conflicted with my environmental DNA was not conducive to optimal relationship. My wife, in her turn, didn't seem to be very satisfied with the move either; and even less so with her job, in spite of doing very well at it. Accustomed to spending the day at home in Hawaii stringing beautiful flower leis to sell them at night, now she spent a big chunk of her days driving on interstate highways to make contact with insurance prospects. I was no longer the only one discontented. Suddenly, it felt as though a wedge had been placed in a gradually widening fracture in our relationship.

By the time she earned a cruise trip to The Bahamas for her sales accomplishments, our marriage hit an iceberg and almost sank in the chilly water of dissatisfaction. Things were not going well, but we managed to get our relationship on a lifeboat and save it from drowning—for the time being.

❧ ❖ ☙

After returning from the old Mexico to New Mexico, I felt an urgent need to create something new. Based on my growing aggravation with my work, it was plainly obvious to me that I was not going to last long in my current job. I was burned out working with pre-teens and their often times difficult parents. Thus, with the professional objective of teaching at the college level, I started looking for employment at both community and private colleges in town. Besides, with the response about my application for the Ph.D. program around the corner, I thought I needed to get a step ahead of my goals. My efforts paid off.

I landed a nightly part-time job with an accredited private university teaching humanities courses (history and elements of dramatic arts). It was a perfect first step because it allowed me to keep my bread and butter day job while making a move in the professional direction I wanted to pursue. Shortly thereafter, I successfully interviewed for a potential full-time position at the local community college for the following academic year. It looked promising as everything seemed to be falling into place in a timely fashion. As for the next step toward my goals, all I could do was wait to hear from the Department of History at the University of New Mexico.

On a Friday evening after a long day at work and yearning for the weekend ahead, I walked to the mailbox next to the condominium main office to pick up the mail. Out of the ordinary, there was only one envelope inside. I looked at it and my hands trembled as I noticed the University of New Mexico stationery. Moved by a combination of burning curiosity and disconcerting trepidation, I held it in my hand for a long time fretfully holding back from opening the envelope to learn about its content. I walked back to my apartment fidgeting with the envelope from one sweaty hand to the other. I was both excited and nervous. Nevertheless, I felt confident that after everything I did—and with great academic results—the likelihood of reading in the first line the word congratulations was very high, indeed. By the time I got to the patio in front of my place, I could not wait any longer. With the key in my hand to open the front door, I slashed it through the envelope and opened it instead. Rapidly unfolding the letter, the key fell to the ground and I didn't even notice.

Agape, I read the letter communicating that my application for the doctoral program in the Department of History at the University of New Mexico had been rejected. I rubbed my eyes, shook my head, and read it again not believing the words in plain black ink in my face. The committee had turned down my candidacy with no further explanation. I read it several times as if by reading it repeatedly the message would change. Of course it didn't; and neither did my heartrending disappointment. Frowning with befuddlement, I put the letter back in the envelope, bent over to pick up the apartment's key, and, instead of entering my home, I went for a walk to process what it felt like an emotional onslaught that assaulted me from my blindside. My academic aspiration had been shot down.

I walked around the condominium complex several times not knowing what to make of the unexpected response. Feeling as if a noose had been tightened around my neck, I had difficulty breathing the dry air as my moist eyes expressed my disappointment. I was in disbelief with the unexpected outcome of my methodical efforts; sad that my academic ambition was thwarted, and even angry at the department's faculty with whom I'd established propitious rapport with. I had done everything within my power to make it happen. I'd planned diligently; I carried out every step of my meticulous strategy; I successfully completed three higher level graduate courses to showcase my academic merit, and I couldn't think of anything else I could have done different or better. I circled around the complex nonstop wondering what could possibly have gone wrong.

Feeling physically, mentally, and emotionally drained, I stopped walking in circles and sat down on a bench in front of the clubhouse. My mind kept mulling over possible reasons for the untoward fate of my educational ambition. Since my academic records were excellent and I demonstrated my scholarship skills in the courses I earned the highest grades, perhaps it'd been the letters of recommendation that I assembled in a hurry. Maybe they were not good enough, especially considering that one of them was not from an academic source (one was from the director of the State of Hawaii Adult Education Program), which in hindsight was a faux pas of mine. No matter how much I tried to figure it out, I could not pinpoint what went astray. I realized it was a fruitless effort to indulge in rationalizations about a fait accompli. What I needed was to move on. Hence, as a strategy for self-recovery, I started scrutinizing all the negative observations I'd gathered during my brief experience in my ill-fated attempt to earn my doctoral degree at the University of New Mexico.

I recalled a particular interaction with a fellow-student that epitomized the intellectual debauchery and the arrogance of academia. I should have taken it as a warning sign of not belonging.

"What's the area of expertise you intend to work on?" A female classmate asked me askance at the end of a class we shared.

I paused probably looking as puzzled as I felt, for she followed through before I had a chance to reply.

"What's the regional and historical time focus of your academic interest?" She asked and her voice echoed a subtle hubristic scorn with my delayed response.

"I'm afraid I haven't decided yet," I replied looking into her eye through her squared black frame glasses. "I suppose I might be an academic generalist."

"Academic generalists are endangered species with very little chance of survival," she remarked with supercilious superiority.

I kept looking at her dismayed with her pretentious arrogance without saying a word.

"I'm specializing in the colonial period in the region of Oaxaca, Mexico, from 1650 to 1800," she volunteered the unrequested information out of her own conceited volition.

"Interesting," I said dishonestly thinking the extreme opposite of what my single-word statement conveyed. With my broad scope of interests and unbridled academic curiosity, I could not fathom limiting my intellectual creativity to one narrow field of study within a limited timeframe, which sounded like mind-numbing drudgery to me.

I should have known what I was getting myself into from the very beginning. The braggadocio I overheard in the department about new research and publications; the military-like rankings of professorship status (instructors, assistants, associates, and tenured); the murky aura of intellectual superiority often bereft of substance; and, as a graduate student, the voluminous amount of readings required in very short periods with no time for critical thinking process to evolve or discuss the materials' content. It was all about quantity not quality; dissemination not assimilation; appearance not meaning; ranking not competence; and yes, publish in inconspicuous journals or perish in the utter irrelevance of your own writings.

What seemed like harsh judgment triggered by resentment had validity backed up by actual research. In the serendipity of the time, I came across an interesting book by Charles J. Sykes (1954–) titled *Prof Scam* that exposes the fallacies of professorship in higher education. Having rejected the Renaissance man and replaced him with the narrow specialist, the Ph.D. degree became what renowned American philosopher William James (1842–1910) cautioned to be "an octopus that would strangle the academy." A few years later, William James would press further labeling the Ph.D. degree as "the Mandarin disease;" a sham and a bauble whereby to decorate the catalogues of universities. I felt both vindicated and ascertained that the world of traditional academia perhaps was not right for me. And yet, I had scholarly ambitions and a ravenous hunger for knowledge that had to be satiated, doctorate degree or not. What's a Renaissance man to do?

My first source of inspiration emerged when I learned about the excellent work of one of the most prominent scholars in the world who, incidentally, does not have the letters Ph.D. added to the end of her name: the prolific British author Karen Armstrong (1944–). Relying on the excellence of her scholarship instead of pretentious academic titles to validate the quality of her work, Ms. Armstrong proved to me that one does not need a Ph.D. to be a bona fide scholar, though the credential is imperative for becoming a professor at a university. As William James pointed out, the Ph.D. is an essential decorative lure to the status of an institution of higher learning credibility. Since my original professional aspiration hinged on a doctorate degree, I had to reevaluate my career objectives. Regardless of what I was going to do next, the idea of becoming a so-called expert on any limited particular subject did not resonate with my expansive intellectual curiosity. Comprehensive learning was my goal, and not the presumption of having narrowly focused knowledge. I didn't want to become a traditional specialist as defined by what I once read: an expert is someone who knows more and more about less and less, until he knows everything about nothing.

However, determined not to abandon my commitment to higher learning, I decided at that disappointing time that I would create my own self-didactic equivalence to the Ph.D. degree. Now that I became aware of not having any interest in limiting the scope of my learning to narrow acquisition of expertise in one subject—or worse yet, a fragmented timeframe of a region, such as “specializing in the colonial period in the region of Oaxaca, Mexico, from 1650 to 1800”—I realized that I could never be a traditional scholar. At last, I’d discovered my true studious nature: more than an academic, I am an intellectual artist; an indestructible Renaissance man with manifold interests ranging from philosophy to physics.

After mulling over the circumstances of my latest disappointment, I stood up and walked back home feeling resigned and convinced that, as it had happened many times in the past, this apparently inauspicious occurrence was the best outcome in disguise. If nothing else, the main motivational factor that had been keeping me put in New Mexico no longer existed. Suddenly, there was an opening to the opportunity to leave this place that was out of sync with my environmental preferences. But as it’d happened in several other instances in my life when I faced the prospect of moving, the question often repeated itself: where to go next?

At that time, all I needed to know was that I was going on a cruise to The Bahamas.

☙❖❧

By the time we went to The Bahamas, our marriage was sailing some rough seas. A combination of factors was at play. Besides being utterly discontent living in the desert, dissatisfied with my job, and disappointed with the outcome of my doctorate degree aspirations, I started developing a strong visceral feeling that B.L. was having an affair. Since I’ve always relied on my acute intuitive power to navigate me through life—in fact, I couldn’t have made thus far without it—I was certain, albeit without substantial evidence yet, that matrimonial infidelity was taking place. Then, one afternoon when a male client of hers called to make arrangements for an appointment supposedly to discuss health insurance policies, I knew right away that my intuition had been corroborated. Of course, at first she denied my suspicion, but it was a matter of time for her to quietly and remorsefully acquiesce to admitting what I already knew. Henceforth, it was fair game. Soon afterwards, I started bedding an attractive young college student from my evening part-time teaching gig, and opened myself up to other sexual affair opportunities. Her being unfaithful cracked the levy holding my marital fidelity in place and the floodgates burst wide open. I became a willing sexually available married man. Thus, as we approached our tenth anniversary and were about to go on a cruise to The Bahamas, our marriage was like a ship stuck in a sandbar with a broken rudder.

All of a sudden nothing seemed to be working out for me. Like the crisis at home, at work the situation was equally bad. A new principal had been hired to transition the fledgling school into its expanding high school years; and he and I just didn't seem to see eye to eye. Although the original head of school, with whom I had a great rapport, made an effort to smooth out the rough edges between the incoming principal and me, the feeble bridge he attempted to build fractured under development. The incoming boss and I seemed to be on opposite banks of a river where a voluminous body of water of incompatibility flowed. Hence, he and I never connected at any reasonable level; to the contrary, his unctuous personality just could not blend with my straightforward nature. It became obvious that my employment days were numbered. However, since I was already displeased with the job and had been setting up a path of transition to higher education institutions, I realized the new principal was but an important antagonistic character in the plot of the play of my life. He was the harbinger of necessary changes to come.

With my marriage heading to the rocks, my academic aspirations abruptly sunk, and my regular job jeopardized by stormy conditions, I began feeling like a shipwreck adrift in a sea of confusion. Something had to give and I wasn't willing to wait much longer to find out what that would be. I'd have to make some decisions and take immediate action. As it happened, the cruise to The Bahamas was a perfect getaway and a timely opportunity for me to sort things out within my inner turmoil.

Arriving in muggy Miami smack in the middle of winter felt brutally hot and humid. If it weren't for the (mostly) English spoken around me, I'd say I was back in a strange version of Latin America. The climate, the people, and the cultural atmosphere all oozed an undeniable Latin flavor that somehow didn't persuade my palate. Perhaps I'd grown accustomed to—and fond of—the Mexican appeal that permeated the entire United States where even in Hawaii the traditional 5 de mayo holiday was celebrated. The Latin America tang of Miami, however, didn't appeal favorably to my senses, for it seemed unoriginal and lacking authenticity. It was as though the Latinos living there suffered some sort of identity crisis; like wanting to be Americans while adamantly holding on to their original national identities. An ethnically and culturally conflicted Latin American population, I thought. After spending a couple of days in Miami, I was ready to get the hot hell out of what I perceived to be a specious representation of the Latin America I knew.

Aboard the cruise line was another disappointment. Although it looked fancy from the outside, the floating hotel was not as nearly as sophisticated as its spurious appearance indicated. The mostly unrefined middle-class crowd, the unimpressively confining accommodations, and the unsavory fancy-looking food, all added up to an unappetizing experience. And to make matters worse, on the very first night of sailing, we navigated unexpected rough seas and a got badly seasick—and so did many other passengers who swarmed the front desk asking for anti-nausea medication. That was the end of the false credibility that large ship stabilizers prevent seasickness.

Regardless of my disillusionment with the circumstances of the cruise, I had some particular goals I wanted to accomplish in my own inner expedition; one of which involved the future of my marriage. Although B.L.'s forays into extramarital adventures had put a major damper in our relationship—and triggered my own incursion into sexual soirées—the fact she displayed genuine repentance for her mischievousness of late, I was willing to meet her in the middle of the reconciliation road, albeit with feeble hopes of patching things up in the long run. In the meantime, as a therapeutic tool for making marital amendments, we engaged in passionate no holds barred sexual activity as if we were a newly married couple in a honeymoon trip.

After a couple of dinner parties laden with tedious speeches recognizing the awarded employees, we were done with the formalities of the business events and free to enjoy ourselves as we wished. For me the fun began when we arrived in Nassau, the capital of The Bahamas. Watching the stunning turquoise water, all I wanted to do was to go for a long swim in the Atlantic Ocean; something I hadn't done in more than a decade. Thus, I stepped off the ship, alone, and went on an exploratory jaunt of both the island and my state of mind.

Soaking in the ineffable pleasure of swimming in the lukewarm water of a beautiful Caribbean island, I recalled the 10 wonderful years I lived in Maui and how happy I was then. As I indulged splashing water in my back strokes beholding a splendid blue sky, I realized I could no longer live in the desert. I had to move out of New Mexico. At that point, not even if an extraordinary full-time employment opportunity arose I'd be persuaded to stay. I was determined to no longer remain in a place that was not conducive to my well being. With my mind moving faster than my limbs in the water, I switched to breast strokes and dove deep down in the clear water. As I followed the light piercing through the emerald green surface all the way to the white sandy bottom, I made up my mind to move to another state where the green color was predominant in the environment. I longed to live in a beautiful place with an abundance of tall trees and large bodies of water, preferably with an ocean nearby. By the time I got up to the surface, I'd speared a most valuable insight: I was going to Oregon; the place I originally intuited to move to when we decided it was time to leave Hawaii. Now, it would be B.L's turn to compromise—and she was in a disadvantageous position to negotiate.

When we returned to Albuquerque, I felt like I had worked out the kinks and doubts that had kept me off-kilter for the last year and a half in the desert. I came back from The Bahamas determined to sail through the storm my life had encountered. With indomitable conviction, I was resolute to make one of the boldest moves I'd ever made.

I was a man on a mission of self-rescue.

Approximately a month before the end of the school year, the subtle animosity between the new school principal and me had turned into overt aversion. Neither one of us was even trying to disguise our mutual dislike anymore. Every now and then I'd catch him sneering at me from afar and I pretended not to notice it. I was aware that he was the boss and I was the one on the short end of the stick. But at that point, I didn't give a rat's ass about it.

Having not secured a full-time college teaching job and with only my nightly part-time gig in place, the forecast for my employment security was precarious at best. Aware that my days at the private school were counted—and without that source of steady income, I wouldn't be able to remain financially afloat for long—I immediately began thinking up a viable alternative strategic plan. In the meantime, B.L., who was dissatisfied with her work and wanted out of the insurance sales business, started cutting down on the number of days she worked weekly. Suddenly, our financial stability took the top rung on the ladder of our priority list of urgent needs to address, followed close by our marital troubles.

At last, the predictably inevitable day arrived. I received a dismissal letter letting me know that my contract would not be renewed for the following school year. The lame excuse was that the school was heading in a more conservative direction, which my progressive stance on education would not fit in. As I finished reading the letter, I could see the new school principal sneering at me in my mind's eye. This time, however, unlike my reaction to the rejection letter from the University of New Mexico, I'd anticipated the news and therefore it didn't faze me in the least. In fact, now I had both a good reason and plenty of motivation to go ahead with my moving out of the desert plans.

Utterly discontent with the dismal circumstances of my life, the prospect of moving to a more suitable environment became an enticing option. It was obvious that I'd already exhausted all the motivations and possibilities that would validate any reason to remain in New Mexico. With no doctoral degree to pursue, no job security, and living in a place I abhorred from day one, it would be foolish to not search for a way out; a viable alternative out of the unspoken dissatisfaction my life had become. I realized it was time to take the most daring step of all my traveling adventures to date; even more so than when I went to Portugal and Los Angeles without knowing anyone. This time around I would have to proceed exactly the same way, but with a significant aggravating factor: I'd have to do it with a family in tow and a child to care for who'd need to be settled and in school soon. Furthermore, there would be no preliminary scouting mission either. I would have to dive into a narrow cove of possibilities with unwavering self-confidence; like a *clavadista de La Quebrada* in Acapulco. But instead of a dive, it would be a drive into the unknown with only my experience and boldness as guidance.

"What's the matter?" B.L. asked me after I summoned her to the kitchen table; just as we'd done in Maui when we were planning to move to the mainland.

"Take a look at this," I said nodding toward a large map of the State of Oregon on the table.

She looked at it with a furrowed brow, then toward me with an expressionless countenance. "What's it supposed to mean?"

"We're going to Oregon," I said with unfaltering determination. "After two years trying to adapt to this region, I've realized what I've known all along: I am not a desert rat and I can no longer survive in this snake pit of a place. There's nothing left for us to do here, and now it's your turn to compromise."

She looked sideways and I noticed her facial muscles unfurling piecemeal. The ensuing silence lasted awhile as she seemed to mull over my words, and likely aware of my dogged resolve.

"Where do we go in Oregon?" She asked turning to look at me with subtle apprehension in the eye.

Another ensuing silence followed her question. Running my hand continuously over my mustache and beard while looking at the map, suddenly I pointed to the region of the mid-Willamette Valley on the map. "Here!" I said with the conviction of someone who knew exactly where he was going.

"Where exactly is here?" She asked and I noticed her voice cracking as she stared at my pointing finger on the map.

"I don't know yet," I replied nonchalantly. "Somewhere in this region. We'll find out when we get there."

I could hear the fast beating of her heart with my intuitive ears. To her credit, however, she knew of my personal history and she had the utmost confidence in my abilities to pull off such an audacious move.

"What about our daughter?" She asked with inherent maternal uneasiness.

"What about what? The school year is over and she'll start fifth grade wherever we end up in Oregon," I replied in offhand manner before realizing she needed some comforting assurance. "Trust me, we'll all be alright and glad we made this move."

"When do we leave?" She asked and her voice now sounded assuaged and somewhat enthused.

"A week after my knee surgery," I said. I'd already planned to take advantage of the last month of my health insurance eligibility to get a second right knee arthroscopic surgery for the damage incurred over years of soccer and tennis playing.

"That's in three weeks," she said sounding surprised.

"Yep, I think we'd better start packing," I said folding the map and putting it back in my briefcase.

The next two weeks turned out to be both hectic and stressful. Soon, the living room was stacked up with cardboard boxes, several of which containing my most valuable earthly belongings:

my books. Except for a few cooking utensils, plates, silverware, and other necessary items of daily use, the apartment was ready to be emptied. Since the only furniture we possessed were an old couch, a couple of lamps, the king size mattress we all slept on, a kitchen table set, my bookshelves, desk and chair, a small moving truck would suffice. However, I wanted to tow my pick-up truck and sell the other car to cover our traveling expenses. After all, there was not much savings in reserve and I had no idea when—or where for that matter—I'd be working again.

Having made all the necessary arrangements ahead of time, I was ready to embark on the next phase of my life. The only thing that didn't quite work out as planned was not being able to sell B.L.'s car in a short period of time. I dropped by most of the used car lots in town and no one showed the slightest interest in purchasing the old Ford Tempo, no matter how much I reduced the price. Now, not only the additional money I was counting on to finance the move was not available, but also the trip would be more fuel costly. She ended up having to drive the car following me along the way; an unexpected change of plan to which we had to adapt at the last moment.

As for my knee surgery, it went well and I was eager to expedite the rehab process right away, for I didn't have the luxury of time. However, what I did not expect was to need a much longer period to recover than what I'd experienced the first surgery some 10 years earlier. Maybe, with the passing of time, my knee didn't heal as expeditiously as it had a decade ago. In any case, the day before we were scheduled to leave, I was limping with a swollen knee and nagging pain. In spite of the additional drawback, I managed to load our belongings in the U-Haul truck, hitch up the two-wheeler car towing carrier with my pick-up truck on it, and ready to embark on arguably the most challenging journey of my life. And yet, having done it successfully several times in the past, I didn't have a modicum of doubt I would make it happen again. I knew that there are myriad forces engaged in the action in which boldness is the bellwether.

My last day in Albuquerque was probably my best since I arrived. Leaving the parched and barren southwest for the lush and wet Pacific Northwest was a welcoming transition. However, my enthusiasm was tempered by a great deal of apprehension about the adventure ahead. Although my previous experiences had primed me for moments like that, the burden of responsibility for the welfare of my daughter and wife weighed heavily on my mind. Moving to a new place with a family without any connections or preparation presented a unique set of challenges I'd never experienced before. Suddenly, my recollections of past achievements on the road teetered on a fine line between the thrill and anxiety of the present moment. It was like a new tennis match you have to play in which the positive results you had in the past are completely irrelevant when you step on the court again. The game may be the same, but the circumstances of the match are not. The only things you can count on are your skills and willpower to be victorious. Nevertheless, the outcome of your efforts will always remain elusive, and you'll never find out the result until the match is over.

The morning of departure was filled with tense anticipation. We were about to hit the road with all our earthly belongings in a moving truck without any idea where we'd end up. With a child under my aegis, this leg of my life's journey was like an important tennis match I could not afford to lose. This would have to be a "Victorious Sunday" like no other. Tossing the ball of chance in the air while swinging the racket of determination in my hand, this time I would have to ace my serve with utmost accuracy.

Driving into the unknown in five stops. This is how I termed this tour of difficulty, which felt to me like a rite of passage into bona fide maturity of being. Although I didn't know exactly where I was going to end up, like a skilled mariner at sea, I had my bearings in place and proper sails geared up for the wind. The first leg of the journey was to drive to the northern border and cross the state line the following morning. After spending the night in the northwest town of Farmington, New Mexico, we headed to Ogden, Utah. Then, there was another long stretch of pavement to Boise, Idaho. The next day, I woke up feeling energized with optimistic motivation, for before the end of another driving day we'd be in the town of The Dalles, on the Oregon bank of the magnanimous Columbia River. Henceforth, the nature of the driving changed. It was no longer about spending the night in some cheap motel. Now we had to find a place to call home.

Driving west toward Portland, I could not stop thinking of what I'd witnessed the day before two miles east of the city of The Dalles. Somehow I just couldn't get the damn dam out of my mind. I'd been perplexed watching that monumental engineering project disturbing with its intrusion the unperturbed flow of the majestic Columbia River—and the salmon that swim upstream to spawn. Keeping the moving truck steady on the middle lane, my mind took an exit wondering about the enormous sacrifices we make to generate the conveniences of industrial-technological civilization. In order to generate the energy we need to keep the entire infrastructure functioning, we create most consequential interferences in the natural balance of life. For cheaper cost of energy, we pay an exorbitant environmental price that is proving to be very costly—and perhaps even deadly in the long run.

With my mind back to the middle lane of my attention, suddenly I gasped when I first saw the snow covered Mount Hood in the near visual distance. Somehow the symmetrical warlock's hat-looking imposing mountain gave me the heebie-jeebies. It felt as though it had a soul and a consciousness of its own that spoke to me in silent recondite language. I struggled to keep my eyes on the road where they belonged, but the impressive sight of what later I'd learn to be a dormant volcano magnetized me as if the Hawaiian goddess of volcanoes, *Pele*, warned me about my new surroundings. Soon, I'd find out that there was much more to the place I chose to call home than I had anticipated.

The Pacific Northwest is not only a region of powerful volcanoes, like the mighty Mount St. Helens that blew up with devastating power on May 18, 1980, but it's also prone to earthquakes, which is my most dreaded natural disaster of all bar none—in a minor symbolic level, the equivalent of my fear of vertigo that can strike with vigorous unpredictability. Even the most potentially destructive natural disasters allow for some warning to prepare. I'd experienced firsthand the warnings and preparations for the fast approaching category 4 hurricane *Iniki* in September of 1992, which wreaked havoc in its ruinous path on the island of Kauai. Nevertheless, all the residents of the state received ample warnings in advance, therefore the opportunity to prepare. But an earthquake is a different beast. And when I learned that the Pacific Northwest was due to what has been coined "the big one," I wondered how and why I chose, out of my own intuitive volition, to settle in a region prone to the natural disaster I feared the most. Perhaps, I'd been unwittingly influenced by my readings of the work of Friedrich Nietzsche (1844–

1900) who advised in his book, *The Gay Science,* to live dangerously: "…the secret for harvesting from existence the greatest fruitfulness and the greatest enjoyment is to live dangerously! Build your cities on the slopes of Vesuvius!" I was about to build my life on similar grounds.

Immersed in my musings, I almost failed to notice that B.L. drove past me on the left lane. As we approached the outskirts of the city of Portland, the traffic got heavier and the signage on the freeway offered guidance to different destinations. I knew we'd have to veer south to head toward the mid-Willamette Valley, therefore I moved to the left lane thinking that was the reason she had passed by me to lead the way. Suddenly, to my astonishment and consternation, she moved to the middle lane and started driving toward Portland as I'm getting ready to get off highway 84 onto the Interstate 5 corridor going south. I freaked out. What was she doing? I honked, yelled, and cursed out loud damning the trouble she was about to cause by going in the wrong direction. At that point, there was no way for me to turn to the middle lane and follow her toward the opposite course of our journey. I blasted the horn uninterruptedly while screaming with extreme anxiety. Somehow she got the message and abruptly turned left at the last minute. Furious, I sped up to pass her and signaled to exit at the next rest stop.

"What the fuck were you doing?" I shouted still shaken by what would have been a tremendously troubling disconnection.

"I'm sorry," she said meekly. "I got distracted listening to a favorite song on the radio,"

"Fuck!" Do you realize how much trouble we'd be in had you gone ahead?" I fumed unable to tame my red-hot irritation. "What would we do had we gone in different directions?"

Suddenly, it dawned on me that not having prepared for the possibility of disconnecting was a major blunder of my planning. We both paused wondering how in the world we'd reconnect while traveling without knowing where we were going. In the pre-cell phone mainstream era and with no reunifying plan in place, the potential mishap could have turned into a royal nightmare. As the skipper of the ship in that audacious voyage, I felt responsible for not having created a contingency plan in case we got separated. The faux pas was on me and I felt guilty about it. With a communication system now in place and the agreement that henceforth she would drive behind me at all times, we proceeded in our journey to settle down somewhere—and hopefully soon.

The plan was to exit the freeway at the main cities along the I5 corridor to check them out as prospective places to put down roots. The first stop was at the state capital city of Salem. It was a quick detour. The town lacked any semblance to urban charm, hometown appeal, and was bereft of the northwest beauty I'd envisioned before coming to Oregon. In fact, there were areas of town that reminded me of the strip malls of Albuquerque, which was a good enough reason to skedaddle at once.

Some 25 miles south of Salem, we got off the freeway to the town of Albany. Although slightly better than Salem, it still did not meet expectations of what I had in mind as a quaint Pacific Northwest town. At that point, based on what I'd researched about Oregon before leaving New Mexico, I thought Eugene bode favorably to being our stay put stop. A hip mid-size city with a progressive reputation tantamount to Berkeley in the Bay area of the 1960s, the hometown of the University of Oregon sounded like a good option to reactivate both my professional and domestic life. However, since we were so close to the small town of

Corvallis, I decided to drive west to check it out, spend the night, and then continue driving south to Eugene the following day. It was a momentous decision that changed the course of my plans.

As soon as we crossed the bridge over the Willamette River leaving Albany city limits, we entered the two-lane road toward the college town of Corvallis, the home of Oregon State University. Driving alongside the river, I immediately experienced a feeling of geographical affinity. The expansive mantle of greenery covering the hills with tall trees; the distinctively shaped Oregon red barns in the small farmlands; the hawks circling high above hunting their midday prey; all of it exuded a bucolic landscape that triggered an enormous feeling of familiarity that I'd known intuitively long before I left Hawaii. The neurons in my brain were firing up in all cylinders, as the endorphins ran through my blood stream like the water flowing on the river I drove nearby. At every mile forward, I sensed that I was going in the right direction.

By the time we arrived in Corvallis I was already bewitched. We checked in at a local motel by the river before going on an exploratory spin around town. It was love at first drive. The charming neighborhoods with streets flanked by beautiful tall trees; the bike lanes painted throughout the pavement; the small college town atmosphere with a beautiful campus; the picturesque parks with manicured vivid green lawns; all of it evoked a home-like feeling I had not experienced in the last two years. Then, when we decided to step out of the car to go for a short stroll, I couldn't help noticing a variety of birds singing, including the distant hooting of owls coming from the green hills. As I rejoiced in auditory pleasure, a train gently whistled through town adding an idyllic tune to the avian symphony. I was enthralled with this place I'd just arrived. And the people who walked by greeting strangers like me with friendly demeanor demonstrated their copacetic lifestyle. By the time I took a deep breath to anchor the entire experience into my being, the fresh air felt like appetizing nourishment for my lungs. I didn't have anything else to do or see. I'd found the place I was looking for.

"We are staying here," I spoke abruptly with uncontroversial determination.

B.L. smiled and nodded in agreement without saying a word. I wondered whether she realized that I was right when I knew, in most uncanny fashion, that we should have come from Maui to Oregon without an untoward 2-year detour through New Mexico. Never again would I go against the clear-cut grain of my intuition, whether she or anyone else agreed with me or not. But at that moment what mattered was that we made it to the right place; and based on my self-guiding Taoist approach, most certainly at the right time. Now we had to get busy and find stable housing.

The following morning, instead of heading to Eugene some 45 miles south, we went searching for permanent lodging. Since it was summer and most students at Oregon State University were out of town, there were quite a few apartments available for rent and we had no problems finding one that suited our needs. A day later, we moved into a cozy two bedroom condo, returned the rental moving truck, and were ready to jumpstart our lives in the heart of the valley; the meaning of the name of our new hometown. A month later, I'd already secured a part-time teaching job at the local community college; B.L. landed a gig at a local boutique, and my daughter was duly enrolled in school for her fifth grade year. We'd established the foundation upon which to build a new life. Now it would be a matter of time for me to reignite my professional aspirations at the age of 40; or so I optimistically thought at the time. Alas, setting up a stable work situation would prove to be a long challenging endeavor.

In spite of the many trials and travails I would endure in the years to come, there was one detail that remained as an undeniable validation to the accuracy of my intuitive power. When some two years earlier in Hawaii I knew, without any evidence, that Oregon was the right place to move to the mainland, I was correct beyond my expectations. It so happened that I would end up living in the heart of the Willamette Valley the longest of all other places I'd ever lived before. My extra-sensorial perception had proven to be eerily accurate, again.

Perhaps, it would be an exaggeration to say that I'd squandered two years of my life in Albuquerque—the equivalent of John Lennon's self-proclaimed "lost weekend" year in L.A. However, I couldn't help wondering what would've been like had we come to Oregon first. It was a moot point, of course, but both my professional and marital challenges rolled over to my new home state just the same. What my self-evident ESP failed to alert me was that I would not find solutions for my quandaries in Oregon either. Evidently, the tribulations of life are not intrinsic to any particular geographical location, but abide deep within us as we carry our emotional baggage wherever we go, like it or not.

❧❖☙

In order to give continuity to my personal edification and professional aspirations, I decided to continue my education on my own terms. At the same time, I'd also pursue my terminal degree through schooling (in my writings on education I've emphasized the unambiguous distinction between schooling and education). With my unquenchable thirst for knowledge unabated, I dedicated myself to researching the various approaches of the educational system. My original idea was to write a book on the results of my findings as a pathway to a doctoral degree in education. However, since I'd already been disillusioned with the traditional institution of academia, I'd lost the desire to go through the application process again, even though I'd only submitted once. At the time, I came across a passage from one of my all-time favorite teachers, Friedrich Nietzsche (1844–1900), whose authoritative statement in his acclaimed book *Thus Spoke Zarathustra* resonated with my own feelings about the academic world: "I have moved from the house of scholars and slammed the door behind me. My soul sat hungry at their table too long. I am not like them, trained to pursue knowledge as if it were nut cracking."

However, I realized that abiding by society's shallow standards of intellectual recognition was important; and that was the reason many a good thinker acquired the terminal degree in order to validate the quality of their scholarly work. Thus, when I found out that several famous pundits and bestselling authors with Ph.D. letters after their names obtained the degree from inconspicuous universities, I didn't hesitate to consider similar approach to facilitate the publication of my own independent research work. Hence, I committed to pursuing my Ph.D. with a twofold purpose in mind: to validate my self-proclaimed intellectual artist status, and as a potential enticement for publication of my writings. Ironically, after investing much of my time and money on the degree, I never used the hubristic title to legitimize the quality of my work, for it felt like a spurious tactic to me.

In due time, I completed the Ph.D. program from the same unassuming university one of the most famous bestseller authors at the time earned his. His übber popular psychologically themed books probably would not have been as well received if it weren't for his pretentious academic recognition, even though the quality of his work stood on its own merit. In my turn, I felt like I had to follow the same pragmatic approach in order to achieve my goals, which was to turn my work into a quality book; my own judgment of my self-didactic doctoral degree. Thus, I officially celebrated my personal graduation the day I signed a book deal contract with a major publishing corporation—and I didn't even bother to add the three solitary letters next to my name on the book cover. However, it was when my book was adopted as required reading in the School of Education at SUNY that I found the academic acknowledgment I wanted to certify my terminal degree. Afterwards, the Ph.D. became as unassuming to me as the university that had issued it. Now, I was ready to pursue my highest educational aspiration: to become a bona fide independent intellectual artist with a multitude of learning interests; a legitimate Renaissance man.

On the job front, however, the battle raged on unabated. Although I'd been able to find a part-time job at the local community college within a month of arriving in Oregon, landing a permanent full-time employment proved to be a veritable challenge. Job announcements that read like a perfect fit to my skills and background were unresponsive to my candidacy. Seldom was I invited for a job interview; and the few that happened didn't pan out. I was growing increasingly frustrated. It felt as though I was battling an employment curse I could not seem to be able to overcome. In the meantime, I kept my head above water with teaching gigs at Oregon State University, a couple of community colleges, and even a short-lived desperation job at a charter community high school. But neither one of these jobs was permanent positions with the highly coveted retirement plans and health benefits, which the latter my family and I never had throughout the many years we shared a household.

While teaching part-time classes at the English Language Institute at OSU, I learned about an excellent opportunity within the university's international department. Never had I come across a job description that read like it'd been tailored for me. Of course, I enthusiastically submitted my application feeling absolutely certain that I was a frontrunner for the job. Seemingly, I was correct as I was invited for an interview. Besides, because I worked at the university in the same building of the international department, I felt that even my local references added a reasonable advantage over the outside candidates. In fact, I was so unequivocally sure that I'd be hired for the job, I would have bet my life's savings on it convinced that I would double my stake. Luck had that on the day I received the letter following the interview, no one had placed a wager on my false sense of certainty. I would have become a pauper heading to the poor house in my early 40s. I was in complete disbelief. The disappointment I experienced receiving the rejection letter from the University of New Mexico paled in comparison. This proved to be the tipping point that got me over the edge of dejection. Begrudgingly, I surrendered to my ill-fated kismet to live off casual work unable to get a permanent job at a time the economy was booming. I was beginning to wonder whether I'd been hexed by some evil eye; a malicious spell of misfortune. I just could not seem to be able to break through.

My wife, on the other hand, was sailing the employment sea with more favorable trade winds. She'd made acquaintances with a lady whose husband was a computer geek who had recently launched a unique software startup company. As their relationship developed, the lady invited B.L. to join the fledgling company. The unexpected well-remunerated turn of events encouraged us to move out of the apartment into a house. Things looked promising again. After a couple of years since arriving in Oregon, there was a possibility for stable employment opportunity, at least for one of us. In fact, even I was commissioned to do some freelance work for the newly founded software company. Then, as if we'd been cursed by the evil gods of labor, within a few months all fell apart as quickly as they'd come together. B.L. and the lady boss had an expected fallout that to this day I still don't understand how or why it happened. All I knew was that, all of a sudden, acrimony was brewing between us and them and almost became litigious. In another untoward turn of events, B.L. and I were back to square one with ever-growing frustrations, disenchantment, and stress-building economic uncertainties—and the unresolved marital issues dormant underneath a shaky ground.

The insidious inability to land a steady full-time job; unpredictable income; no health insurance, and years of disappointing experiences started accumulating until it reached an unbearable level. The stress in our household was building up piecemeal. At a time when conservative politicians ballyhooed about "family values," we were one of the millions of American families whose unstable economic situation was eroding the foundation of whatever family values they were preaching from the pulpit of hypocrisy. As the head of the family, I was hit particularly hard. I was exceedingly stressed out and it was spilling over to my already troubled marriage. I became irritable, nagging, impatient, and garrulous. I was not well.

The weather was not favorable for smooth sailing. I could see the billowing clouds of a looming storm in the horizon. Although I strove to keep my family vessel on course, it was clear that we were heading for the rocks.

Seven years had gone by quickly since we moved to Oregon. Within this timeframe, I'd put so much energy and effort into making something happen in my professional career with nothing substantial to show for. Other than part-time jobs and occasional gigs to get by, a full-time permanent position eluded me like a shadow I could not hold on to. Now past my mid-forties and with a high school senior daughter, I felt as though time had passed me by leaving me behind where I started. Still without a steady job, reliable income, health insurance, and, perhaps worse of all, a stable career I could be proud of, it seemed that the main reason I'd left Hawaii for had failed miserably. Although I never lacked an iota of personal self-esteem; much to the contrary, what I endured and overcame in my travels made me very proud of my individual accomplishments, my professional self-worth was badly battered and bruised. My obstinate unsuccessful pursuit of a gratifying career had reached rock-bottom—and so had my marriage.

With my high achieving daughter moving out and away to attend college, the eve of the empty nest era had arrived. Coincidentally or not, it was also the time that B.L. had learned about the renowned Camino de Santiago; the footpath where people go searching for purpose they can't find where they are at. Enthused about the medieval route where international pilgrims walk hundreds of miles in search of some existential meaning, she began delving into the possibility of embarking on the journey. Being a Taoist to the core, I espoused the truth of the verse 26 of the *Tao Te Ching*, which states that "a wise man can travel all over the world without leaving his backyard;" in other words, the path to self-discovery is nowhere but within. But I was the only Taoist in the household, therefore my viewpoint was irrelevant to anyone but myself. In my turn, I had a lot of backyard walking to do in order to sort things out in my life. Already feeling glum because of my daughter's departure in addition to everything else I was going through at the time, I was in a particularly vulnerable position. In maritime analogy, I was navigating some rough seas and I could not afford to lose another crucial deckhand to help me sail my vessel to a haven ashore. Instead, B.L. thought it was an opportune time to jump ship and swim away to some idyllic island of her own. Then, she made what I considered to be an irreverent proposal.

"I think we should take a break," B.L. said without looking at me as we sat across the dining table.

"What do you mean take a break?" I asked.

She paused before lifting her chin to look me in the eye. "I think it'll be best for us if we separate for a while; take a break from this difficult routine we've been through."

"And what exactly do you have in mind?" I asked suspecting I already knew the answer.

"I want to walk the Camino de Santiago to find out where I'm at in my life," she said.

"And I suppose I should stay here waiting for your realizations to find out whether or not we'll get back together at a later date," I replied sardonically not liking where the conversation was going.

She lowered her head without saying a word.

"I'll tell you what. I want to be supportive of your needs, even though you're not taking mine into consideration. Next week, we'll go to the courthouse and file for an amicable divorce. Since we don't have any property to wrangle over and our daughter is no longer a child, it should be a fairly easy and simple process," I said determined to carry out the action. "After the paperwork has been filed, you are free to go wherever you want."

"But what if we want to get back together later?" She asked looking at me dubiously as if she were unsure of the arrangement.

"Getting married is as easy as 1,2,3; it's getting divorced that's a real bitch to disentangle. If we decide to get back together again later, we will talk about it then," I said convinced that reunification never would happen. "But from the moment you walk out the door, I want to make sure I'm a divorced man free to live my life as I wish, and you just the same."

The following week we headed to the courthouse to file the divorce paperwork after an 18-year marriage. Although I resented both the timing and the circumstances of her ludicrous proposal to go traveling while I sorted out on my own the mess my life had become, I tried to make it as seamless as possible. Wanting to bail out when I was struggling to put my life together didn't sit well with me. Besides, coming up with the suggestion to break up at the time my daughter was leaving home, it made me feel like our family life was all about her child and not me. But I wasn't railing against her. Soon, I'd be following my personal path while she walked her own Camino.

"You go ahead and sign it first," I said handing her the pen.

"Oh no, you're the man in the relationship; you're the one who must go first," she said almost laughing as we bantered with each other at such a momentous time in the courthouse.

The court clerk looked utterly baffled witnessing the most bizarre marriage dissolution spectacle she'd probably ever seen. It is safe to surmise that we were the exception rather than the norm of divorce cases. And by the disoriented expression in the clerk's contorted face, I was assured of my assumption. But in fairness to the disreputable institution of divorce, we didn't have property or assets to divvy up and fight over. I suppose adding money to the mix makes it more likely to ignite the keg of contention. In our case, however, it was a genuinely amicable divorce. In fact, we even went out for dinner after signing the divorce papers to discuss the upcoming changes in our individual separate lives.

"One day you'll look back and realize this was the best that could have happened to you," she said as we sat across from each other at the dining table in a favorite restaurant. "Not having to account for anyone but yourself will set you free in a new way; like you used to before we met. You've invested so much of yourself into caring for your family. And now with the heavy burden of responsibility off your shoulder, you shall feel lighter than a feather and be able to fly as high as you want."

I hearkened her words as I once did from another woman in my distant past. Like that time decades ago back in Rio, it was obvious to me that B.L. was speaking from inspiration (in-spirit); and her statement, too, would prove to be right years hence. Light as a feather would allow me to fly to new horizons; and embracing the change would be the wings that would take me the distance.

We continued enjoying our oddly celebratory dinner blending casual talk with more serious conversation. Suddenly, another slant of topic was introduced via body language. We started looking at each other amorously. The truth was that in spite of our marital challenges along the way, we did love and care for each other, which made it even more out of the ordinary the fact that we were getting divorced. But at that moment, and for another couple of months, we were still a married couple and behaving as such. From gazing at her lined eye to touching her hand lying on the white tablecloth, the thermodynamic of the moment heated up as we decided to close the evening. Next thing I remember we were engaging in passionate sexual intercourse in the sacrosanct space of our home; a place that was about to disintegrate in the aftermath of our soon-to-be sanctioned divorce.

Lying exhaustedly satisfied next to her, I wondered what the court clerk would think if she knew about the ensuing moments she'd witnessed at the courthouse.

Like I'd experienced numerous times in the past, there I was on the move again. This time, however, it felt completely different from all the other times I set sail elsewhere. This moving went much further beyond sheer relocation; it was a radical life change. Unlike the last two times we moved as a family, this time we were each going in different directions: my daughter to the University of Oregon in Eugene; my now ex-wife off to Europe to walk the Camino de Santiago; and I, well, I didn't have the slightest idea of where I was going—physically or otherwise. Suddenly, I found myself on my own without my family, work, friends, or anything that would grant me the slightest sense of pride, security, or comfort. At the age of 48, I had to reinvent myself under unprecedented difficult circumstances.

Facing what had become a familiar sight, I looked at the cardboard boxes stacked up against the living room wall wondering how many more times I'd have to do this in my life. Initially, the plan was to move them into an apartment for the three months before my daughter went to college and B.L. to Europe. As for me, I still had to find a place to live and a job to support myself. The former was not easy but with serendipitous luck it happened, eventually. The latter, however, would prove once again to be a veritable challenge that would take months to come to fruition.

After checking out several places that either did not meet my basic standards of livability or my budget, I was feeling hard-pressed to find a place to live in a hurry. Out of desperation, I started looking for any kind of shelter aware that I could only lower my standards but not exceed my budget. Sentient of my limiting financial parameters, I ended up seeing some truly awful places that would have decimated my soul into smithereens of desolation. I had to find a decent habitat to call home; otherwise I would have a hard time surviving such difficult change.

Then, as it'd always happened in my life, providence came to my rescue. On a Tuesday afternoon, I decided to check out the classified section of the newspaper where an inconspicuous tiny ad in the midst of many listings called my attention. Like a little island in a sea of advertisements, the listing of a small cabin in the woods in the outskirts of town seemed like the ideal atoll to rest and regroup in the midst of a storm of change. I immediately called the contact number and within half-hour I was there checking it out. It was the perfect place for my transitioning into the next phase of my life. A small, cozy, quaint, and lovely one-bedroom cabin surrounded by trees in a park-like setting outside of town was exactly what I needed. Furthermore, it was within my budget and well above my minimum standards of livability. I'd found a good home; and that has always been sine qua non for my wellbeing.

After getting rid of most of our furniture—the selling of our intimacy-infused king-size bed to a very strange fellow somehow made me feel quite uncomfortable—we were ready to do part at last. I rented a small moving truck for a day intending to move B.L. and my daughter into their place in the morning, and then move my belongings into mine in the afternoon. It was in the morning that a most bizarre occurrence took place.

"I'm going to take these boxes on the dolly to the apartment and I'll be right back," B.L. said before dashing away while I arranged items for the next load.

Inside the truck's container with my back to the open door, I absent-mindedly kept shifting boxes around trying not to think too much about what was actually happening. Suddenly, I was brought back to the present moment in the most unusual and profound way. Sensing an almost palpable energy coming from behind me, I turned around and I was stunned with what my eyes encountered. There, gazing at me with loving eyes and a quasi-angelic expression, the woman who used to be my wife expressed an unspoken pungent emotion. Caught by surprise, I looked back into her eye trying to make sense of the unexpected incidence. After a long awkward moment of silence, she gently verbalized what her eyes were already saying all along.

"I love you so much; so much," she muttered barely moving her lips.

I kept staring at her wondering how all of it made any sense. Why in the world were we getting divorced if love was still an element in the equation of our relationship? The only answer that made sense to me was because, for some reason beyond my ken, the time of our union had expired; our coming together had fulfilled its purpose. Evidently, now we each needed to move on separate ways for reasons I could not comprehend at the time.

Once the last box was moved in their transitional residence, it was time to bid farewell; one of my most dreaded moments in any occasion, particularly that one. As far as my ex-wife was concerned, I suppose I handled it better than I anticipated. But saying goodbye to my daughter was awkward and hurtful to both of us. I made an extraordinary effort not to break down while noticing the sorrow in her saddened eyes. Attempting to expedite the growing emotional discomfort, I embraced her with reassuring fatherly love, kissed her on the forehead, and dashed out the door desperately yearning to release tears as if a full bladder had occupied my lacrimal glands. Then, sitting on the moving truck driver's seat, I wept uninterruptedly until I regained a modicum of emotional stability to be able to drive safely.

The final step of this distressing transformational process was to load the truck with my belongings and move to my new place. Under any other circumstances, I'd probably be very excited and elated to be moving into a cozy cabin in the woods, which was the first time in my adult life I had my own living space that was not a boat—not counting a couple of months stay in Laguna Beach. Unfortunately, the sad state of affairs didn't give way to any jubilation. Instead, just as I did hours earlier on the truck driver's seat, I shed tears realizing that henceforth I'd be alone; without my family, a job, or the expectation of positive possibilities in the near future. I was in for some rough sailing ahead.

The next morning marked the beginning of a very trying period with signs of many more challenges to come. And it started out in the most hypocritically ironic way. Firstly, when I drove to the post-office to retrieve my mail, my old beat-up pick-up truck showed, for the first time, signs of malfunctioning as the calipers on the front wheels started getting stuck hindering the motion of the vehicle. I was about to have transportation problems—and unexpected expenses. But that was not the hypocritical element. The real sardonic reason was inside my P.O. Box in the form of a letter from the county courthouse.

Puzzled thinking how quickly the divorce documents had been processed, I opened the envelope right away. As I read it, I was stunned with the content of the 12-page document requesting additional information in order to process the divorce paperwork.

Considering ours was a most amicable divorce, with no financial conflicts, an 18-year-old college-bound daughter, and no prevailing animosity whatsoever between the parties, the questions listed on the document were absurd and even insulting. From co-parenting inquiries to wanting to know how the "child" would be provided with health insurance, I was appalled and incensed with the latter question, which I deemed to be an insolent request. For many years in a roll, none of us had ever had access to health care; and now that the family fell apart, the judicial system demanded to know how the parents were going to provide health care for an adult child with what had been a financially prohibitive resource to our family. Where was the judicial system when my child, wife, or I were ill and we could not afford health care services? Angered by what I took as an affront, I felt like tearing the preposterous letter and tossing it in the trashcan. But since I needed the final divorce document, I contained the urge to react to my indignation. Besides, I had more immediate pressing issues of concern to deal with.

The following morning my aggravations went from bad to worse. Firstly, the faulty calipers on the front wheels of my truck took a descending turn. Now the wheels were sticking together as if they were welded to the drums. They heated up so badly that I had to stop every now then and wait for them cool off before being able to drive again for a few more miles. After several stops along the way, finally I was able to make it to my regular tennis match with my buddies; my brief moment of solace in the midst of the chaos my life had become—and about to be aggravated further. In the middle of the second set, I launched to reach for a drop shot and a misstep sent my body eastward while my twice surgically repaired knee headed west. I fell over the net grimacing in pain. Limping to the sideline, I looked at my swollen up knee throbbing like a high diastolic heart pressure, and I had no doubt I'd damaged it really bad. Based on the increasing discomfort, I was convinced that I'd likely torn my ACL. I could not believe my misfortune. Feeling excruciating pain at the slight stepping on the throttle, somehow I managed to drive home safely. Without health insurance or money to spare, now I had two problems that demanded my immediate attention; and both involved my ability to move to make something happen: my knee health and my car functionality. And when I thought my adversities were daunting enough, it got even worse the next day.

I'd just finished reading an interesting book from an author I knew very little about. Thus, I decided to check it out online to learn about him and other books he might have written. After a quick search I found his website. As soon as I landed on the homepage, a window popped up inviting me to learn more about his work. Since it was exactly what I was looking for, I clicked on the link and inadvertently opened a wicked Pandora's Box. A series of windows kept flashing on and off one after the other until the computer screen turned pitch black. My computer had been infected with a nasty virus that made me feel sick to my stomach. Now, my most important tool for job searching and communication was out of commission. I screamed out loud my frustration to no avail. As if not having a healthy knee and a functioning car to move about were not challenging enough, now my essential device for communicating with the outside world vanished at the click of a button. Utterly infuriated with the last inauspicious occurrence, I powered off the now defunct computer and went straight to bed lamenting my misfortunes of late and cried myself to sleep.

Deep asleep, I dreamed that I was surfing at Ho'okipa Beach Park when a series of monstrous waves headed in my direction.

Scared out of my wits, I desperately paddled out to avoid being gulped up by the mountain of water before me. And just like on the day it actually happened, feeling exhausted and hopeless, I surrendered to death with resignation. At that point in my dream I realized that, in genuine Nietzschean fashion, what had not killed me then had made me stronger now. Somehow I felt self-assured that I was going to overcome the allegorical waves that were currently crashing over me. Although in entirely unrelated conditions, I knew I was going to triumph over my troubles again.

A couple of months had passed since I'd moved into my cabin in the woods. Although I was still struggling mightily, I was able to count my blessings under the circumstances I was embroiled in. I'd found an independent mechanic who fixed the calipers of my pick-up truck for a fraction of the estimates I received from several shops. One of my tennis buddies who happened to be the IT director of the local community college debugged my computer for free. And the most concerning issue of all, my knee, which I thought had been severely damaged, healed on its own after numerous rounds of ice packs, hours of elevation, a slew of anti-inflammatory medication, and an inexhaustible amount of positive thinking. I was grateful it was likely an ACL sprain and not a tear. As for the match of life, though I was still far behind on the scoreboard, I was getting back in the game.

After months of unsuccessful job searching, I was beginning to feel the monetary pinch in my savings account balance. Although I loved my new home in the woods and the town I'd been living since moving to Oregon, I started feeling the pressure to having to apply for jobs wherever they happened to be. Thus, when I came across an administrative position job announcement at Portland State University that my credentials were suited for, I submitted my application hesitantly and with conflicting feelings. Then, with a mix of excitement and consternation, I was invited for an all-day interview on campus; some 2½-hour drive from my cabin in the woods.

On the drive back home after the terribly tiresome interview, I moped about the entire process and its potential consequences if I were to be offered the position. Not only the job itself sounded like an uninteresting drudgery, but worse yet, I'd have to move to the city and rent some small apartment in an area I knew no one. I'd have to leave my newfound comfy sanctuary in the woods and start a new life doing something I didn't want to do in a place I didn't want to be. And yet, the pressure to find work and make money was mounting up with the signing of every check I wrote to pay my bills.

Afflicted with contradictory sentiments of relief and distress, I did not get a job offer. I would have to continue job hunting for months to come, which now I felt obliged to apply for employment opportunities out of state. It was a real grind. However, as I'd experienced numerous challenging situations since leaving my country of origin, I realized that each new trial presents its own disturbing characteristics requiring a whole new set of adaptation skills. I was in for an unprecedented round of adversities.

Frustrated, disillusioned, and uptight, I decided to surrender to my kismet and stop fretting about what I could not control. Instead of worrying about the untoward circumstances of my life, I budgeted my limited resources calculating how far I could dig into the well of my savings before it would run dry. I estimated I had another year until my finances hit rock bottom. In the meantime, I was determined to tap on my previous life experiences—

my valuable inner resources, that is—and do what I'd done so many other times in my life: take a leap of faith. Not only would I not curtail what I deemed to be essential expenses such as my gym membership, but I'd also live with unwavering confidence that some unseen magical forces were acting in my behalf. I committed to stacking up all my chips on the gambling table of life; or as a favorite poet of mine, Charles Bukowski (1920–1994) said in an inspiring poem about self-reliance (*Nobody but You*), "wager your life as you struggle; damn the odds; damn the price. Only you can save yourself."

Following my own philosophical credence, I was determined to live in earnest by the Taoist principle of *wu wei*: doing everything by doing nothing—not forcing the outcome of my actions, but flowing with the spontaneous unfolding motion of the Tao. After all, as I'd learned in my studies of Taoism, "the true character of *wu wei* is not mere inactivity, but perfect action, because it is act without activity."

To my delightful astonishment, an immediate welcoming change came about unexpectedly.

❧❖☙

At the time when it became evident that my marital dissolution was but inevitable, I began fantasizing about having affairs with beautiful young women; perhaps even engage in a lasting relationship with one. I suppose that the proverbial midlife crisis had something to do with it. However, the real motivational factor igniting my newly found romantic aspiration was based on verifiable evidence. Although I was past my mid-forties, I couldn't help but notice how much attention I was getting from women more than half my age. One day when a very young and attractive woman openly flirted with me in a bookstore while I browsed books, I became aware that my own sex-appeal stocks still held some value on the dating marketplace. From that day onward, I was determined to pursue affairs with young women once I disentangled from my failing marriage.

Fast forward a couple of years since that afternoon in the bookstore, I realized that my longing to be in a relationship with a young woman would not be as simple as I'd fantasized. Although I was still getting plenty of nubile interest laden with flirtatious glances and smiles, I realized that my chances of nurturing a new relationship with an attractive mademoiselle were close to nil. After all, what young woman would want to get involved with a broke and unemployed 48-year-old divorced man? But with so much more pressing issues driving the focus of my attention, my romantic fantasy took the backseat as I rode on the winding bumpy road of the challenges at hand.

Remaining true to my commitment to living by the principles of *wu wei*, I went to the gym daily as exercising proved to be an excellent outlet for my pent-up mind and emotions. I worked out for hours on end to the point of complete physical exhaustion. Then, I went home, cooked a meal I washed down with plenty of cheap red wine, smoked my digestive pipe, searched for jobs online, and passed out in bed reading a book while listening to the healing music of J.S. Bach (1685–1750). In spite of the unstable circumstances of my life, I was actually living a quality daily routine of sleeping in, hiking in the woods, playing tennis, exercising, and enjoying my freedom from family responsibilities and economic function drudgeries. Within this ideal living scenario, the only things missing were a source of income and the companionship and touch of a woman. Although the former would be a long time coming, the latter came about when I expected the least and needed the most.

After breaking out some serious sweat on the treadmill, I walked to the water fountain to hydrate myself. Wiping off the perspiration from my drenched face with a towel, I had to wait a moment until another gym patron finished slurping from the drinking water spout. As soon as she turned around, our eyes casually connected as if a magnetic field of energy pulled us into a vortex of mutual interest. We remained quietly looking into each other's eyes for what it felt like an interminable time.

"Excuse me," she finally broke the silence while flashing a timid pearly smile before walking away.

Smitten, I beheld the gracious movement of her petite shaped body moving like a female feline; a sexy kitten in black leotard that accentuated her roundish buttocks that captivated my sex-deprived imagination. With the clear image of her bright blue eyes radiating in my recent memory, I could see the contour of her beautiful youthful face in my mind's eye as if she were still standing in front of me. The fair tone of her soft-looking skin; the cascading straight blond hair adorning her alluring facial features, and the overall magnetism of her womanhood held me helplessly spellbound.

"Do you mind if I have some water?" A brawny young man asked me as I stood motionless by the water fountain long after she was out of sight.

I ended up walking away without drinking any water. I felt as though she'd satiated my thirst while leaving me hungry for getting to know her. She was petite, young, blond, sexy, and beautiful; the immaculate prototype of my romantic fantasies. And even though my common sense assured me I didn't have the slightest chance of hooking up with her, both the look in her eyes and the ensuing smile assured me otherwise. Henceforth, I had another motivation to come to the gym daily. I wanted to see her again; and the next time it happened, I would approach her with determined Latin lover bravado.

A week had gone by and I was beginning to get antsy and impatient. I was yearning to see that Aphrodite's daughter again, gaze into her alluring blue eyes, and feel the touch of her hand. Then, to my effusive delight, one evening she showed up more beautiful than ever; and to my surprise, she approached me and initiated the conversation.

"You're so nimble," she spoke to me casually catching me by surprise while I did my stretching routine. Holding my left leg up with the right solidly planted on the floor, my impressive balancing pose caught her attention when she walked in the backroom of the health club.

"And you're so beautiful," I blurted out without even thinking. It came out so naturally that I was perplexed with my spontaneity.

Like the first time we met at the water fountain, we stood silently gazing into each other's eyes for the longest pleasant moment that cannot be measured by traditional standards. Then, she smiled at me with an impish twinkle in the eye. I reciprocated in kind, and just like that we became a couple in the making. It was the beginning of one of the most unique and bittersweet romantic relationships of my life.

D. was a beautiful and intelligent 26-year-old woman completing her graduate studies at the University of Oregon. Well travelled, trilingual, and with open-minded intellectual curiosity, we hit it off from the get-go and became an official couple after our very first date; a long walk on the promenade by the riverside. The following day, we spent talking on the phone all night long—

amidst very lengthy moments of silent connection—until the Sun rose and we decided to meet at a local French coffee shop for breakfast. After that morning, we both knew that something meaningful was unfolding.

We were getting emotionally closer by the day, and within a couple of weeks we were, I suppose, in love. Feeling insecure and vulnerable as a 48-year-old divorced, broke, and unemployed man, having a much younger beautiful woman show a genuine interest in me was a tremendous morale booster. She was a God-sent gift to lift my spirit at a time of great personal distress. However, her most important role in my life would come many months later when we were no longer together. In the meantime, she kept disclosing subtle and disturbing aspects of an obscured part of her nature that I'd never experienced before with anyone.

One evening, she called to ask me to join her for the night in a place she was house sitting for a friend. Of course, I agreed right away thinking this was going to be the night we would make love for the first time. I arrived at the address within half-hour after hanging up the phone.

After spending a lovely relaxed time talking and laughing while drinking Pinot Noir, I ensconced around her making the first move in preparation for the main act of the evening. Because it was so obvious she wanted intimacy as much as I did, I was taken aback with her totally unexpected reaction.

"What are you doing?" She asked pushing me away with a furled face that screamed disgruntlement.

I immediately pulled my arms off her and moved back away to the other side of the couch completely befuddled. Looking at her eyebrows almost joining together above her clearly aggravated eyes, I was utterly flummoxed with whatever was going on that I could not comprehend. Suddenly, out of the blue, the beautiful, smart, and pleasant D. reacted so temperamentally that I wondered whether I'd unwittingly done or said something wrong. Since we had made out several times in the past, this had nothing to do with placing my arms around her. Maybe I said something that upset her, though I had no idea what it could have been. In fact, I was absolutely certain I had not done or said anything worthy of such a short-fused reaction. Mystified by her odd behavior, I apologized, stood up, and walked away without saying another word. I waited hoping she'd eventually realize how absurd her abrupt reaction was, and, in her turn, would apologize to me. Not a chance. I went to one of the bedrooms and fell asleep, alone, wondering what had just happened.

It was my first experience ever with what later would prove to be a significant mental health disturbance. In the following weeks, I began observing how her email messages drastically transitioned from poetic paragraphs expressing her love for me to blitzkriegs of disgruntled statements. However, besides her unpredictable behavior, she was, most of the time, a pleasant companion; a girlfriend I was yet to have sex with.

When an opportunity came up for me to go on a trip by myself, I jumped on it with much anticipation. With a surplus of air miles points and a burning desire to visit my former home state of Hawaii, I decided to attend the renowned Maui Writers Conference. I contacted a friend who was glad to put me up for a week, and soon I was packed and ready to spend some quality time with Mamma Maui. At that time, my relationship with D. was flying high, though she was still holding off the sex, which puzzled me since she was, without a shadow of a doubt, as eager to do it as I was. Although I was clueless to her reasons for postponing the inevitable, I respected her stance and patiently waited for the right moment and she felt ready. Meanwhile, when I was in Maui we talked daily on the phone; always exchanging loving and passionate words with each other. In spite of her occasional emotional let downs, I remained patient and willing to be there for her, as she was for me in a way she wasn't aware of. But by golly, I really wanted to have sex with her.

When I came back from Maui, our sex life erupted like the Kilauea volcano spewing smoldering red lava of passion over our relationship—and eventually burning down my masculine pride.

☙❖❧

I had taken the redeye flight from Kahului Airport to San Francisco. By the time I arrived at PDX in Oregon, my sleep deprivation started catching up with me. Aside from the interspersed naps I took on the airplane, I had barely slept at all. Nevertheless, I was so amped up about seeing D. again that I felt energized.

"I'll be there in 15 minutes," D. said when I called her from the shuttle drop-off hotel lobby. She sounded as excited to see me as I was to embrace her.

As soon as I saw her old white Honda Civic turning around the corner, my heart started pounding inside my chest as if it were a drum beating for a long waited pow-wow that was about to begin. As she got closer, I could see her gleeful shiny smile sending rays of joy my way. Somehow I felt like my coming back from Maui was the beginning of a renewed phase in our relationship.

"It's so good to see you," I said after embracing her with both my arms and lips.

"You must be exhausted and famished," she said after kissing me. "C'mon, let's go home and I'll fix you something to eat."

Oddly, I didn't feel like someone who'd barely slept or ate in a long time; to the contrary, I felt as wide awake and fed as if I'd slept all night and eaten a hearty meal. The sheer joy of sitting on the passenger's seat talking with her stimulated me like a hot cup of Sumatra coffee. And every time we stopped at a red traffic light, I held her right hand with my left as we caressed each other's fingers. A simple, ephemeral, and yet most complex experience of elation.

As soon as we entered my cabin, I dropped the luggage on the small living room floor, picked her up in my arms, and walked to the adjacent bedroom where my bed had waited a long time for this moment. As the fire of our passion was ignited with fervent kisses that heated up our crescendo desire, we undressed with impatient eagerness to connect our bodies in carnal bondage. Lying naked and aroused like Adam and Eve about to eat the forbidden fruit of love, she reached inside her purse and handed me a condom she insisted I put it on.

"You must wear this," she said interrupting the spontaneity of the moment.

I snatched it out of her hand in one swoop, unwrapped the damn thing, and hurriedly rolled it down my erected manhood eager to penetrate her nubile genitals. Obviously, she had concerns about unwanted pregnancy and was prepared to avoid it; or so I thought.

We made love with unbridled abandon—four times! After spending all day in bed, by late afternoon we had the urge to do it again, but her genitals were so sore that she couldn't do it again. I'd never felt as sexually accomplished as I did then. There I was, a 48-year-old man fucking the brains out of a 26-year-old cutie willing and able to surrender to me. Never mind that I barely slept after hours of long travel. I was possessed by the spirit of Dionysus; the manifestation of Don Juan incarnated in the sexual man I'd been all my life. I was satisfied, fulfilled, and yes, very proud.

The next evening she showed up at my door unannounced.

"I got something for you," she said as soon as I opened the door surprised to see her. "It's pink and I'm wearing it under my white dress. Would you like to see it?"

Suddenly, I realized the pressure was on. It seemed that her sore genitals had recovered rather swiftly and she came back hungry for more. In hindsight, I should have withheld my sexuality as she did to me when she had an outburst of bad temper while house sitting. But since when does a proud Latin lover say no to a beautiful young woman yearning to be ravished? Never! And sometimes the Latin lover can pay a hefty price for his macho hubris. Even though I felt pressurized, I managed, with some degree of angst and struggle, to make love with her twice with a great deal of performance anxiety, which backfired on me psychologically in the months to come. Somehow the pressure to perform at the level I had done the day before affected my self-confidence in my sexual prowess and stamina. But that ended up being the least of my concerns.

A few weeks later, she asked me to accompany her to what I thought to be a most unusual and unexpected request.

"You want me to go with you to a Planned Parenthood clinic?" I asked feeling concerned that one of the many condoms I used might have failed.

"Yes, I want you to be there with me when I hear the good news and learn what I've been so sure all along," she said.

"So sure of what?" I asked beginning to feel apprehensive.

"Just come with me, please," she insisted clearly not wanting to elaborate on details.

I had a hard time sleeping the next couple of nights before the dreaded appointment. I was convinced it had something to do with pregnancy test, and the thought of a positive result terrified me. How in the world would I, a 48-year-old recently divorced, broke, and unemployed man sire a child with a young woman out of wedlock? Taking care of me had been plenty challenging enough. At that point in my life, I had neither the financial nor the emotional stability to take on such a gargantuan responsibility. Although it ended up not being what I feared, it was equally alarming in its own way.

"It's negative," the doctor said as D. grinned at me with unconcealed contentment. "In fact, everything looks very well and healthy with you."

The supposedly good news left me extremely upset and disturbed. D. had neglected to tell me that she'd had a sexual encounter several months before meeting me with someone who might have been potentially exposed to the HIV virus when she was travelling in West Africa. Although she insisted in taking precautions, I was extremely upset with her for withdrawing such important information from me. Somehow that incident affected me psychologically to the point of affecting my sexual performance confidence. Even though it was all in the clear now, I started thinking about it every time we had sex, which made me uncomfortably nervous. Things got even worse after her next episode of mental health breakdown. It happened when we were making out naked on the living room floor of my place in a prelude (foreplay) to another ecstatic love-making session. All of a sudden, like an earthquake making the floor tremble, she abruptly stood up and glared at me with that same crazed expression she displayed in the house sitting incident.

"I'm leaving right now," she blurted out sounding very upset for no apparent reason. I looked at her nodding my head sideways trying to figure out what could possibly have triggered such an irrational behavior in such an inopportune time. It didn't make any sense no matter how I tried to rationalize it.

Watching her hastily putting her clothes on, I stared at her agape unable to comprehend what was going on. At that moment, I realized there was something terribly wrong with her, and I didn't think I could be of any help. Then, as she stormed out of my place slamming the door while knocking a picture frame off the wall, I lay on the floor wondering how flawed my romantic fantasy of having a relationship with a beautiful young woman was proving to be. I recalled the first time I went to her home and how taken aback I was with her messy and utterly disheveled bedroom. It looked like a hurricane had swept through it leaving her belongings scattered on the floor in its wake. On that night she walked out on me snappishly when we were about to have sex, I speculated that the image I had in mind of her chaotic bedroom was symbolic of the inner chamber of her mind.

The next day she called me in the morning as if nothing significant had happened. Other than apologizing for her impulsive departure, she didn't make any reference to a justifiable reason for such erratic behavior. Like many of her email messages to me in which a livid paragraph would lead to loving poetic words, D.'s behavior was disturbingly unpredictable; and that had a troubling impact both on our now shaky relationship, as well as on my sexual performance. The following times we got together, I was so pent-up and concerned about if or when she'd snap that I became unable to get an erection with her again, which devastated my hitherto proud Latin lover ego. Suddenly, she went from being a source of support to my battered mid-life crisis to a burdensome emotional liability. Alas, my fantasy of having a relationship with a beautiful young woman turned into a curse that eclipsed my optimistic light behind a shadow of hopelessness.

By the sixth month of our turbulent relationship, the end of my fantasy came to a close. In spite of all the troubles and travails of our brief dating time, we still had feelings for each other. However, I had a life to put back together and she, for better or for worse, could not fit in my plans of rebuilding stable living conditions. Thus, without excuses or fanfare, I broke up with D. Shortly afterwards she traveled out of the country for undetermined sojourn abroad and I'd never see her again.

Although both the breakup and disillusionment exerted a heavy toll on my downtrodden self, I was immensely grateful for the experience. Indeed, D. played a fundamental dual role in my life; not only at a time when I was down and out and desperately needed a boost of confidence, but even more so in the upcoming near future events. In the short term of our relationship, her interest in me enhanced my morale when I had reached rock bottom. However, it was in the long run that she proved to make a most valuable contribution to my future. Once my frivolous fantasy was (partially) fulfilled, I realized the vacuity of youth and beauty as a baseline upon which to build a worthwhile relationship. Had I not met D., I know I would have never given up my longing for dating a beautiful young woman. But once my desire for appealing appearance dissipated in the fog of illusion, it closed the door of superficial pretense at the same time it opened up the gates for unbounded possibilities.

Hence, as time went by, I welcomed the prospect of dating a very attractive woman who happened to be a few years older than I. At a gradual steady pace, we would develop a most meaningful relationship that transcended into complex psychological factors that greatly contributed to strengthening our loving bond. And if finding love after divorce past the half-century mark of our lives were not exceptional enough, neither she nor I could have ever imagined that we'd have the best sex of our lives in our fifties and sixties. What a pleasurable surprise!

A few months after D. was out of my life, I'd finally gotten over the hump of the break-up and ready to move on to the next phase of my love life.

Meanwhile, my struggle with unemployment persisted unabated. As frustration with my job search rocked my boat with ongoing disappointments brought about by adverse winds of misfortunes, I decided to change the coordinates of my course. I realized that I needed to put myself out to make one-on-one acquaintances if I were to get any positive results. Thus, I started attending social organizations and business meetings hoping to establish professional connections. It paid off. I met someone who owned and operated a publishing business that showed interest in hiring me, albeit at an entry level position far below my qualifications. Desperate for any kind of work, I unhesitatingly accepted it determined to turn it into a springboard to a better situation down the line; either within his company or elsewhere.

It took only a couple of months for me to realize that whatever advancement within the company I was hoping for would not happen any time soon. Besides, the boss proved to be a real drag and the job a factual drudgery. The silver lining of the unpromising circumstance was his willingness to allow me to choose any reasonable title for my position, which was printed on my business card. Picking out "Communications Director" to embellish my credentials, I began promoting myself as a bona fide communications professional. Without wasting any time, I resumed applying for jobs in the field inserting the business card along with my résumé. With unexpected rapidity, soon I landed an interview for an excellent paying job that was going to change my kismet and catapult me to a new professional and financial status.

"The fact that you were already employed as an experienced communications director weighed heavily on my decision," the CEO of the company that hired me commented casually at the signing of my employment papers.

My strategy had paid off handsomely. Now, at 49-years-old, for the first time in my life—not counting my flower business in Hawaii—I had a well-remunerated job that gave me both personal and professional satisfaction that was not in the field of education. In the carrying out of my duties, I was surprised to learn that I was a schmoozer extraordinaire, which I exercised with joy and aplomb. I was hobnobbing with politicians, business and community leaders, among other movers and shakers in the capital city of the State of Oregon. I established beneficial connections, friendships, and liaisons with the media, government, and a wide range of organizations. I was developing a slew of communication materials, writing grants, producing promotional videos, and involved in all sorts of creative projects. After a long arduous search for work, at last I had a good paying job in a professional field I enjoyed and was proud of.

Living in my low rent cabin in the woods, a 45-minute commute to work, now I was in a stable financial situation in my life. However, even though my work search had taken a favorable turn, there was still one missing link on the chain of my good fortune: I missed having a woman in my life; someone with whom I could hang out and cuddle after a passionate round of mind-blowing sex. Hence, I took on an active stance and started searching for my prized female companion with the same determination I engaged in my pursuit of employment.

Just as supermarkets were one of my favorite hookup spots in my mid-twenties in Los Angeles, I realized in my late forties that gyms were the places where opportunities to make acquaintance with women abounded—I'd already met a few, including D. A safe and social environment, the health club I frequented favored approaching suitable prospects in casual style. It so happened that sometimes I was the one being targeted.

"I've noticed you doing this exercise before. Those are very interesting motions you seem to be able to do for a very long time," an attractive woman in her late 30s remarked as I practiced my own version of aquatic qigong in the gym's swimming pool.

Noticing the undeniable hitting-on-me-tone-of-voice, as well as the subtle words choice of her statement ("interesting motions you seem to be able to do for a very long time"), I cut short my routine to give her my undivided attention.

A couple of hours later, her naked body was straddling mine as I introduced her to my interesting motions; my unique version of sexual qigong. Never in my life had I gotten laid so fast after meeting someone. Immediately after our small talk in the swimming pool, I invited her over for dinner in my cabin, which she obliged promptly. But before I even had a chance to fix us a bite to eat, she made it really clear that she was more interested in having the sexual main course in bed than dinner at the table. In fact, we didn't have dinner at all. She seemed perfectly satisfied with the bodily banquet served in bed. It was as though her carnal appetite had been satiated and the nutritional needs of her physical body were numbed in the process. In my turn, other than rewarding my Latin lover ego by exhausting her with pleasure, I was impressed with neither the sex nor the companionship. And unlike her, I was starved for both food and meaning.

"I should get going," she said putting her clothes on while I stood naked by the stove. "I don't want to get home too late and let my kids wondering why I've been taking so long."

"Of course not," I said feeling relieved with her wanting to leave right away. "We'll keep in touch."

We never did. After that evening, I only saw her once again many weeks later at the health club when we cordially conversed as if we'd never had an intimate encounter.

After that disappointing rendezvous, I decided to take a different approach; one that I'd never taken before: online dating. I logged on to a social network connecting people of all sorts of sexual orientation and perused through the "women seeking men" category. It was a most bizarre experience. After evaluating several posts, I selected one of an attractive young woman whose descriptive spiel appealed to me. She presented herself as college educated, worldly traveled, and with an interest in tennis; all of which were right up my alley. We made arrangements for a dining date in town that turned out to be an indigestive annoyance and a major disappointment. It was one of the most tedious and uneventful dates I've ever had. And to make matters worse, she was not at all pretty in person, had never attended college, and barely ever stepped outside the state's line. And as far as tennis is concerned, she was absolutely clueless about the game.

"Why did you falsely embellish your profile description?" I asked unable to contain my irritation with her falsehoods and the wasting of my time.

"Because catfishing works," she replied nonchalantly. "It's after meeting in person that we see where it goes."

Obviously, with her it went nowhere fast. And when I found out what catfishing was (the process of luring someone into a relationship by means of a fictional online persona), my interest in looking for a girlfriend online was over.

Disillusioned with the whole dating scene, I decided to put all my attention on my new job, my independent studies, and the writing projects I'd taken on my spare time. I worked, I studied, I wrote, I played tennis, and I exercised; and that was the scope of my daily life. Although I still yearned for an affectionate woman, I was content with the way my life was moving along. Then, when I finally let go of looking for what I wanted, I eventually met the woman who would become my loving life companion for many years to come.

Once again in my life, the Taoist principle of *wu wei* (doing everything by doing nothing) proved to be the most effective approach to live by.

☙❖❧

The first time I saw her walking on the treadmill I was smitten. Wearing black leggings under a short skirt and a flesh-hugging pink top that accentuated her curvaceous mid-section, I gawked at her as she stared at the television monitor on the wall completely oblivious to my uninhibited attention. After weighing myself on the scale at the end of the room, I walked back in front of her ogling as before and receiving an equally indifferent response. I was unfazed. At the health club, I knew by experience that it would be a matter of time till we crossed paths again.

There was something about that attractive mature woman that tickled my interest to get to know her. In addition to being a beautifully shaped older woman, she exuded some loving maternal energy that captivated my attention. Perhaps, it was the suppressed motherless boy inside of me with an unfulfilled Oedipus complex that longed to have a motherly-figure in my life. To me, at least in my initial perception, she seemed to embody the dual role of passionate lover and loving mother in one female package; an ideal combination in a woman I'd never experienced before. Both physically and emotionally aroused, I was determined to get to know her as soon as an opportunity arose.

The next time I saw her, she was exercising on a pull-down weight bar. With no one around, I positioned myself right next to her pretending to work out on the adjacent equipment while not-so-discretely undressing her with my coveting eyes. But as she did before when I walked by intently staring at her, she remained indifferent to my audacious gawking as if I were not even there. Feeling dispirited with my failed attempt to get her attention, I backed off wondering whether she was in a committed relationship or just didn't want to give me the time of day. But until I found out the reason for her unambiguous indifference, I was in no mood to give up.

By sheer serendipity, a few days later I accidentally came across her at the same water fountain I'd met D. several months earlier. In an almost identical situation, she was finishing drinking water when I showed up for my turn. As she turned around, my eyes were on stand-by mode to greet hers. This was the opportunity I'd been waiting for and I was not going to squander it.

"I knew that sooner or later I'd have a chance to talk with you," I said zeroing in her right eye. "I've been trying to get your attention for a long time wondering if you'd ever notice me."

"Notice you? How could I have not?" She replied wilily.

From that terse exchange of words in a few seconds in time, the minutes, hours, days, weeks, months, and years that followed were imbued with growing loving feelings and indelible memories. A.G. and I would become best friends and, against the odds of time, the greatest lovers either she or I ever had. Although our intimacy was initially ignited by potent mutual physical attraction, it was perpetuated through the years by an extraordinary spontaneous chemistry that cannot be fabricated. Furthermore, there were deeply rooted psychological factors that cemented our long-lasting—and very sexually charged—relationship.

Both of us were recently divorcees and eager to experiment something new at the latter stage of our lives. After the day we exchanged our first words, we grew closer and more intimate at a steady pace. Soon and without even noticing, we were in a serious relationship in which we spent most of all our free time together. Every Friday evening, which I fondly nicknamed *Fabulous Friday*, I went to her place after work to dine and wine in nights of unfettered passionately fabulous sex through the entire weekend. It was at that time, in my early fifties, that I, for the first time in my Latin lover life, engaged in seven long-lasting and highly fulfilling intercourses in a 48-hour period. That was the ultimate barometer gauging the intensity of our sexual chemistry. Never in my wildest pubescent dreams would I have imagined that I'd break my sexual endurance record in my 50s. A.G. and I were mid-centenarians making love like two horny adolescents who'd just discovered the joys of sex. Indeed, in the earlier years of our relationship we had sex all the time; and there were legitimate reasons for our sexual indulgence.

A.G. had just ended a 33-year-marriage of misery in which she felt trapped in unbecoming circumstances. Coming from a goodie-two-shoes upbringing in the San Francisco Bay Area, she was raised to be a loyal housewife, devoted mother, and a faithful religious woman. Thus, at the tender age of twenty-one, she married a man from the Middle East, who misled her into believing he'd provide her with a life of international travels and luxury.

Instead, she ended up in a small town in Oregon catering to her middle-class electronic engineer husband and their three troubled children in a lackluster domestic life. Per her own account—aside the enjoyment of her motherhood role—her daily existence was a miserable routine of drudgery, gloom, and dissatisfaction with multiple aspects of her life. Among a laundry list of discontent, she endured three decades plus of frustrating and unfulfilled sex life in an utterly unhappy marriage, which had a heavy toll on a highly sensual woman. Uncertain whether she'd be able to make it on her own—and gaslighted into believing she would not—she felt shackled to a dismal matrimonial sentence. But when emotional despair superseded the anxiety of financial insecurity, she divorced her husband after her children moved out of the house determined to reinvent herself and jumpstart her life anew.

In my turn, not only had I been divorced well over a year, but also had recently endured a disappointing romantic experience with a beautiful, young, and troubled woman with whom I had a difficult emotional relationship and traumatizing sexual experience. Consequently, my short amorous liaison with D. left me utterly disillusioned with youth and beauty as preferential standards for a sought-after desirable relationship. Thus, meeting A.G., an older woman with whom I got along very well and enjoyed an extraordinarily fulfilling sex life, turned out to be a life changing event. The combination of deep psychological factors and a physical chemistry that transcended the parameters of traditional sexuality, we ended up enjoying the best sex of our lives in our 50s and 60s—and sometimes it manifested in the most intensely sublime manner.

On a cold winter night while making out in front of the fireplace, A.G. and I engaged in what can only be described as a "kissing intercourse." Connected through our mouths as if our lips and tongues were genitals of the same gender, we were consumed in each other's mouth as if feeding our souls with unrestrained ecstasy. The dynamic kinetic energy that our kissing generated was nothing short of transcendental. We kissed with such abandon that time seemed to have come to a standstill. Whether it was dozens of minutes or multiple hours, I could not determine even as a wild guess how long we kissed, for the depth and length of our oral sensual connection remains unfathomable to my comprehension to this day. Never had I experienced a kiss that equated a bona fide sexual performance.

After overcoming the challenges of divorce and the trauma of a troubled relationship with a beautiful young woman, in the mid-centenarian stage of my life I found a loving and stable relationship with an older woman who fulfilled emotional, physical, and psychological aspects of my being. At last, I had a maternal presence that enveloped me with a special kind of love I'd never had before. Besides, the long-repressed Oedipus complex I'd directed toward my stepmother in my puberty was now fully liberated. Now I was free to give in to indulgence in my sexual fantasies without guilt or regrets. My long hidden and repressed secret sexual desires, which had haunted me in my adolescence and throughout my young adulthood, at last were put to rest for good. In one woman I found my best friend, best lover, and best mother. And in some peculiar way, the past 16 years we've been together feels as elusive as the time that passed incognito that evening when we kissed by the fireplace.

Now, as a mid-sexagenarian embarking on the final stretch of my life's journey, I reflect on my travels over land and sea that led me to the United States where I became an American citizen. With an immeasurable sense of gratitude to my adopted motherland where I've rebuilt my life, raised a family, established numerous enduring friendships with my fellow citizens, and served the communities where I've lived, I feel like a legitimate kin of the national family. Aware of my responsibilities and civil duties, I've striven to be a worthy member of the American society and an exemplary citizen of the United States of America, both at home and abroad. And on an individual level, I am imbued with a gratifying feeling of self-fulfillment for everything I've learned and accomplished since setting out on my extraordinary international expedition.

Alas, my self-perception of belonging is not always synched with certain narrow-mindedly prejudicial concepts. Many times I've wished my (mostly conservative and ignorant) native born fellow citizens could even vaguely understand how difficult it is to be an immigrant. To be deracinated from one's original homeland and culture is a harrowing progression that takes many years to overcome. And once the long acculturation process has been cemented into the immigrant's new cultural identity, his country and culture of origin can become quasi-foreign to him. Indeed, being a step-citizen can be a challenging experience. Perhaps, because I've dealt with the issue of discrimination as a stepson in my childhood, I'm particularly sensitive to unfounded prejudice on the basis of native born justification. Either as a stepson or step-citizen, I've always felt that I should be recognized on the basis of my merits alone, for any other means of validation is an act of injustice. And even though the 14th Amendment of the United States Constitution grants equal rights to all native or naturalized citizens, bigotry toward the immigrant does not reflect the legal constitutional rights of this noble document.

Prejudicial ignorance and jingoism aside, I am and always will consider myself to be a bona fide American citizen, regardless of my naturalization status. In fact, I embody the values Americans are proud of: I bravely launched myself into the world in the pursuit of happiness; I became an immigrant who had nothing but inner resources and an inexorable desire to make something out of my life; I managed to put myself to college all the way to graduate school on my own efforts and expenses; I became an educator and a writer of books in my second language—and one of my books was adopted as required reading in the School of Education of a major American university—and I made valuable contributions to the communities where I've lived. I am, indeed, an American immigrant success story.

Although by traditional societal standards of success—financial status, that is—I haven't amassed any significant amount of money to be considered a paragon of achievement, the extraordinary wealth of life experience that I've accumulated in my adventurous journey makes me feel like a most prosperous sovereign in the kingdom of my being. And as I am now ready to wrap up the last chapters of the book of my life with a great sense of pride and accomplishment, I get to define the meaning of success on my own terms.

From a childhood marked by the greatest of all losses to mature adulthood of inestimable gains, I feel as successful as any man could possibly be, whatever his measuring standards happen to be. Now I can take inventory of my life assured that I have absolutely no regrets; to the contrary, I harbor but a strong feeling of triumph as I look ahead to the final stretch of my earthly journey with great anticipation. As the inexorable passing of time ticks on toward the most dreaded unknown of all, I welcome the future as a new adventure that must be undertaken like all the others I've encountered in my lifetime. Courage, faith, self-reliance, and tenacity, all of which were paramount to sustaining me in the course of my globetrotting escapades, they shall remain as the contextual principles of the foundation upon which I'll always stand until the end of my human experience.

But regardless of what lies ahead beyond the limits of my ephemeral biological existence, I feel empowered to take on the next leg of the extraordinary cosmic voyage of my soul. And I, whatever this lonely personal pronoun may mean among billions of other human beings passing through this planet adrift in an unfathomably immense and ever-expanding Universe, I am aware to be but a quantum of consciousness and a scintilla of love exuding from the perennial mystery of Life.

Like a skillful skipper of a vessel sailing against the wind, I shall navigate through the rest of my life's journey with the same determination and confidence that led me to new beginnings that never seem to end…

About the Author

Sebastian de Assis is a writer, teacher, philosopher, intellectual artist, and a consummate bibliophile with an unquenchable thirst for acquiring knowledge.

A graduate of the University of Hawai'i at Manoa and California State University at Dominguez Hills, he has lived in several countries and traveled extensively through Europe, South and North America, Africa, and the United States. He is fluent in Spanish, Portuguese, and French.

He lives in Oregon where he reads and writes in his personal library while listening to J. S. Bach, Miles Davis, and other inspiring music that nurtures his spirit.

For more information about the author and his work visit www.sebastiandeassis.com.

www.ingramcontent.com/pod-product-compliance
Lightning Source LLC
Chambersburg PA
CBHW020453030426
42337CB00011B/102
* 9 7 8 1 7 3 2 3 2 8 5 0 1 *